DATE DUE

SCHOOL DESEGREGATION

PERSPECTIVES IN SOCIAL PSYCHOLOGY

A Series of Texts and Monographs • Edited by Elliot Aronson

INTRINSIC MOTIVATION
  By Edward L. Deci • 1975

SCHOOL DESEGREGATION
  By Harold B. Gerard and Norman Miller • 1975

A Continuation Order Plan is available for this series. A continuation order will bring delivery of each new volume immediately upon publication. Volumes are billed only upon actual shipment. For further information please contact the publisher.

SCHOOL DESEGREGATION

A LONG-TERM STUDY

Harold B. Gerard
University of California, Los Angeles

and

Norman Miller
University of Southern California

PLENUM PRESS • NEW YORK AND LONDON

Library of Congress Cataloging in Publication Data

Gerard, Harold Benjamin, 1923-
  School desegregation.

  (Perspectives in social psychology)
  Includes bibliographies and index.
  1. School integration — United States — Addresses, essays, lectures. I. Miller, Norman, 1933-   joint author. II. Title.
LC214.2.G47   370.19'342   75-28037
ISBN 0-306-34402-5

©1975 Plenum Press, New York
A Division of Plenum Publishing Corporation
227 West 17th Street, New York, N.Y. 10011

United Kingdom edition published by Plenum Press, London
A Division of Plenum Publishing Company, Ltd.
Davis House (4th Floor), 8 Scrubs Lane, Harlesden, London, NW10 6SE, England

Printed in the United States of America

Contributors

Lois Biener, University of Massachusetts, Boston
Tora Kay Bikson, University of California, Los Angeles
Edward S. Conolley, University of Southern California, Los Angeles
Desy S. Gerard, University of California, Los Angeles
Harold B. Gerard, University of California, Los Angeles
Jacqueline D. Goodchilds, University of California, Los Angeles
Duane Green, University of California, Los Angeles
James A. Green, Los Angeles County Mental Health Services
Irving G. Hendrick, University of California at Riverside
Terrence D. Jackson, University of California, Los Angeles
Eugene B. Johnson, Brooklyn College, City University of New York
Norman Miller, University of Southern California, Los Angeles
Vivian Tong Nagy, Veterans Administration Outpatient Clinic,
    Los Angeles
David Redfearn, University of California, Los Angeles
Harry Singer, University of California at Riverside
Michel Thelia, University of California, Los Angeles
Erhan Yasar, Middle East Technical University, Ankara, Turkey
Merle Linda Zabrack, University of Southern California, Los Angeles

Contents

Introduction

HAROLD B. GERARD AND NORMAN MILLER

In the fall of 1965, when the school board of the Riverside Unified School District made its momentous decision to desegregate the elementary schools in Riverside, both of us were faculty members in the psychology department on the Riverside campus of the University of California. The riots in Watts had occurred the previous August and the shock waves were being felt around the country. Although the black population of Riverside at the time was only 6% or 7%, people were apprehensive. A story appeared in the local paper, *The Riverside Press Enterprise*, about several Blacks who were watching the burning and looting in Watts on TV. One of them, excited by what he saw, exclaimed, "Man—let's burn here, too." The others in the bar were more level-headed and fortunately dissuaded him from following his impulse. Barely two weeks later, however, someone set fire to one of the buildings of Lowell School, in the eastside ghetto area. Nothing was left of the building but a charred shell. People in Riverside, of all ethnic groups, were generally edgy in the face of a seemingly volatile situation. Agitation by minority parents for improved education for their children seemed to be reinforced by the general unrest.

We had followed the action in the school district closely and when the desegregation decision was made, we felt that it represented a unique opportunity for social scientists to study the progress of the desegregation program. And in spite of the fact that one of us had met

HAROLD B. GERARD • University of California, Los Angeles, California. NORMAN MILLER • University of Southern California, Los Angeles, California.

with frustration in attempting to arrange to study the effects of a bussing program in New Haven, Connecticut, the preceding year, we both believed that social scientists had a social responsibility to try to assess the effects of planned social changes. Further, we felt that the schools should be armed with as much information as possible as to what consequences might follow from the decision to desegregate.

A search of the literature yielded only two studies that had been done prior to that time, which itself shocked us. With all the talk and furor about desegregation both before and after the historic 1954 *Brown vs. Board of Education* decision, we would have thought that social scientists, especially those working in the education field, would have carried out some studies of the problem. The two previous studies, one in Louisville, Kentucky, and the other in Washington, D.C., were not very informative. The data from both were fraught with problems that made interpretation of the results difficult. At the time of the school board's decision, James Coleman was still in the process of collecting his data on a nationwide sample of schools. His study was not designed to investigate the effects of an intervention that suddenly and drastically changed the entire complexion of a school district. Coleman's children were, by and large, in neighborhood schools or in feeder schools where a tradition of either segregation or integration was longstanding.

Being dismayed by the lack of knowledge in the area, we felt a strong sense of urgency to learn something about the problem. We began to formulate a tentative plan to follow a small sample of minority children through the elementary grades to determine how they fared in the new school situation. Since some funding would be necessary, we approached several private foundations for a relatively small amount of money. The Rockefeller Foundation came to our aid with a small grant, which they subsequently increased. The regents of the University of California, upon learning about our plans and about the Rockefeller grant, offered to match the money we had already received.

A number of other people on the Riverside campus, Jane Mercer in the Sociology Department, Fred Gearing in Anthropology, and Harry Singer and Thomas Carter in Education, felt that here was an opportunity for people in different departments to join forces to study an issue of overriding local and national importance. Robert Docter, who is now a very visible member of the Los Angeles Board of Education, was at that time associated with the California State Department of Education. He got wind of our plans and proceeded to convince us to raise our sights and study all of the minority children involved in the desegregation program as well as a sample of "Anglos" in the receiving schools. If we agreed to do that, he promised that he would attempt to provide us with a sizable grant from the McAteer Fund of the Division of Compensatory Education. This grant did materialize, so we proceeded to gear ourselves for a large-scale study. The first data were collected in the spring of 1966.

The upper echelon administration of the Riverside School District were eager to help. We do not have enough words to thank Bruce Miller, who was then Superintendent of Schools; Ray Berry, the Associate Superintendent at the time, who later became Superintendent; Mabel Purl, the chief psychologist; and Jess E. Wall, the Director of Intergroup Relations. The research would not have been possible without their full support and cooperation. We are especially grateful to Ray Berry for his statesmanship, patience, and forebearance during the entire course of our study.

Up until that time, both of us had worked almost exclusively in the psychological laboratory and were unprepared for the trauma of an interdisciplinary, interinstitutional study of a very hot social issue about which neither we nor anybody else knew very much. Rather than rushing into the study with a broad-gauge, atheoretical shotgun, we felt we ought to have some perspective, however vague, to guide us. As we point out in Chapter 1, many of the proponents of desegregation believed that the lack of achievement of minority children stemmed from a motivational or value deficit and that entry into the majority "Anglo" classroom would somehow reduce or compensate for that deficit. If these people were right, we were, in effect, dealing with issues in personality development and change. This model of "value mediation of achievement" and the assumed susceptibility of values to social influence became our underlying focus. With retrospective wisdom we would take a different approach were we to begin again. At the time, however, those most intimately involved with the problem seemed to favor that type of approach. The early work of Pettigrew and especially Katz emphasized the importance of these aspects of personality. When the Coleman report, which was published shortly after we began our research, also gave prominence to the lateral transmission of values as the mechanism mediating beneficial effects of integration, we certainly felt reassured about the wisdom of our research strategy, which would enable us to test this model carefully.

From the time we were assured of McAteer funding we had six weeks to mount the study if we were to succeed in taking premeasurements before the school year ended. Although a small percentage of the children had of necessity been desegregated because of the burning of Lowell School, full-scale desegregation was to be implemented that fall. Neither of us realized how large a chunk we had bitten off. Again, we went to the literature for help. We combed the relevant journals and books for information about how achievement-related values develop in children and for appropriate measures that could be administered and readministered in order to detect the motivational changes, which we were just about sure would occur. Again we found very little help. As you will see in the chapters that follow, we were able to utilize or adapt some existing instruments, but we also found ourselves in a situation in which we had to bootstrap many of the measures.

Had it not been for Jane Mercer, we probably would not have been able to get out into the field at all. Her organizational ability and sheer savvy about all phases of field methods were critical to our getting under way. We will be eternally grateful to her for the monumental effort she put in on the study. The two of us and the other UC–Riverside faculty members on our School Study Executive Committee, as we called it, were interested in different things. We each hoped to find answers in the data to our own specific questions. The nature of the study necessitated that we cooperate closely with one another, with our individual interests built into the instruments we were using.

It was clear to us at the outset that we were not interested simply in short-term effects but in long-term ones as well. In the desegregation research field, we were in the unique position of having taken extensive premeasures on most of the children involved in the study. We also had administered a battery of tests that provided us with a number of perspectives on what might be happening to individual children as they moved through the grades. Continued McAteer funding could not be assured, so we decided to seek federal support. We approached the National Institute for Child Health and Human Development and the U.S. Office of Education and were eventually successful. Both the NICHHD and the U.S. Office of Education underwrote the study for five years, with most of the funding coming from NICHHD. After this money ran out in 1971, the NICHHD provided an additional 18 months of support. The linguistic analysis, some of which is reported in Chapter 9, seemed to take on a life of its own under the general direction of Michel

Thelia, so we applied for some additional funding from the National Science Foundation, which we received. Without this long-term support from those agencies, the important longitudinal analysis could never have been done. Finally, we gratefully acknowledge a Summer Research Award from the Haynes Foundation to Norman Miller. This greatly facilitated the completion of the final manuscript.

This report represents the first volume of what will be a two-volume work. A considerable amount of analysis remains to be done. In the second volume we hope to present additional findings on speech changes, teacher bias, the effect of the minority child's physical attractiveness, the effect on the minority child of contact by his parents with the larger "Anglo" community, and a multivariate correlational overview of the study as a whole. The second volume should follow this one in about a year. The reason for publishing this partial report now is our feeling of urgency in apprising school people, other research workers, and the public at large of our basic findings, which we believe are important. Ours is the most thoroughgoing study of school desegregation in a single school district. To delay publication any longer would represent a disservice to all interested parties.

Many people besides those listed in the frontispiece contributed to this volume, some in small and others in large ways. Peter Lenz worked with us nearly from the beginning helping to design the data reduction and statistical package that developed over the course of several years. Officially his title was Programmer, but he did much more than just write programs. A person whose contribution cannot be overestimated was Jeanne Thornburg who oversaw much of the administration of the project and dealt with the many, many headaches. Through much of the period of data collection and analysis we had two secretaries; first, Carol Hausman and then Susan Cole. We were fortunate indeed that both of them were efficient and well organized and kept us from getting embroiled in many of the work-a-day details. Daniel Christianaz was second in command in the computer room. His seemingly boundless, creative energy was an important ingredient in keeping the analysis going, especially after Peter Lenz left to take up farming. In the later stages of the work William McGarvey and Geoffrey Maruyama provided invaluable help. Their contribution will be acknowledged fully in the second volume. Others who have helped along the way are Toni Falbo, Marika Farkas, Asher Koriat, Susan Rakow, Thomas Wong, and Jerry Zadny. We also wish to thank Donald T. Campbell for valuable suggestions on earlier versions of the manuscript. Finally, we wish to express our gratitude and appreciation to Gary Westman for carefully preparing a most comprehensive index.

To do research on a controversial issue such as desegregation is a touchy affair. Whatever conclusions one reaches, they will elicit attack from some quarter. Even before the study was fully under way we had to contend with middle-of-the-night crank phone calls. We were looked upon by some of the members of the local John Birch Society chapter as possible perpetrators of a communist plot hatched in Washington (for real)! Some members of the local Mexican-American community regarded us with suspicion. And so it went.

When the results were in, interpretation was fraught with difficulties, many of which are described in Chapter 3. There was virtually no similarity with the usual arena in which we work: the carefully controlled laboratory experiment in which the task involves linking some relatively straightforward manipulations of stimulus conditions to one or at most a few response measures. But even a laboratory study can create a tempest involving alternative and counteralternative interpretations. One can imagine, then, the cauldron our results have stirred up and will stir up even further after publication. Our main criterion (or response) variable was academic achievement. We feel pretty secure about the conclusions reached in Chapter 4, regarding achievement changes, but on what should be a relatively straightforward matter we have already been charged with possible misreading of the achievement results. Let the reader judge for himself on that score. That problem is a relatively simple one, though. The larger and much knottier issue concerns the factors, variables, circumstances, and processes that might mediate changes in achievement where they do occur. Interpreting a lack of change is even more troublesome. As any laboratory worker knows, positive results are many times easier to interpret than no effect at all. Negative results might mean that the manipulation did not take, that the response measure was no good—that it was insensitive to actual changes in attitude that may have occurred—or that the hypothesis under test is not tenable, all of which is certainly an ambiguous state of affairs. Field research is much, much worse. So many possible influences can confound the effects of an intervention in the "real world." It boggles the mind to contemplate them. No wonder most social psychologists have staunchly attempted to remain chaste in their pristine laboratories. But we were the fools who rushed in! In doing so we did, however, anticipate a trend in social psychology of disenchantment with the laboratory and a growing concern with problems of social "relevance."

Our experience has taught us at least two things. First, it is possible to learn something from a field study and that the findings can be valuable in stimulating us to think more deeply about theoretical issues—shades of Kurt Lewin. Second, the laboratory does have a firm place in our science—certainly as a court of last resort. The real world *is* too complex to comprehend fully—even after painstaking analysis in which one attempts to exercise statistical control over possible confounding variables. There is just too much going on. We would have liked to be able to dictate conditions to the school district: random assignment of children, teachers, and administrators; unchanging curricula; constant class sizes; the use of the same teaching methods and consistent practice regarding such issues as ability grouping; and finally, keeping all of these conditions the same after as before desegregation. If we want to assess the effects of desegregation, *per se*, these other factors must be controlled. Of course, we were not able to influence these decisions, and it's altogether proper that we were not. Desegregation does require a great deal of social engineering to make it work, and the school district was committed to making it work in Riverside. Most of what was done was probably based on good sense. Certainly there was no research available to back up the many decisions that were made about the allocation of children, about programs, about teacher training, etc. The problem for us, of course, is to interpret changes in the main output variable—achievement—in terms of this overall change program we have called desegregation, in which the schools did whatever seemed necessary to make the program work.

A "desegregation program" in one community will take on a different character than a program in another community. Riverside's program involved one-way bussing of minority children into previously "all-Anglo" (or nearly so) schools. Although there were other options, options that have been employed elsewhere, this was probably the most feasible method, given the social conditions in Riverside in the fall of 1966. One-way bussing has been depicted as "tokenism" by some. *Tokenism* must in some sense mean actions that are designed to assuage those who protest but at the same time minimize any "real" social change. Thus insincerity must be one of the critical ingredients of tokenism. At this point a distinction must be drawn between tokenism and other considerations such as, for instance, the minimum minority–majority ratio needed for beneficial desegregation effects. The Riverside desegregation program can hardly be depicted as tokenism when viewed in terms of these distinctions. Indeed, the very fact that the desegregation program was initiated as early as 1965 and eliminated completely the *de facto* segregation that did exist in Riverside adequately counters any potential charge of tokenism. But more importantly, the Riverside school system honestly attempted to implement a program in which minority children would eventually be integrated throughout the entire district. Whether the number of minority children added to previously "all-Anglo" classrooms was minimally sufficient or less than optimal from the standpoint of social-psychological and educational considerations is an entirely separate point. In Riverside an even distribution of the 20% minority population among the various schools could only result in a relatively small number of minority children in a single classroom. Following desegregation a Black boy might well find himself to be the only Black male in a class perhaps consisting of three Mexican-American children, a Black girl, and 20 or so Whites. Were these numbers or proportions shown to be inadequate in terms of anticipated beneficial effects, it would not impugn the motives and admirable aspirations of the Riverside School Board, Superintendent, and community. To put the Riverside situation into perspective, of the nine school systems studied by Crain in 1968, in *no* school anywhere in the nine systems did the Black population increase by more than 5% after desegregation. In Riverside, as well as in other cities in the Southwest, it seems reasonable to include Mexican-Americans as minorities. If so, then the elementary schools in Riverside increased their minority percentage by considerably more than 5%. At the same time, the influx of federal and state money showed an overall increase during the years following desegregation. While occasional blunders did occur in this or that instance, such as segregated reading groups in a particular classroom, internal segregation was clearly being discouraged by the central school administration. Nevertheless, we should keep in mind that the program we studied was in a very real sense one of a kind. We do, however, feel that certain of our conclusions have general value because of the simple fact that children, teachers, and parents everywhere (especially everywhere in the United States) have certain things in common. Most importantly, they are people.

1

The Study

Harold B. Gerard

In the long-term study of the desegregation of a school district in southern California that this volume reports, we found a clear and startling difference between Anglo[1] and minority (Black and Mexican-American) children in the relationship between IQ and achievement, which is shown in Figure 1.1. Wechsler IQ scores for the nearly 1800 children who participated in the study were plotted as quartiles against verbal achievement. The parameters of the achievement score distribution were adjusted to match those of the IQ distribution, that is, to have a mean of 100 and a standard deviation of 15. The figure shows in very bold relief that for any given IQ level, minority children do more poorly than Anglos and, furthermore, that this "achievement gap" increases with increasing IQ. The relationship depicted in the figure may, in part, be due to statistical regression, especially for the Q_1 Anglos and the Q_4 minority children, since overall there is a substantial measured IQ difference favoring Anglos (see Chapter 5). The clear Anglo-minority achievement differences for the Q_2 and Q_3 scores do, however, argue for an effect over and above regression. Furthermore, the regression coefficient of achievement on IQ, assessed within each ethnic group, is significantly higher for Anglos (.67) than for either Blacks (.45) or Mexican-Americans (.47).

---

[1] *Anglo* is often used in the Southwest to distinguish majority group members from Mexican-Americans. For want of a better label we shall use *Anglo* in this and the chapters that follow. When, however, we compare children in the White majority group with Blacks, we will, as is customary, refer to them as "Whites."

Harold B. Gerard • University of California, Los Angeles, California.

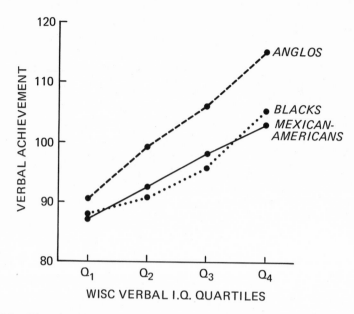

Figure 1.1. IQ and achievement: comparison of the 1800 Anglo and minority children who participated in this study.

If those who argue that IQ tests are biased to favor Anglos (Eells, 1951; Hunt, 1967) are correct, the situation is even worse than that depicted in the figure. That is, an IQ test bias favoring Anglos implies that a minority child with the same native intelligence as an Anglo child would tend to score lower on the IQ test than the Anglo child. If we assume that such a bias exists, it follows that if a minority child and an Anglo child receive the same IQ score, the minority child will tend to have more native intelligence, that is, he is genotypically more intelligent. If this is so, Figure 1.1 actually underestimates the achievement gap.

Minority children thus appear to be somehow blocked in realizing their achievement potential, an effect that is cumulative with age. As Chapter 4 shows, the overall achievement difference between ethnic groups is quite small to start with, but the "achievement gap" between the Anglo and the minority children widens markedly as the children progress through the grades. The gap, which in first grade is only 0.2 of a grade equivalent, widens to approximately 2.5 grades by the time the children have reached sixth grade![2] This occurs under both segregated and desegregated circumstances. In spite of the tendency for the variance in scores to increase in the later grades, the difference between the first- and sixth-grade gaps is highly significant statistically. Although no one to our knowledge has looked at the achievement gap with long-term *longitudinal* data, our results are consistent with other evidence, such as that provided by the Equal Educational Opportunity Survey (Coleman, 1966). The EEOS data, which are cross-sectional, show the gap widening to more than 3.0 grade equivalents by the time children are ready to graduate from high school. Other studies (e.g., Vane, 1966) find similar differences. Again, the real situation is actually worse than implied by the data, since the high school dropout rate for Blacks (and Mexican-Americans, as well), especially in urban ghettos, is far higher than it is for Anglos. Since those children who finish high school tend to be more academically talented than those who do not finish, the twelfth-grade gap is less than it would be if equal proportions of minority and Anglo children reached twelfth grade.

It seems most reasonable to present progress through the grades by the three ethnic groups in terms of grade-equivalent performance on achievement tests, since these scores reflect the actual relative accomplishment of the children in the school district measured against national norms. As children move through the grades, grade-equivalent scores typically become more dispersed, reflecting the fact that children benefit differentially from the school curriculum (and presumably from extracurricular exposure as well). By and large, children tend to maintain their relative standing as they progress through the grades (Vane, 1966), so that if the data were presented as percentile scores, the widening gap between Anglos and minority children would not appear to be as dramatic. This, however, would not be an accurate reflection of what the children knew relative to what they are expected to know in each grade.

Jensen (1970) argues that rather than the scores being presented

---

[2] A serious question is at issue here, since our minority students were from two distinct ethnic backgrounds, Black and Mexican-American. Both groups, however, were clearly socioeconomically disadvantaged and to approximately the same extent, although the Mexican-Americans were somewhat lower in socioeconomic status. If we can argue that achievement deficits are strongly related to disadvantaged socioeconomic status (Lewis, 1967; Jencks, 1972; Whiteman, Brown, & Deutsch, 1967), then it seems reasonable to consider the percentage of minorities in the classroom to be based on the sum of the number of children from both minority groups.

as grade equivalents, the means for each of the minority groups at each grade are better presented in terms of the number of standard deviation units (calculated from the dispersion of the Anglo scores) of discrepancy from the Anglo mean. The Coleman (1966) study presents achievement data both in terms of grade equivalents and standard deviation units without any rationale that would make one preferable to the other. In analyzing data from another school district in California, Jensen found that minority children, by and large, tend to maintain a constant 1.0 standard deviation gap below the Anglo mean. From this fact he argued that the schools themselves do not disadvantage minority children. The argument that since children who perform poorly initially remain relatively poor performers, the schools have done their part, seems to miss the essential function of a school curriculum, which is to prepare the child for life by teaching him what he ought to know.

It thus seems that it is possible to present group achievement data with or without an initial gap (Jensen is able to "eliminate" the initial gap entirely by correcting achievement for the regression coefficient of achievement on IQ!) or with or without a "progressive achievement gap," depending on the point of view one wants to advance. We have chosen grade equivalents, since we believe they describe best what the groups know on the average, relative to each other and relative to national norms.

Segregation and the Achievement Gap

This shocking waste of human potential has been blamed on the alleged disparity in educational opportunity between segregated Anglo and minority schools, as exemplified by Section 402 of the Civil Rights Act of 1964, which authorized a survey (eventuating in the EEOS) "concerning the lack of availability of equal educational opportunities for individuals by reason of race, color, religion, or national origin." The EEOS showed, unexpectedly, that such was not the case (see especially the illuminating discussion by Mosteller and Moynihan, 1972) as measured by the quality of school facilities and teachers available to both groups. The EEOS data do reveal a positive relationship between the percentage of Whites in his classroom and the achievement of a Black child (Commission on Civil Rights, 1967, p. 90, 102; McPartland, 1969). Since presumably a large proportion of the children participating in the EEOS, especially those in the elementary grades, were attending neighborhood schools, we cannot draw conclusions from those data about the anticipated effects of desegregation, which typically involves out-of-neighborhood bussing. Black parents who live in predominantly White neighborhoods may be different from those living in the Black ghetto in ways that bear on their children's academic achievement. Furthermore, as pointed out by St. John (1971) and others, the percentage of Whites in the classroom may be an effect rather than a cause of the Black pupil's achievement. That is, a high-achieving Black pupil is more likely than a low-achieving one to be placed in a predominantly White classroom, since many schools track by ability. This hypothesis is supported by the fact that in the EEOS data the relationship between achievement and the percentage of Whites holds for classroom but not for the percentage of Whites in the school (McPartland, 1969). If there is substance to the assumed effects of classroom ethnic composition, we had a situation *par excellence* in the school district we studied for producing salutary effects on the minority child's achievement, since when desegregation was complete the typical minority child found himself in a classroom in which approximately 80% of his peers were Anglo. According to Pettigrew (1969), a 20–40% minority group is ideal.[3]

The EEOS data also reveal a relationship, which was also subsequently questioned by St. John and Lewis (1971), between Black achievement and the socioeconomic status (SES) of the White peer group in the school. Our own data bearing on such effects are reported in Chapter 4.

The Home as an Arena of Influence

Where shall we look for clues as to what keeps the lid on the minority child's achievement? That it is not simply minority group status is clear from an examination of the performance of other minority groups, such as Orientals and Jews, two groups that do very well academically. There are two sources of influence that are likely candidates: the home and the classroom. It is undoubtedly true that in Oriental and Jewish homes high achievement is encouraged and rewarded. That this is not the case in Black and Mexican-American

---

[3] See footnote p. 11.

families is certainly part of the stereotype generally held of both groups, although our data (as we shall see in Chapter 12) and those collected by the EEOS tend not to support the stereotype fully. The EEOS Black children were more likely than Anglo children to report that their parents wanted them to do well in school. These findings could very well be an artifact of the testing situation. Since in the EEOS testing the child's teacher administered the test schedule, he may have been anxious to put his best foot forward.

In his review of the effects of family background on the development of cognitive skills, Jencks (1972) concluded that such factors as the educational attainment of the parents, the father's occupation, and family income all appear to correlate with the child's IQ and cognitive skills test scores, but the mechanisms that mediate the relationship are not clear. After considering the evidence regarding a possible hereditary link at the beginning of the chain, Jencks argued, as have others in the past, that given the facts of life in the United States, it is virtually impossible, from test scores alone, to pin down the possible existence of different intelligence genotypes between Blacks and Whites (it is somewhat easier, on the basis of twin studies, to demonstrate hereditary differences among Whites or among Blacks). Even if Black–White genotype differences do exist, unadulterated by differences in cultural overlay—Jensen notwithstanding—their effect on test scores is probably small relative to differences in native intelligence within both the Black and the White groups. The literature is reviewed more fully in Chapter 5.

Assumptions Underlying Desegregation Policy

Let us now examine some of the assumptions, both explicit and implicit, underlying the expectation that desegregation will have salutary effects on minority pupils. We think it is possible to assess the tenability of those assumptions by means of our data and those collected by others and to identify conditions that may and conditions that may not produce a desirable effect. The set of assumptions we describe is probably not exhaustive, nor would all proponents of desegregation endorse all of them. Some of the assumptions are more typically held by laymen, others by more sophisticated educators and social scientists, and still others by policy makers.

1. *The achievement gap is not due to a difference in native ability between Blacks and Whites.* As we have indicated above, the evidence here is very fuzzy and will remain fuzzy in the foreseeable future. We may eventually be able to identify the genotypes for intelligence in the germ plasm, which may indeed reveal racial differences. The genetic structure underlying intelligence is, however, undoubtedly quite complex, involving many genes and their interactions, which manifest as different intelligence phenotypes (Bodmer, 1972). Therefore, even when such identification is possible, it will still be difficult to make unequivocal statements regarding innate racial superiority or inferiority.

Even if intelligence differences do exist that favor one group or the other, within-group variation is huge relative to variation between groups. This holds for both IQ and achievement. It is therefore safe to assume that racial groups do not differ markedly in the proportion of their children who can profit from similar schooling.

It is extremely unlikely that the huge achievement gap that exists is due primarily to differences in native ability. Therefore, desegregation proponents insist that if we provide Black children[4] with the same opportunities as White children, their achievement will come up to par. They further argue that it is virtually impossible, because of social, political, and funding problems, to maintain separate but equal schools (although the EEOS data argue otherwise). It is also, however, quixotic to assume that merely placing a Black and a White child in the same classroom provides both with the same opportunity to learn. Most thoughtful proponents of desegregation would agree that such an assumption is naïve. There is more to the classroom situation than meets the eye. Chapters 10 and 11 examine the subtle effects of the social-psychological climate in the classroom on the minority child's achievement.

2. *The achievement gap is due to a difference in orientation toward educational attainment within the Black and the White communities.* This orientation is, of course, internalized by the children in those two communities, mostly through contact with their parents (Jencks, 1972; Whiteman, Brown, & Deutsch, 1967). A subassumption

---

[4] What we say about Blacks could also probably be said about Mexican-Americans. Our discussion, however, will focus mostly on Blacks since most of the previous concern and evidence has to do with Black performance, evidence on Mexican-Americans being sparse.

here is that *White values stress academic achievement more than do Black values.*

Studies of achievement need and achievement-related values in the Black community have produced mixed and sometimes perplexing results. Direct measures of achievement motivation typically show that of Blacks at all age levels as being unrealistically high (Coleman, 1966; Katz, 1968; Gordon, 1965; Boyd, 1952), whereas indirect measures such as those derived from projective test protocols and from psychiatric interviews reveal Blacks to have lower motivation than Whites (Rosen, 1959; Kardiner & Ovesery, 1962; Mussen, 1953; Mingione, 1965) and to show considerable anxiety and depression and a sense of futility. These latter manifestations are interpreted as being the result of uncommonly high aspirations among Blacks, coupled with their inability to achieve, given both their lack of training and the societal barriers that are difficult for most to surmount. Measures of self-esteem reveal a similar pattern. Questionnaire items calling for general, direct self-evaluative statements show Blacks to be on a par with Whites, whereas measures that tap below this self-presentational surface reveal marked negative self-feelings along with considerable disturbance.

Rosen (1959) argues that achievement does not depend simply upon the desire to achieve but that the child must learn to defer gratification and must develop realistic educational and vocational aspirations, which are primarily fostered in the home. There appears to be a disparity among parents at lower socioeconomic levels (which includes the majority of Blacks) between the aspirations they have for their children and their views of how those aspirations are to be realized (Weiner & Murray, 1963; Drake, 1965). Ausubel (1958) found evidence for the same disparity among Black children whom they report as aiming high but not being able to muster the wherewithal actually to strive for lofty goals. Thus the aspirations of both Black parents and their children are not functionally related to the path involved in eventually realizing high status. There is also evidence suggesting that Black parents may have unrealistically high desires for their children but have lowered sights regarding how high up the professional and economic ladder they actually expect their children to climb (Weiner & Murray, 1963).

Implied in the above discrepancy between desire and expectation is the assumption that part of the stigma of lower social status is a lack of personal efficacy in realizing academic and vocational goals. The syndrome of societal disadvantage includes this sense of helplessness and an inability to exercise control over circumstance (Battle & Rotter, 1963; Smith, 1968; Epps, 1969). The lower-class motivational orientation thus consists of poorly articulated goals along with low sense of control over one's fate.

3. *Achievement orientation deficits are reversible and are easier to reverse the younger the child.* Since it is difficult to design and implement a value change program in the home, the best place to get to the child is in the classroom. The evidence for the reversibility of values is sparse. For example, programs that have attempted to reduce prejudice have met with only minimal success. Some of the findings reported in Chapters 6, 7, and 8 bear on this problem.

4. *Social influence will occur in any group, so that the norms of conduct, beliefs, and values of the majority will influence the minority.* There is a large body of evidence from the social-psychological laboratory that such is the case. (See especially Chapters 9, 10, 11, and 12 in Jones & Gerard, 1967.) One study in particular (Gerard, 1954) found much greater influence by the majority upon the minority than vice versa. Many proponents of desegregation argue that as long as the Black students in a given classroom are in a minority, majority White influence over the minority will prevail, thus changing the achievement-related conduct, the beliefs, and the values of the Black children in the class. Evidence from the laboratory typically involves beliefs and values to which the experimental subject does not have a deep commitment. There is no systematic evidence supporting majority influence on deep-lying values. The recent broad-based but anecdotal evidence of the effectiveness of T-groups and encounter groups does, however, offer some hope for the possibility of changing strongly held values in a group context.

Reanalysis of the EEOS data (U.S. Commission on Civil Rights, 1967; McPartland, 1969) has provided some possible indirect evidence for majority influence on the minority. The data show a correlation between the proportion of Whites in his classroom and the achievement of the Black child. If we assume that "percentage White" influences the Black child's achievement (and not that the higher-achieving Black child is more likely to be placed in a class with a large proportion of Whites), then attitude and behavior change by the Black child in response to prevailing White norms might be the mediating process. These changes would presumably come about through cross-racial comparison (Pettigrew, 1969).

5. A crucial next assumption is that *there are no strong barriers*

to communication. In order for White values to prevail, intensive communication of some sort is necessary. This assumption implies that there is a fluid social structure in the classroom: that the racial subgroups will not segregate themselves into work and friendship cliques. This assumption raises the issue of desegregation versus integration. Often when a school district is desegregated, some form of ability tracking is instituted that tends to reinstate segregation, thus defeating the original purpose of desegregation. Under such circumstances, invidious comparison is likely to occur between the "fast" and the "slow" children. Furthermore, when any group of children, regardless of their ethnic identity, is bussed into a school, they are less likely to develop friendship ties with the children in the receiving school than with children in their own neighborhood. Thus by virtue of their inability to maintain contact after school and on weekends, children who are bussed or driven by car from a distance will find it relatively difficult to break into the friendship structure of the receiving school. The social structure of the classroom as described in Chapter 10 presents data relative to this assumption.

6. *Salutary effects will also be mediated by teachers' influences, which will tend to normalize achievement in the classroom.* The teacher will tend to teach up to the Anglos and the minority children will then pull themselves up to that level in order to stay in the running. This assumption is predicated on assumption 1, namely, that basic ability differences do not exist. That this normalization does not occur is clear from our data. Wilson (1963) contends that the data from his Berkeley study do reflect some normalization of instruction.

7. The previous assumption is based on a more fundamental assumption that is part of the American ethos, namely, that *competition is good and will lead to improved performance.* There is no doubt that under certain circumstances competition will result in an increase in the competitor's level of aspiration. Studies that have demonstrated such an effect have typically involved a relatively small performance difference between the competitors (see Jones & Gerard, 1967, Chapter 10, for a review of that research). Katz (1967) has argued that the higher standard represented by the performance of his White peers will act as a spur to the Black child. There is reason to believe that when a performance discrepancy is large, as is often the case between Black and White pupils, "bootstrapping" will not occur (the lower performer will not use the high performers as a comparison referent and will therefore not exert himself in order to raise his performance level).

8. An assumption related to and supporting the two previous assumptions is that *if the performance standard for a person is raised, he will improve in order to meet the new standard.* In order for this to occur, however, the person must both be motivated to reach the new standard and not have it exceed his grasp, so to speak. In other words, the situation has to be somehow tractable. There would be considerable disagreement among both psychologists and educators as to the most effective method for optimally programming successively higher performance goals. The work of Atkinson and his colleagues (see Chapter 9 in Atkinson, 1964) reveals subtle relationships among the relative strengths of the person's motivation to succeed, his motivation to avoid failure, and his goal-setting behavior. Setting overly high standards for the minority child may induce expectations of failure, which may, in turn, cause him to withdraw because of his fear of failure.

9. *Teachers will treat children similarly regardless of ethnic background.* This assumption implicitly underlies assumption 6. At best, it assumes that the teacher's ethnic attitudes will not unduly affect the minority child's performance. That this is not the case is clearly attested to in our data from both direct and indirect measures of teacher bias (see Chapter 11). A recent classroom study by Rubovitz and Maehr (1973) provides additional evidence that teachers tend to be more positively disposed toward Whites than toward Black children.

According to Katz (1967) self-reinforcement as well as self-discouragement are consequences of social learning, a process mediated by social reinforcement and modeling. This theory gives us reason to expect that under certain conditions desegregation can have a beneficial effect on the motivation of minority children. Teachers in predominantly Black schools tend to be more punitive and rejecting of pupils regardless of their academic performance (Clark, 1965; Davidson & Lang, 1968; Gottlieb, 1966). It is possible that positive reinforcement of minority children is more frequent when most of the class is composed of middle-class Anglo children. Chapter 11, which discusses the effect of teacher bias, and Chapter 10, which concerns peer group acceptance, present evidence that bears on this assumption.

10. *Desegregation will increase the minority child's self-esteem.* Katz's argument, outlined above, would predict such an effect. Katz has also argued that when the minority child finds that he is being treated like everybody else, he will no longer feel marginal, which, in turn, will reduce or even eliminate any self-derogating tendencies he may have

had. Chapters 6 and 7 present new evidence on the effects of self-esteem on level of aspiration.

11. Increased self-esteem will lead to increased achievement. Since goal-setting depends upon expectations of success or failure, and since self-esteem can be translated into such expectations, high self-esteem will lead to the setting of higher goals and subsequent improved performance. This assumption is also examined in Chapters 6 and 7.

The assumptions above that have to do with contact and teacher attitudes are captured by Amir (1969), who, writing from the perspective of an Israeli in assessing the effects of culture contact, delineated a complex of factors that may promote both favorable and unfavorable intergroup contact. Amir built upon the earlier discussion of contact by Allport (1954). In addition to the necessity of equal status within the contact situation, the outcome is influenced positively by such factors as the degree of intimacy of the contact, the extent of support by authority figures and the broader social climate, the pleasantness or "rewardingness" of the contact, the interaction between members of the different subgroups in functional activities, and the development of common goals that supersede subcultural differences. Negative effects may result from intergroup competition, tension-laden involuntary participation in the contact, the loss of prestige by one group during the contact, subcultural standards that are in conflict, and a belief that one group or another is of lesser ability. Amir cited a considerable amount of evidence in support of his contentions. Given this array of positive and negative influences, he suggests that we should not be surprised if intergroup contact between adults or children produces no general or consistent change in ethnic attitudes.

Carithers (1970) concluded that we lack knowledge of "what happens to whom under what conditions of school desegregation" (p. 43) and stressed the need for an approach that will take a more differentiated look at the school community and the individuals in it, which was one of the intentions of our study.

Amir's list of factors suggests some necessary qualifications of the assumptions we have discussed. Contact per se is not enough; rather it is the quality of the contact that is important. Given the outcome of the recent American experience with desegregation, it would appear that this obvious conclusion has been overlooked by policy makers and school administrators. An abiding optimism may have led some proponents of desegregation to assume that the previously all-White classroom would be welcoming and nurturant to the minority child, which has by and large not been the case. We believe that our data shed some light on the problem, which has been obscured by politicizing and invective.

One last word by way of summary. Much has been written about the conditions of contact necessary for successful desegregation. Little serious concern, however, has been given to the psychological processes that might mediate the relationship between variation in those conditions and the achievement of minority children. If we are eventually to exercise control over the circumstances that condition the well-being and the achievement of schoolchildren, we must develop an understanding of the causal nexus that promotes or inhibits school success. Our assumptions represent at attempt to spell out alternative but not necessarily mutually exclusive processes.

The outline of three such processes can be distinguished, each depending on the realization of certain conditions of contact. The simplest of these involves the minority child's raising his level of aspiration by virtue of a presumably more advanced curriculum and the higher performance standards in the desegregated as compared with the segregated classroom. This has also been referred to as "normalization of instruction." Many, but by no means all, desegregation proponents fail to take into account the delicate balance that undoubtedly exists between goals that are realistic and those that are not, as well as the kind of climate (e.g., absence of threat) that must exist in order for minority children to raise their level of aspiration.

A second process detailed by some of our assumptions is one of lateral value transmission, by which the minority child comes to adopt the prevalent majority group values. These values are presumed to be those associated with striving for excellence. Whereas in the first process improved performance is prompted by the presence of higher performance standards, the second process is mediated by a change in the child as a result of exposure to majority group norms, which, in turn, is assumed to induce striving.

The third process is also mediated by a change in the minority child—in his self-esteem—by virtue of his belief that he is being treated in the same way as are the majority children. This process is one that depends on the behavior of authority figures—his teacher and the school administration.

Each process is assumed to be engendered by a different feature of the contact situation, the raised performance standard, the higher achievement value norms of the majority peer group, or the positive attitudes of authority figures. One, two, or all three processes may operate in the classroom. Our study, as reported in the chapters that follow, can be seen as providing evidence of the extent to which these processes occurred in the desegregated classrooms in Riverside.

Chapter 2 provides some historical perspective and a flavor of the events leading up to and ensuing from the desegregation decision of the Riverside California School District Board of Education. Chapter 3 was designed to give an overall picture of the study's research design and its limitations. Chapter 4 is on short- and long-term achievement effects, and Chapter 5 is on IQ and its relationship to achievement. We then attempt to examine, in a series of three interrelated chapters, the effects of desegregation on attitudes and values and the way in which these personality predispositions might possibly mediate achievement. Chapter 9 attempts to examine linguistic changes and also reports an attempt to develop and use a measure of speech anxiety. The effects of the social and cultural context on the course of desegregation are reported in the three succeeding chapters, one attempting to examine the influence of teacher attitudes, the second concerned with the social structure of the classroom, and the third looking at factors in the parents' background. The final chapter attempts to summarize the study within the context of a broad societal perspective.

In this report of the data, the general focus is an attempt to examine initial ethnic differences on the particular variables in question, the effect of desegregation on these variables, and in turn, their influence on achievement.

References

Allport, G. W. *The nature of prejudice.* Cambridge, Mass.: Addison-Wesley, 1954.

Amir, Y. Contact hypothesis in ethnic relations. *Psychological Bulletin,* 1969, *71,* 319–342.

Atkinson, J. W. *An introduction to achievement motivation.* New York: Van Nostrand, 1964.

Ausubel, D. P. Ego development among segregated Negro children. *Mental Hygiene,* 1958, *42,* 362–369.

Battle, E. S. & Rotter, J. B. Children's feelings of personal control as related to social class and ethnic group. *Journal of Personality,* 1963, *31,* 482–490.

Bodmer, W. F. Race and IQ: The genetic background. In K. Richardson and D. Spears (Eds.), *Race and intelligence*. Baltimore: Penguin, 1972.

Boyd, G. F. The levels of aspiration of White and Negro children in a nonsegregated school. *Journal of Social Psychology*, 1952, *36*, 191–196.

Carithers, M. School desegregation and racial cleavage, 1954–1970: A review of the literature. *Journal of Social Issues*, 1970, *26*, 32–43.

Clark, K. B. *Dark ghetto*. New York: Harper & Row, 1965.

Coleman, J. S., & staff. Equality of educational opportunity. Washington, D.C.: U.S. Department of Health, Education, and Welfare, U.S. Government Printing Office, 1966.

Davidson, J. L., & Lang, G. Children's perceptions of their teachers' feelings toward them related to self perception, school achievement, and behavior. *Journal of Experimental Education*, 1968, *29*, 107–118.

Drake, St. C. The social and economic status of the Negro in the United States. *Daedelus*, 1965, *94*, 771–814.

Eells, K. W. *Intelligence and cultural differences: A study of cultural learning and problem solving*. Chicago: University of Chicago Press, 1951.

Epps, E. G. Correlates of academic achievement among northern and southern Negro students. *Journal of Social Issues*, 1969, *25*, 55–70.

Gerard, H. B. The effect of different dimensions of disagreement upon the communication process in small groups. *Human Relations*, 1954, *6*, 249–271.

Gordon, E. C. Characteristics of socially disadvantaged children. *Review of Educational Research*, 1965, *35*, 377–388.

Gottlieb, D. Teaching and students: The views of Negro and White teachers. In S. W. Webster (Ed.), *The disadvantaged learner*. San Francisco: Chandler, 1966.

Hunt, J. McV. Environment, development and scholastic achievement. In M. Deutsch, I. Katz, and A. R. Jensen (Eds.) *Social class, race, and psychological development*. New York: Holt, Rhinehart, and Winston, 1967.

Hunt, J. McV. The psychological basis for preschool cultural enrichment programs. In M. Deutsch, I. Katz, and A. Jensen (Eds.), *Social class, race and psychological development*. New York: Holt, Rinehart, and Winston, 1968.

Jencks, C., *Inequality: a reassessment of the effects of family and schooling in America*. New York: Basic Books, 1972.

Jensen, A. R. Do schools cheat minority children? Paper delivered in the Seminar Series on Education, Rand Corporation, Santa Monica, California, 1970.

Jones, E. E., & Gerard, H. B. *Foundations of social psychology*. New York: John Wiley & Sons, 1967.

Kardiner, A. & Ovesey, L. *The mark of oppression*. Cleveland: Meridian Books, 1962.

Katz, I. Socialization of academic motivation. In D. Levine (Ed.), *Nebraska symposium on motivation*. Lincoln: University of Nebraska Press, 1967.

Katz, I. Factors influencing Negro performance in the desegregated school. In M. Deutsch, I. Katz, and A. Jensen (Eds.), *Social class, race, and psychological development*. New York: Holt, Rinehart, and Winston, 1968.

McPartland, J. The relative influence of school and of classroom desegregation on the academic achievement of ninth grade Negro students. *Journal of Social Issues,* 1969, *25,* No. 3, 93–102.

Mingione, A. Need for achievement in Negro and White children. *Journal of Consulting Psychology,* 1965, *29,* 108–111.

Mosteller, F., and Moynihan, D. P. (Eds.). *On equality of educational opportunities.* New York: Random House, 1972.

Mussen, P. H. Differences between the TAT responses of Negro and White boys. *Journal of Consulting Psychology,* 1953, *17,* 373–376.

Pettigrew, T. F. The Negro in education: Problems and proposals. In I. Katz and P. Gurin (Eds.), *Race and the social sciences.* New York: Basic Books, 1969.

Rosen, B. C. Race, ethnicity, and achievement. *American Sociological Review,* 1959, *25,* 47–60.

Rubovitz, R. C., & Maehr, M. L. Pygmalion Black and White. *Journal of Personality and Social Psychology,* 1973, *25,* 210–218.

Smith, M. B. Competence and socialization. In J. A. Clausen (Ed.), *Socialization and Society.* Boston: Little Brown, 1968.

St. John, N. Desegregation and minority group performance. *Review of Educational Research,* 1971, *40,* 111–134.

St. John, N., & Lewis, R. The influence of school racial context on academic achievement. *Social Problems,* Summer 1971.

U.S. Commission on Civil Rights. Racial isolation in the public schools: A report. Washington, D.C.: U.S. Government Printing Office, 1967.

Vane, J. R. Relation of early school achievement to high school achievement when race, intelligence, and socioeconomic factors are equated. *Psychology in the Schools,* 1966, *3,* 124–129.

Weiner, M., & Murray, W. Another look at the culturally deprived and the levels of aspirations. *Journal of Educational Sociology,* 1963, *36,* 319–21.

Whiteman, M., Brown, B., & Deutsch, M. Some effects of social class and race on children's language and intellectual abilities. In M. Deutsch et al (Eds.) *The Disadvantaged Child.* New York: Basic Books, 1967.

Wilson, A. Social stratification and academic achievement. In A. Harry Passow (Ed.), *Education in depressed areas.* New York: Teachers College, Columbia University, 1963.

2

The Historical Setting

Irving G. Hendrick

Early in the present century the public schools were asked to serve as the principal agency for inducting the youth of European immigrants into the social and economic ways of a new land. More recently, institutionalized education has been given an opportunity to contribute toward improving the quality of life for the non-European grandchildren and great-grandchildren of those Americans who were not principal beneficiaries of the earlier thrust. A key difference is that the present challenge also requires a basic restructuring of attitudes and policies across the entire social order, a process likely to produce mental anguish among both majority and minority elements of the population. Schools historically have been expected to serve as agencies for social preservation and for inducting youth into the ways of society. In the present they are also being called upon to help produce a basic reform in the way Americans behave toward one another—a rare and fateful challenge indeed.

Following the historic Brown decision of the U.S. Supreme Court in 1954, school authorities were slowly forced into an awareness that racially separate schooling cannot result in education of equal quality. The decade following that decision did not, on the other hand, produce anything like a national commitment to integration. Not unlike other social objectives, it became a desirable end in the minds of many, providing the price—economic, political, and emotional—was not too great.

Irving G. Hendrick • University of California at Riverside, Riverside, California.

The Riverside Unified School District in southern California became one of those rare places where the price and other conditions were
right for change. It was not the first school system in America to
develop and implement a plan for the total desegregation and eventual
integration of children in its schools. What is somewhat surprising, and
a commentary as much on national reluctance in this area as on
Riverside's progressive attitude, is that its school integration decision of
October 25, 1965, entitled it to a couple of other "firsts." It became, for
example, the first school system in a city exceeding 100,000 in population, and with a total kindergarten through grade 12 enrollment of more
than 20,000 to develop and implement a full-scale plan.[1] Another
unique feature of the Riverside experience was that the administration
and board were able to develop and adopt this plan within seven weeks
after being confronted with a petition from minority parents vigorously
requesting integration. Given the hostile social and political reaction to
court-ordered desegregation in northern as well as southern communities during the early seventies, the quick and comparatively simple
resolution of the segregation issue in Riverside appears almost spec-
tacular.

A reasonable understanding of Riverside's success in desegregating
its schools must be based upon a knowledge of some characteristics of
the local community, of the goals adopted and means employed to accomplish them by national and local forces pressing for integration, of
the social view and larger philosophical orientation of school officials
responsible for making policy, and of the political dynamics operating
between the school board and the larger local community.

The Community Setting

Located approximately 60 miles east of Los Angeles, in the
Riverside–San Bernardino–Ontario metropolitan area, an area with a

---

[1] The commonly used differentiation between desegregation and integration is used
throughout this article; i.e., *desegregation* refers to the physical process of bringing
ethnic groups together in the same classrooms, while *integration* refers to the much
more complex process of comfortable social interaction. *Racial balance* appears to have
many and variable meanings. As used here it refers to a school with a maximum
minority enrollment of less than 50%. Ideally each school in a racially balanced district
would not deviate more than 10% from the district average (Greenfield, 1967).

population slightly in excess of 1,100,000, Riverside's own population was estimated at 133,200 in 1965. Although the boundaries of the school district and the city are not contiguous, the population of the school district approximates that of the city. The total school enrollment for the 1965–66 term was 25,374, spread among 3 senior highs, 5 junior highs, 27 elementary schools, and 1 school for physically handicapped youth.

During this same year, 1965–66, the minority enrollment of the Riverside schools stood at 16.71%, including 6.09% Blacks, 9.96% Mexican-Americans, and 0.66% other minorities. By 1973–74 all figures had increased; 27% total minority, 10% Black, 15% Mexican-American, and 2% other minorities. In 1966–67, the state minority average was 20.49% for districts of comparable size, i.e., those with enrollments between 20,000 and 49,999. Riverside enrolled slightly more Black and slightly fewer Mexican-American pupils than other California districts in its size classification (California State Department of Education, 1967). Clearly the total number of minority students was small enough to permit students of the majority group to be the dominant group in virtually all schools.

Basically Riverside was viewed as a pleasant residential town of moderate Republican persuasion. Its economy, based heavily on the citrus industry and lacking in industrial development until after World War II, came to support only a relatively modest number of minority citizens. By 1960 Blacks constituted 4.7% of the total population and Mexican-Americans, 8.5% (U.S. Census Bureau, 1961). Consistent with the national pattern, racial and ethnic discrimination in the areas of employment, housing, schooling, and social relationships were all part of the city's history.

By the mid-1960s, although an isolated minority property holder or two could be found residing in most of Riverside's residential areas, Riverside was still a city of marked segregation. Research conducted by Joan W. Moore and Frank G. Mittelbach, in conjunction with the Mexican-American Study Project at UCLA, found Riverside ranking third among 13 California cities in terms of Black and Mexican-American segregation as measured by an index of residential dissimilarity. Measured by degree of overall residential segregation, Riverside was found to be at very nearly the same level as Los Angeles, but considerably more segregated than San Francisco, Oakland, or San Diego. The same study also found Mexican-Americans to be more rigidly segregated than Blacks in the southwestern states (Moore & Mittlebach, 1966).

Not unlike other communities, the deliberate gerrymandering of attendance areas to exclude minority students from certain public schools was practiced in Riverside many times over until the early 1950s. Separation of Mexican-American children was assumed to be legal and was practiced in California prior to 1946.[2] Legal segregation of Black children, on the other hand, had not been sanctioned under California law since 1890.

Two of Riverside's three elementary schools with minority enrollments of virtually 100% in 1965, Irving and Casa Blanca, had been recognized as minority schools for over 40 years. The third, Lowell, although located less than a half mile south of Irving, had served the city as a school for Anglo children from 1911 until the early 1950s, when it became desegregated. Both served the eastside area of the city, while Casa Blanca served a distinctive Mexican-American settlement by the same name located a little more than three miles southwest of the eastside.

The boundaries separating Lowell from Irving had been adjusted periodically between 1911 and 1952 for the purpose of maintaining the homogeneous racial composition of the two schools. The few Anglo children who by chance continued to live in the Irving area found little difficulty enrolling at Lowell. Between 1950 and 1961, during a decade of rapid growth, shifts in residential living patterns and a series of school district boundary decisions changed the eastside picture dramatically. As the Anglo population continued to grow to the west and the south of the Lowell area, new schools were opened to accommodate them, thereby effectively desegregating Lowell. Finally, with the opening of Alcott School in 1961, Lowell's minority population jumped dramatically from 50% to 90%. In spite of its eventual development into a segregated minority neighborhood, the Lowell area's history, location, and socioeconomic status remained comparatively higher than that of either Irving or Casa Blanca.

Although the eastside, especially that part of it within the Irving School attendance area, was populated by more Mexican-Americans

---

[2] Overt segregation of Mexican-American children, never having been written into the law, was ruled illegal in the district court decision of *Mendez vs. Westminster School District of Orange County* in 1946.

than Blacks by 1950,[3] the distinctly Mexican-American *barrio* in town
was Casa Blanca. Over a period of 44 years, Casa Blanca School
developed into a significant community entity with a closer relationship
between the people of the community and the school than was typical of
other elementary schools in Riverside. Prior to 1952 it was, in effect, a
kind of minority island with nonminority children on all four of its sides
attending other Riverside schools, principally Palm. More than a
school, it seemed almost a kind of Anglo-American consulate to the
people of Casa Blanca. For 41 of those years the school was headed by
the same principal, Mabra B. Madden. If it served as more than a
center of elementary grade instruction for children, it was because its
leader served as more than a school principal.

Madden was helpful on many fronts, sometimes urging parents to
use hospitals, directing them to the appropriate public and private
agencies for needed assistance or service, helping them find employment,
occasionally paying a telephone bill or offering other limited service
himself, and acting as a notary public, a marital counselor, an amateur
attorney, and an unofficial mayor for the people of Casa Blanca.
Particularly during the earlier years, but continuing to some extent
through 1964, a number of parents became dependent upon his helping
hand. Others were less involved, and a few, particularly in the later
years, even resented what they considered to be a kind of benevolent pa-
tronship cultivated by the principal.

Through the course of more than four decades the quality of life in
Casa Blanca changed for the better as the population became less dependent upon harvesting crops for a living. By the mid-1950s, instead of
opening school in September with one-third of the pupils registered, as
had been the case during the twenties and thirties, the school began
with nearly its full enrollment. Illiteracy had been greatly reduced, and
community pride increased. An active minority within the community,
now including a few Blacks, became vigorous advocates of community
improvements. So far had the community come by the mid-1950s that
the *Saturday Evening Post* featured an article concerning Casa Blanca
entitled, "The Slum That Rebelled" (Taylor, 1956).

Although the minority schools had been discriminated against over
several decades in tangible ways relating to physical facilities and staff

[3] According to the Riverside *Press* of February 15, 1950, Irving enrolled 173 Blacks, 320
Mexican-Americans, and 5 "various" pupils during the 1949–50 term.

assignments, by the fifties most discrimination of this sort was ending. Segregation remained as Lowell was about to join Irving and Casa Blanca as totally minority institutions. The opening of Victoria School in 1955 and Emerson School in 1956 cut deep into Lowell's enrollment of Caucasian pupils. The opening of Alcott School in 1961 came close to evacuating them from Lowell; approximately 35 remained out of a total projected enrollment of 356. The board and top-level administration were no longer attempting to implement a segregationist policy, but neither were they willing to adopt a policy that would deliberately avoid segregation. The fact that the new neighborhoods were all Anglo, while older neighborhoods, such as the one surrounding Lowell School, were nearly all minority, was of little concern. It was acknowledged by 1961 that gerrymandering school boundaries in order to preserve segregation was wrong. It was also assumed that setting boundaries for the specific purpose of achieving integration was wrong or, at best, a highly questionable practice.

A Growing Awareness of Segregation

The decision to place the boundary between Lowell and Alcott schools at the Tequesquite Arroyo, thereby immediately transforming Lowell from a school with approximate racial balance to one almost totally minority, produced a polite howl of protest from Black and Anglo residents of the Lowell area. From this time forward, segregated schooling would be an issue in Riverside. The protest did lead to the appointment of a joint school board–community study committee, recommendations from which stimulated board adoption of an ineffectual voluntary transfer policy. Although implemented immediately, it was not until 1963–64 that four Black children requested and received transfers out of Lowell. Perhaps more important than the policy was the opportunity it provided for several board members, including the future president of the board, as well as key members of the administration, to become familiar with an emerging social and educational issue.

In October 1962, soon after the State Board of Education's decision requiring local school authorities to "exert all effort to avoid and eliminate segregation of children on account of race or color," Riverside Superintendent Bruce Miller initiated a study of school boundaries and attendance areas. By March the district's policy on boundaries was amended to permit "ethnic composition of the residents near the school, the student body, and the adjacent schools and school areas" to be considered for the purpose of avoiding *de facto* segregation (from the minutes of the school board meeting of March 18, 1963). In concrete terms it led to some relatively minor adjustments in the boundaries of a few elementary and secondary schools over the next three years.

The early sixties in America witnessed the rise of two notable devices intended to ease the pain of inferior segregated schooling for minority students. The transfer policy was one; compensatory education programs the other. Compensatory education, without integration, did not produce significant results in Riverside. It lasted as an official district program for two years, was never funded adequately, and in a sense was not even given a chance to fail. The new programs that were implemented, while only minimally effective, did touch the minority pupils in the three *de facto* segregated schools. The transfer policy to provide "integrated" experiences had not even touched its target group.

From a community relations standpoint at least, the steps taken by the school district regarding compensatory education between 1961 and 1964 did appear to be having some payoff. On May 16, 1964, the Board of Education received an award for "outstanding service to the community in acknowledgement of and sincere efforts toward resolution of the problem of defacto segregation in Riverside" from the Riverside branch of the NAACP. The 1964–65 school year witnessed a continuance of communication and cordial relations with the minority community, but no major shifts in board policy. At a meeting between minority community leaders and school officials on September 15, 1964, several significant suggestions relating to the problems of *de facto* segregation were made by the leaders present: "Do not let compensatory education be a substitute for real integration. Continue program, but work on defacto segregation also." "Aim toward closing Casa Blanca and placing students in adjacent schools." "Plan future schools in such a way as to permit closing of Casa Blanca." "Seek funds from the Office of Education for desegregation." "Don't be too concerned with feelings of the community in closing a school. There would not be much resistance to closing Irving and Lowell, even if parents had to provide some transportation." "Enlarge attendance area of Emerson to maintain racial balance."

The 11 months that followed witnessed the rise of increased disillusionment on the part of concerned Black parents. The compensatory education program was not producing the desired results, class size was not being reduced as rapidly as had been hoped, and the transfer policy was not being administered to the liking of some eastside parents. Once discussion began on what should, could, and would be done, minority aspirations and hopes, followed shortly by disappointments and even bitterness, developed at a far faster pace than the school system's willingness and ability to institute the changes. On May 17, 1965, Associate Superintendent Berry's "Supplemental Report on Instruction, 1964–65" was presented to the board but was not discussed. Noticeable among the points made in the context of his brief discussion on improving educational programs for economically and educationally disadvantaged youth, was the following statement:

> Considerable thought and effort should continue to be found, not only on how to improve programs in defacto segregated schools, but how to eliminate the schools themselves.

As far as the board and the superintendent were concerned, this problem was one that the district would continue to keep abreast of and work to solve, but not one that demanded any immediate and substantive corrective attention; certainly not one that demanded an immediate policy of school desegregation. By summer's end, 1965, school officials had shown practically no disposition to change the virtually totally segregated conditions at Casa Blanca (99.8% minority), Irving (100% minority), and Lowell (97.2% minority). Unlike the opening of 1964, "one of the smoothest" Superintendent Miller had ever experienced, the 1965 beginning would be hectic.

A Policy Whose Time Had Arrived: Events Leading to Desegregation

The direct factors that led to desegregation in Riverside were local and are not particularly difficult to determine. The indirect factors were both local and national in nature and are somewhat more difficult to assess with the same confidence. The mid-sixties in America was a time when educational researchers were beginning to return increasingly gloomy evaluation reports concerning the effectiveness of compensatory education programs, but it was the period prior to the school district decentralization and community control thrusts that were to develop in Black communities before the end of the decade. It also marked a time when direct protest activity seemed capable of stimulating desired changes. Three and a half weeks before the confrontation in Riverside over segregated schooling, the riots in south-central Los Angeles (Watts) were acquiring national attention and even closer local attention. During the early days of September 1965, before direct confrontation occurred locally, the city newspapers carried articles headed "Racial Violence Erupts in North, South Cities," "Two Inquiries Underway into Los Angeles Riots," "Greene County Schools Off Limits to Dr. King for Demonstrations," "Mississippi Governor Calls Out Troops to Prevent Riots," "Negroes Turned Away by Two Alabama Schools," and "Boston Negro Pupils Move to White Schools." Reports such as these, presumably capable of stimulating thought and fear in school and city officials, coupled with a general legal mandate against *de facto* segregation, served to set the historical stage for Riverside's action.

Although no court action was involved, the integration decision would be explained, and to some extent defended by the board, on the grounds that the district was under legal obligation to act.[4] In California the State Board of Education stated on June 14, 1962, that "the policy of elimination of existing segregation and thoughtful curbing any tendency toward its growth must be given serious and thoughtful consideration by all persons involved at all levels." On the other hand, it was also plain to see that federal and state pressure was not yet sufficient to force school systems to adopt desegregation plans. In the absence of either intense local pressure or court orders, most districts were able to sit tight and do nothing.

General dissatisfaction with the schools on the part of Riverside's Black parents sustained the desegregation drive, but a specific grievance initiated it. On Wednesday, September 1, a small group of Black women met to discuss their complaints against the schools, particularly what they perceived as harassment in obtaining transfers out of Lowell. None of those present were active in local civil rights organizations. The most concrete decision coming out of their informal get-together on Wednesday was to hold a larger meeting on Friday evening, September

[4] The most relevant legal decision influencing the board as of 1965 was probably *Taylor vs. Board of Education of City School District of New Rochelle,* 191 F. Supplement (1961), 181.

3, at which time men would be in attendance, and, it was hoped, a more concrete plan of action would be formulated. Community "action type people," plus two city officials—the mayor and city councilman from the eastside—were in attendance. Those Black citizens believed to be opposed to direct action were excluded. Some NAACP members were present as individuals, but since this was being shaped as a movement of parents, organizational representation was deliberately avoided.[5] Besides, the local NAACP chapter could not be counted on to wage a vigorous direct-action campaign for desegregation.

It was at this Friday meeting that a decision was reached to circulate a petition calling for the closing of Lowell and Irving schools and to push rapidly for complete integration of the school system. Old and new grievances were aired. Tempers flared. Militant comments were followed by more moderate ones. Determination, followed by vacillation, followed again by determination, was the order of the evening. Through it all there arose a commitment to accomplish something tangible. A simple show of good faith by the board, or what Robert Crain identified as "symbolic equality," would not suffice (see Crain, 1968, p. 111). In spite of reservations expressed by some middle-class Blacks, a petition drive was agreed upon. If support appeared adequate, the result of their success, a signed petition, would be presented to the school board on the following Tuesday, September 7. The petition itself was simple and direct:

> We, the undersigned parents of the Riverside school district, do hereby petition the Riverside School Board to take affirmative steps to improve the educational opportunities for minorities and to eliminate segregation in city schools by closing Lowell and Irving Schools and by reassigning these students to other schools in the area which have previously had less than 10% minority group students.

By Monday evening, September 6, as community leaders prepared to confront the school board at 4:00 p.m. the following day, they were armed with a small bundle of petitions containing 396 signatures. As events unfolded during the night, they were to have much more going for them. Shortly before 4:00 a.m. on Tuesday, September 7, a deliberately set fire swept through the old building of Lowell School, lay-

---

[5] Black men and women whose previous behavior had led the organizers to think of them as subservient to the White power structure—i.e., those thought to be "Uncle Toms" and "handkerchief heads"—were not invited.

ing waste to six classrooms and the auditorium, thereby displacing 143 pupils who were scheduled to begin classes on the following Monday. The question of who started the fire was never answered, nor was it particularly relevant to either school authorities or the petitioners for integration. The fact of the fire was relevant to all. Fear of "another Watts," coupled with the fact that 143 students were now without classrooms, proved a great incentive to action.

Meeting that Tuesday afternoon, the board received the petitions and listened to the petitioners. Without a clear idea of the district's capacity to absorb students from two segregated schools, the board was not about to agree on the permanent transfer of all Lowell and Irving pupils to other schools. It did agree to hold a special meeting on Monday, September 13, to consider the requests further, and it accepted the superintendent's recommendation to put Lowell on double sessions temporarily. The meeting was obviously not pleasant for the board, and it was decidedly unpleasant for the superintendent.

Accusations, some overstated but almost all valid, were hurled. Segregated schools offered inferior education.[6] School officials had gerrymandered school boundaries in order to segregate minority pupils. They had made exceptions to their own rules, permitting children from the majority group to attend majority schools, even when living in a minority district. Compensatory education represented "separate but equal" education, but it was not equal; it was a "paper tiger." The transfer policy was impractical for most Black families, and besides, most Blacks had trouble getting transfers.

The board's willingness to accept Superintendent Miller's recommendation of putting Lowell students on double sessions served to increase the fury of Lowell parents and helped stimulate a decision by them to boycott the schools. This form of pressure touched a sensitive nerve at school headquarters. Early on Wednesday both the superintendent and the board president tried unsuccessfully to make contact with the boycott leaders. It was clear that the boycott organizers

---

[6] Some teachers at Lowell and Irving took this charge personally and were offended by it. On some occasions it was implied that since the schools were inferior, the teachers must be inferior, too. Such assertions were particularly invalid in the case of Lowell School. There half of the faculty held master's degrees, two teachers were bilingual, one spoke three languages, two were considered districtwide experts in the teaching of reading, and one was an expert in speech therapy.

were not going to initiate contacts with school officials. "We have no intention of going to them. We have been talking to them three years and getting nowhere," remarked a Black mother to a *Press* reporter (Riverside *Press*, September 9, 1965).

That same morning the superintendent was persuaded by two members of his own staff and the board president that double sessions at Lowell were neither wise nor necessary. This concession was revealed to boycott leaders by the board president, Arthur L. Littleworth, later in the day at an eastside home that was doubling as boycott headquarters. Maintaining steadfastly that theirs was a community movement, the boycott leaders would agree to nothing on their own. They did arrange for Littleworth and other school officials to meet with eastside parents at Irving School on Friday evening, September 10. The extra two days gave the administration time to make a feasibility study, the contents of which were revealed by Littleworth at the Friday meeting.

Children in grades kindergarten through 3 at Lowell would be transported by bus at district expense to seven schools with low minority enrollments. There they would be integrated into established classes. The entire problem of segregation would be studied. No plans were being formulated to replace the old Lowell building on its present site. On the contrary, it would be logical to phase the remainder of the school out in future plans. Any future move toward integration would include Irving and Casa Blanca.

Questions, assertions, and impassioned pleas by members of the community grew more and more hostile as the evening progressed. Many speakers demanded complete integration immediately. One pointed out that Irving was a perfectly good school and could well be shared by Anglo students. Bussing had been used for segregation purposes prior to 1961; now it could be used to aid integration. The dominant sentiment among the approximately 200 citizens in attendance that evening was clearly running in favor of maintaining maximum pressure on the board by moving ahead with boycott plans. One impassioned critic asserted, "You cannot lose your momentum. He wants you to go home and feel they are going to do something when they are not going to do anything" (Riverside *Press*, September 11, 1965). As the level of anger heightened, the chairman suggested that Littleworth leave, a course he gladly followed.

The second weekend of the crisis began badly for school officials.

The Friday night meeting had been a disaster from their perspective. Possibly the most awesome sign of all was that Superintendent Miller had been advised not to attend the Friday evening gathering and was thus forced to remain at home with hurt pride. As the symbol of an intensely distrusted school authority, he represented to some much of what was wrong with the schools. On the other hand, Associate Superintendent Berry, who inside of three years would be superintendent himself, possessed greater rapport with the minority community, partly the result of personality factors, but also because of having worked more closely and directly with eastside parents over a period of several years.

During the week of September 7 and the weekend that followed, meeting after meeting was held, followed by still more meetings. In addition to numerous personal contacts between administrators and board members, between school officials and city officials, and between school officials and the boycott leaders, several group meetings were held in a sometimes frantic attempt to avoid trouble on the opening day of school, Monday, September 13. City fathers were most concerned about the possibility of violence, while the schoolmen were still trying desperately to avert a boycott that could result in a serious loss of state revenue if school attendance dropped drastically over a protracted period of time.

In spite of considerable local effort, and even assistance in intergroup relations from the State Department of Education, Monday, September 13, marked the beginning and the ending of a peaceful boycott. So far as pressure was concerned, the actual holding of "freedom school" classes for some 200 children probably was not necessary. The administration and board did not alter their plans after seeing the boycott classes in session, but they certainly had made some alterations in the process of trying to head off the meeting of those classes in the first place. Each party in the struggle had less than a full understanding of where the other stood. Furthermore, each had certain role expectations it felt obligated to play out. The boycott leaders did not really believe that the board was already committed to integration, but even if they had been convinced, it would have been difficult to call the plan off once it had gained momentum in the Black community. Fear of being accused of having been taken in by the White power structure assured that the movement's leaders would want the school to operate at least one day. When the boycott was called off in the evening of September 13, it was done for practical reasons and not before considerable discussion by many. For their part, the board members did not know that the boycott movement would be hard pressed to sustain even a week of operation.

At its meeting on September 13 the board agreed that a comprehensive plan for desegregating the schools should be prepared by the superintendent's office and submitted to the board not later than the second meeting in October. In the course of discussion prior to that action several Black citizens again spoke in favor of cross-bussing Anglo students into Irving School. The principal boycott leaders were not at all interested in pushing a cross-bussing plan. They felt, and with precise accuracy, that Littleworth considered it unthinkable. Nothing could have done more to arouse Anglo counterpressure than an active consideration of the idea. Riverside, after all, was not known for its liberal social and political views. Limitations imposed by political realities aside, a cross-bussing plan probably would not have been feasible in Riverside anyway. Only 3 of the 26 elementary schools were predominately minority, and of these only 1 was a totally adequate facility. Furthermore, minority children comprised less than 20% of the total school-age population in an area of nearly 70 square miles.

Without the petition–fire–boycott sequence it is clear that the board would not have been as receptive to change as it was now inclined to be. Desegregation, if it had proceeded at all, would have been far slower. Superintendent Miller called the fire a great "catalyst" to action.[7] One of his closest associates in the administration acknowledged that "the fire made integration possible, while the freedom schools and the loud meetings helped." Another intimate associate, when asked to evaluate what difference the fire made, responded even more succinctly: "Total." It had, after all, displaced children in need of classrooms, led to the recovery of damages from fire insurance coverage (thereby permitting the money to be used for construction elsewhere), provided a good reason for closing a school that the board had considered closing in 1961, and helped to stimulate the board to active consideration of an integration plan. Even apart from the social, educational, and moral questions concerning desegregation, transporting students in the Lowell attendance area to other schools suddenly made good business sense.

In planning his announcement of a limited bussing program on September 13, Littleworth encountered no opposition from other

---

[7] Statement made to the author by Bruce Miller on May 22, 1968.

members on the board. As an attorney he was well aware of the legal issues involved in *de facto* segregation, not to mention the larger issue of justice. During the seven weeks between Labor Day and October 25, 1965, he proved highly effective in offering moral leadership as well as in demonstrating political skill. As a middle-of-the-road board on most social and educational issues, the members had not been disposed to move very far ahead of the community they served. Their willingness to espouse integration put them somewhat ahead on that issue.

Adoption and Implementation of an Integration Plan

Three key groups had a hand in formulating the *Proposed Master Plan for School Integration,* which was presented to the board for consideration on October 18: the administration, an "Advisory Committee for Integrated Schools," and the board itself. The appointment of community advisory groups is a typical approach employed by boards seeking to produce a consensus. It worked well in this case. Both the advisory committee and the board helped to determine the direction of the plan, with the administration preparing the actual document. It was clear from what had already developed by September 13 that the closing of Lowell School and extensive pupil transportation would constitute major elements in the plan. It was not yet clear in terms of formal policy whether Irving would remain open for children whose parents preferred having them attend a nearby school; whether Anglo children would be bussed into Irving; how soon Casa Blanca would be desegregated; or indeed, how soon full desegregation would begin at Lowell.

Of all the issues, only the one dealing with Casa Blanca proved really troubling. Opposition in the Casa Blanca community to the closing of the school was almost unanimous at first. Superintendent Miller and his staff knew that the board would not require Anglo children to be bussed into Irving. They were also fairly certain that the advisory committee and the board would accept a clean break with segregation, specifically the closing of Irving as an elementary school.

By October 18, a *Proposed Master Plan for School Integration* was presented to the board by Superintendent Miller for discussion, and a week later it was adopted. Its heart, a "Proposed Plan for Integration," was all spelled out on a single page. As expected, it called for the closing of Lowell and Irving schools by September 1966. The Irving facility, however, would remain open for special programs, such as Head Start classes, a special reading clinic, and adult education. Approximately 126 pupils at Emerson, a school with 55% minority enrollment at the time, would be transported to two predominately Anglo schools, thereby reducing Emerson's racial imbalance.

The complicated problem of integration for Casa Blanca children was handled more gingerly. A citizens' committee on Casa Blanca would be formed to study the problem and make a recommendation by May 1, 1966. Nevertheless the plan itself declared that some concrete steps were to be taken for the reduction of segregation there by September 1966. Boundary changes, resulting in a one-third reduction in the number of students attending Casa Blanca, were to be made by September 1966, unless the committee could propose a better plan. If the committee's proposal for 1966–67 failed to cover the entire community, beginning that year transportation would be provided at district expense to students whose parents preferred that they attend an integrated school.

Transitional education, the adaptation of compensatory education to an integrated setting, was also a part of the plan. Tutorial help, remedial reading classes, improved counseling procedures, and various kinds of vocational retraining programs were all to have their place. The administration declared its intent to submit applications for appropriate federal funds to help defray the costs of all special programs. Moreover, if adopted, the plan would commit the district to the continued prevention of segregation. School boundaries would be changed and "other adjustments" made to ensure that segregated schools would not develop in the future.

In all, 565 pupils would be transferred by September 1966. This would be in addition to those relocated in September 1965 as a direct result of the Lowell fire and the demands of minority parents. Nineteen additional classrooms would be needed, four of which were already available at the schools to be designated "receiving schools." Nine would be portables already owned by the district, which could be moved to the receiving schools. Six would have to be built. After the classroom shifting was completed, no receiving school was expected to have fewer than 8.5% nor more than 17.8% minority students.

The capital outlay involved in new classrooms was estimated at approximately $200,000, almost all of which could be made up by the recovery of $159,000 in insurance from the Lowell fire, plus the revenue received from the sale of the Lowell site.[8] Bus transportation called for in the plan would cost an estimated $45,700 during 1966–67, but approximately $35,000 would be saved from reduced operational expenses coming as a direct result of desegregation. According to the *Proposed Master Plan for School Integration,* the net operating cost to the district would be $10,000–$11,000 per year.

The passing of even seven weeks between September 6 and October 25 permitted Anglo citizens, concentrated in one affluent neighborhood, to collect some three times as many signatures opposing integration as were contained in the original petition of minority citizens. By the time of the October 18 and 25 meetings of the board, the opposition's voice was at least equal to that of those favoring integration. Nevertheless, by eliminating the issue of cross-bussing and by moving rapidly, the board was able to accomplish a remarkable feat by 1965 standards. President Littleworth knew that the board would have to allow enough time for the issue to be discussed—but not enough time for the opposition to gain an upper hand.

In spite of the intense short-term frustrations experienced by Black parents and school officials, the overall political dynamics of the Riverside experience were comparatively simple. To begin, the school board was still able to function along its traditional line of consensus politics, a common pattern among rural and suburban school districts (Iannaccone & Lutz, 1970). Incumbent defeat had not been experienced in the last decade. On the integration question, as on other substantive issues, the socially and ideologically homogeneous board was able to remain unified. This proved an advantage to the board president in that he was able to communicate with boycott leaders relatively freely, secure in the knowledge that his fellow board members would support him.

At the same time, the board had established an enviable record for not permitting itself to become isolated from the community at large, something that has proved a hazard—perhaps even a pattern—for inbred boards. Also fortunate was the fact that neither the superintendent nor the board president felt his leadership seriously threatened by the other. Some of the political advantages were the result of the superintendent and the board president's skill; others are attributable to

[8] On November 7, 1966, the board sold the Lowell Elementary School property to a church for $36,200; *Minutes,* November 7, 1966. The eventual cost of moving four classrooms from Lowell to neighboring Alcott was $56,000; *Minutes,* May 16, 1966.

local circumstances not controlled by either. The absence of any sustained opposition to the eventual desegregation plan was partially the result of accrued goodwill enjoyed by the school system in the larger community. Even opponents of desegregation were prepared to allow school officials one small mistake. Since the financial cost promised to be modest, and since bussing of Anglo students was not involved, opponents were never given the grounds to become terribly exercised in their opposition. School desegregation was simply a hard issue to oppose when it involved such a minimal inconvenience and cost to the majority community.

Even though done for defensible reasons, one-way bussing made it obvious that minority children would have to bear the brunt of the adjustment problems accompanying desegregation. It would be they, after all, who would be leaving familiar surroundings and traveling to unfamiliar ones. Not all Black families on the eastside were readily willing to make this sacrifice, but for the most part they were convinced that desegregation would result in improved education for their children. The Casa Blanca community, on the other hand, was determined to retain their community school. Early in November 1965 Superintendent Miller appointed a 40-member Casa Blanca Study Committee, composed mainly of Casa Blanca residents, to recommend how best to integrate children from that area. After five meetings with the superintendent and members of his staff, the committee appeared convinced that closing the school by 1967 was in the best interests of Casa Blanca children. The skill and personal diplomacy of the superintendent had paid off. Nevertheless a deep-seated opposition to the closing remained.

The initial plan for physically integrating approximately 264 kindergarten and primary grade children from Lowell and Irving in September 1965 was far from optimal. Since it was handled by grade level, children of the same family in the elementary grades were sometimes split into two or more schools. Desegregation by grade level was not the kind of plan adopted for implementation in September 1966. In drawing up the basic plan, each elementary school with a minority enrollment lower than the 16.7% district average was designated as a potential receiving school. Space available was not a criterion. Only 3 schools with fewer than 16.7% minority children were not included among the receiving schools, 2 because they had already been employed as receiving schools in February 1966, and a third because its enrollment had already reached the designated 1000-student maximum for elementary schools. The other 11 schools were all designated receiving schools after rough estimates were made regarding the number of pupils each could accommodate. To a large extent, that number was based on how many children would be required to bring each school's minority percentage close to the district average.

Once the approximate number of students appropriate for each school to receive was determined the next task was to match children to schools by block areas. The homes of pupils were located on a map, and then they were divided, block by block, into groups approximating a number already determined as appropriate for each receiving school. In effect, where formerly one geographic area—most of the eastside—was divided into 2 school attendance areas, Lowell and Irving, that same area was now being divided into 12 attendance areas.[9] The boundaries, while as subject to change as any other school boundaries, were intended to be permanent. With the exception of the children who formerly attended Lowell but who had recently become a part of an expanded Alcott neighborhood, students would no longer be attending "neighborhood" schools. They would, on the other hand, still be attending school with neighbors. In terms of actual distance, the furthest any student was bussed to school was seven miles. The average distance was slightly over half that.

Obviously it would make little sense for the district to expend this much work on the mechanics of integration, only to see the effort lost on the classroom level. Accordingly, each principal was notified well in advance of the opening day of school concerning the number and grade levels of the pupils his school would be receiving. Although the mechanics of moving pupils presented the school system with some substantive administrative problems, the issue of encouraging social integration was—and is—far more formidable. Studies by Irwin Katz (1967) and other social psychologists have affirmed that the quality of interpersonal relations is a particularly vital element in the educational success of minority children. Assuming the truth of this assertion, it would be difficult to overemphasize the crucial role played by principals and teachers in assuring the success of integration.

The decision to desegregate the Riverside schools and move toward integration compelled the district to deal more effectively than had been

---

[9] Pachappa School served 2 of the 12 geographical divisions.

the case previously with individual differences in attitudes and rates of learning among students. Traditional ability grouping clearly would not accomplish the goal. Early efforts to prepare teachers and principals for integration included holding a series of in-service education activities, utilizing the assistance of school–community aides to work with both parents and teachers, adopting numerous special instructional programs for children with learning problems, introducing new curriculum materials for the purpose of reducing the potential of alienation and encouraging learning, and, perhaps most important of all, attempting to seek creative solutions to instructional problems through a program of participatory management. Some lapses in implementation notwithstanding, the success of these efforts remains to be seen, although the absence of obviously negative results in the lives and the academic achievement of minority and majority pupils is clear.

The Riverside School Study

The administration and the board were aware that a careful analysis of the social and educational results of the integration program would be required in order to maintain credibility with the public. The means for accomplishing this was to be a full-scale evaluation of integration as it affected the children. Rarely are social scientists presented with an opportunity to engage in a comprehensive study of integration's effects within the same school system. Almost never would a coincidence of life permit this to be accomplished in a home city. The unique opportunity became immediately apparent to six faculty members at the University of California at Riverside.[10] What emerged was the Riverside School Study, approved by the Board of Education on February 7, 1966. The study, as a joint venture between the schools and the

---

[10] Over the years the institutional affiliations of some of the original six who instigated and conducted the university's side of the study have changed. Jane R. Mercer (sociology) and Harry Singer (education) are still at UCR. Harold Gerard (social psychology) is now affiliated with UCLA, while Norman Miller (social psychology) is at the University of Southern California. Thomas P. Carter and Frederick O. Gearing changed institutional affiliations and terminated their involvement with the study in 1967 and 1968, respectively. The author's own affiliation began shortly after the study was initiated and lasted until January 1969.

university, included both university faculty and school district personnel as project directors.

Although no local school funds were involved, the venture was able to secure adequate financial assistance from several sources. In November 1965, soon after the board made its decision to integrate the schools, Harold Gerard, a university social psychologist, began to explore not only research possibilities with the school district but sources of financial support as well. Two foundations were approached that month; one, the Rockefeller Foundation, made an initial award of $15,000, and a beginning was at hand. A grant of $25,000 from the regents of the University of California and an additional $10,000 from the Rockefeller Foundation helped markedly in launching the early collection of data. Largely as a result of inquiries originated by Thomas P. Carter of the university's education department, the California State Department of Education was approached formally for support. After 1966 state McAteer funds and a substantial grant from the National Institute of Health sustained the study.[11]

The intent of those who joined together to form the Riverside School Study was to make a large, longitudinal study of the growth and development of normal children in an increasingly integrated setting. Their prime purpose was to study the short- and long-term effects of desegregation and eventual integration on the academic achievement, the motivation, the peer group adjustment, and the emotional adjustment of minority group children being desegregated in the fall of 1966 and majority group children already attending the receiving schools. Data have been acquired through a wide variety of means, including tests, teacher ratings of students, teacher self-ratings, teacher interviews, principal interviews, child interviews, parent interviews, school records on the child, and direct observation.

All children attending Lowell, Irving, and Casa Blanca schools during the 1965–66 term were included in the study, as were those transferred out of kindergarten through third grades at Lowell, and out of kindergarten at Irving in September 1965, a year before general integration. A random sample of 698 Anglo children from the 11 receiving schools was also included. Since the basic research design was longi-

---

[11] After 1970 the part of the study remaining in Riverside was largely subsumed under the Program for Research in Multi-ethnic Education (PRIME) directed by Jane R. Mercer.

tudinal, intending to measure behavioral and attitudinal change over time, it was absolutely essential that a premeasure be made of children, their families, and teachers during the spring and summer of 1966. "After" measures were first taken in the spring and summer of 1967, with others taken at regular intervals thereafter. Altogether, 1731 children participated in the study, including roughly 41% Anglo, 37% Mexican-American, and 23% Black.

An acknowledged weakness of the design is the absence of a control group, thus making it more difficult to isolate the extent to which changes in children's attitudes and behavior are the result of integration. Nevertheless, it was felt that the selection of children who experienced similar amounts of desegregated schooling but at different points in time would make possible a reasonable estimate of the amount of change resulting from the integration experience and the amount attributable to changes in the larger environmental context. A second problem, and one that has been completely unavoidable, concerns a gradual erosion in the size of the sample group. This limitation was considered in the beginning, and the original sample size was increased to account for it. Still, the smallness of the minority group sample at some schools severely limits the number of comparisons that can be made between schools. One further problem from a strictly experimental point of view is a virtue in almost every other sense. Although the study was designed to continue for at least six years, the schools did not continue their 1966 instructional programs just to avoid confounding the researchers. In the case of at least a few schools, instructional change was substantial.

Some Social and Political Observations

Not all of the social and political ramifications of the integration program lent themselves to immediate scientific analysis. One of the more intriguing social issues—and one that holds long-term implications for the society at large—is the relationship between integrated schooling and integrated housing. Once children are assigned to schools outside of their segregated residential areas, one might assume that some minority parents would be disposed to purchase homes in the area of their children's new school. Given an adequate family income, relatively open housing, and the absence of racial tensions, there is good reason to believe that increasingly integrated housing will become an important long-range result of school desegregation.

Although the evidence from Riverside shows some migration of Black families into integrated housing developments, preliminary indications are that the movement has not been dramatic. By the beginning of the 1971–72 term, at least 44 school-age children from 15 Black families had moved out of the heavily minority eastside and Casa Blanca areas into predominantly Anglo residential areas within the same school system. In virtually all cases the moves were made while the students were attending secondary schools.[12] Recent interviews with parents whose children were desegregated in 1966 reveal little about the precise number who actually moved. They do indicate that a majority of parents, 54% Black and 77% Mexican-American, believe that "desegregation has opened the door for residential integration to occur." One may reasonably infer that the higher percentage for Mexican-Americans is related to their relatively greater success in finding integrated housing (Russell & Nielson, 1973, pp. 128–129).

In terms of the integration program's political impact on the careers of the superintendent, his staff, and the school board, the effects were largely positive or neutral. Board president Arthur Littleworth was one of three recipients of the Riverside Civic League's award as "Outstanding Citizen" for 1966. By its pioneering action in 1965 the local board won favorable recognition from the State Board of Education and the State Commission on Equal Opportunities in Education. In May 1966 the Department of Classroom Teachers of the National Education Association presented the district with an award of "distinctive merit" for its efforts in the area of school integration.

The administration likewise suffered virtually no ill effects. On June 30, 1968, Superintendent Bruce Miller retired a happy man after 38 years as a school administrator. His last several years had been challenging, but they were also his most distinguished and rewarding years. Of the several key school officials, he did come the closest to be-

---

[12] These preliminary findings, applicable only to Black families who made moves from heavily segregated to predominantly White areas, are based on data analyzed by J. Douglas Wolf, a student in the Graduate School of Administration, UCR, during the spring of 1972. Further analysis of the data, including interviews with Mexican-American as well as Black families, is being planned by Mabel Purl, Director of Research for the Riverside Unified School District.

coming a tragic figure over the school segregation issue. Although his position with the board and the larger community was perfectly secure, he was aware that many eastside parents did not hold him in high regard. As the school system's real and symbolic head, he absorbed most of the ill will generated from the two weeks of crisis in September 1965. Yet his adaptability and political astuteness, combined with a supportive, homogeneous board, permitted him to pull through unscathed. The new superintendent, E. Raymond Berry, had worked closely with Miller, the board, and minority leaders since coming to Riverside in 1960. He had been closely identified with the integration program and was one of its earliest advocates, and if anything, his career may have been enhanced by it.

Although the first tax override election following the decision to integrate lost miserably (58% opposed), other signs at the polls were favorable. Both the board president and the board clerk rolled up 2 to 1 majorities over their single challenger at an election held one year after the decision. Then, on May 23, 1967, the second try at a tax override succeeded by a narrow margin. It is doubtful that racial desegregation was a significant issue in any of the three elections, with the important exception of the Casa Blanca and certain Anglo upper-middle-class precincts in the first election. The Mexican-American community, usually supportive of the schools on money questions, voted overwhelmingly against the first tax measure: 38% in favor. By 1967 that community had apparently forgiven the district. This time the vote was 72.3% in favor, with a large percentage not voting.

Retrospect

In reflecting upon the integration question nationally and locally since 1965, it is apparent that not all changes have been progressive ones. Voluntary integration plans have virtually disappeared from the American scene. A few additional communities were able to adopt racial balance plans before the decade of the sixties ended, doubtlessly the most notable of these being the one implemented in Berkeley, California.[13] Accelerated action by the federal government through 1970

[13] The boldness of the Berkeley plan has been publicized in numerous sources. Although it was implemented in a school district somewhat smaller than Riverside and occurred two years later than the Riverside plan, it was accomplished in a district with a considerably higher percentage of minority students and featured bussing for majority as well as minority students.

produced a substantial increase in the number of Black children attending racially mixed schools, albeit almost all of the improvement was in the South. Nationally 50.2% of the Black children were attending schools with 80–100% minority enrollment in 1970. Two years earlier that figure had stood at 68%.[14]

As federal courts in both the North and the South maintained pressure on segregated school systems, some additional court-ordered desegregation continued through 1971.[15] Pasadena (1970) and San Francisco (1971) were two California school systems that carried out court-ordered plans. Although desegregated education was coming a bit closer to reality, community fear and hostility was growing rather than diminishing. Reflecting, and in some cases stimulating, the fears of their constituents, politicians chose to represent the reassignment of students to desegregated schools as "bussing," or even more forebodingly as "forced bussing." Thus by 1971 it was apparent that most Anglo-Americans were holding dear to the neighborhood school concept. "Bussing," which for 50 years had been used merely as a *means* of getting children to public and private schools, even to neighborhood schools, was suddenly elevated to center stage in the educational enterprise. In 1972 63% of the California electorate approved an amendment to their state's constitution prohibiting the assigning of students to any school on account of race.

On the surface at least, the quality of education a child received appeared to take a back seat to the bussing issue. Sadly for the advocates of integrated education, given the tightening pinch on funding for education and an awareness of the complexities involved, it was also becoming increasingly difficult for them to assure parents—especially disturbed Anglo parents—that their children would experience short-term benefits from attendance at a desegregated school. Perhaps the most optimistic interpretation one could give of the nation's attitude toward school integration by the early seventies was little different from that observed in the Riverside community during the mid-sixties. It was being accepted as a worthwhile social and educational objective, but

[14] Statistics prepared by Office of Civil Rights, U.S. Department of Health, Education, and Welfare, January 1971, as quoted from *Integrated Education, 9* (March–April 1971), 40–43.

[15] The most significant single case was *Swann vs. Charlotte-Mecklenburg Board of Education* (1971), in which the Supreme Court attempted to set up guidelines for achieving school desegregation, an action that supported the means developed by lower courts over the previous four years.

only under the conditions of the most modest expense of money, effort, and convenience.[16]

A most important criterion of success for any policy requiring substantial sociological adjustments is the extent to which that policy is approved by those most directly affected by it. In Riverside the commitment to integration has been retained by the school system and presumably by the community as well. As elsewhere, the level of commitment has been tested continually by the perceived costs.

Anglo, Mexican-American, and Black parents of students desegregated in 1966 are firm in their opinion that the city is a better place because of desegregation. Further 91% of the 334 parents interviewed by Russell and Nielsen in 1973 favored continuing desegregation under the existing or an alternative plan. Although a bare majority of those parents, (51%) claimed to have favored desegregation prior to its implementation, 62% viewed it favorably in 1973. Attitudes of Anglos changed hardly at all and those of Blacks improved slightly, while the perception of Mexican-Americans improved dramatically, 39% favoring desegregation before the policy was implemented and 64% favoring it in 1973. On the other hand, even though minority students alone have been assigned to schools outside of their immediate neighborhoods, 80% of the Anglo parents were opposed to assigning students to schools in order to achieve racial balance (Russell & Nielsen, 1973, p. 104).

Looking back nine years, one can see that the political process involved in bringing about desegregation in Riverside was direct and relatively uncomplicated, while the historical conditions in which the decision was framed were optimum for decisive action. Community conflict had been averted in 1965 largely through avoidance of the highly charged issue of bussing Anglo children. Nevertheless, in the very first year of implementation, 2 of the 26 elementary schools were closed, 11 increased their percentage of minority students by more than 5%, and 2 others declined by more than that amount. Ultimately, the success of school integration will be determined by the educational performance of the students affected by it and by the larger issue of how effectively it contributes to social and economic justice. Necessarily, one cannot

---

[16] In spite of the recent furor over "bussing," according to a Harris survey conducted late in 1970, 55% of those polled favored integrating the nation's schools without further delay in order to comply with the Supreme Court's ruling; *Integrated Education, 9* (March–April, 1971), 50.

reasonably expect early and dramatic results on such complex issues as justification for continuing the pursuit.

References

California State Department of Education, Office of Compensatory Education, Bureau of Intergroup Relations. *Racial and ethnic survey of California public schools. Part One: Distribution of pupils, fall, 1966.* Sacramento, 1967.

Crain, R. L. *The politics of school desegregation.* Chicago: Aldine Publishing Co., 1968.

Greenfield, M. What is racial balance? *The Reporter*, March 23, 1967, *36*, 20–26.

Iannaccone, L., & Lutz, F. W. *Politics, power and policy: The governing of local school districts.* Columbus, Ohio: Charles E. Merrill, 1970.

Katz, I. The socialization of academic motivation in minority group children. In D. Levine (Ed.), *Nebraska Symposium on Motivation.* Lincoln, Neb.: University of Nebraska Press, 1967.

Moore, J. W., & Mittelbach, F. G. Residential segregation in the urban southwest. *Mexican-American Study Project, Advance Report 4.* Unpublished manuscript, Division of Research, Graduate School of Business Administration, UCLA, June, 1966.

Russell, H. M. H., & Nielson, R. S. Parental attitude toward school desegregation and bussing: A longitudinal study. Unpublished doctoral dissertation, United States International University, 1973.

Segregation of races in public schools and its relation to the fourteenth amendment. *Illinois Law Review*, September–October, 1947, *42*, 545–546.

Taylor, F. J. The slum that rebelled. *Saturday Evening Post*, April 21, 1956, *228*, 32–33, 136–138.

U.S. Census Bureau, *U.S. census of population and housing: 1960, San Bernardino, Riverside, and Ontario, California, PHC (1)*-135. Washington, D.C.: U.S. Government Printing Office, 1961.

3

The Overall Research Design and Some Methodical Considerations

DAVID REDFEARN AND HAROLD B. GERARD

In the following pages we will briefly describe the design and methodology of the study. This description will include an outline of the procedures used to include minority and Anglo schoolchildren in the sample, a consideration of the major experimental comparisons that are feasible within the limits of the design, and a discussion of some design problems.

The study is not a true experiment since we had no control over the assignment of children to the receiving schools and to the classrooms within those schools. Such control would have enabled us to approximate random assignment. More importantly, there was also no adequate comparison group that remained segregated, against which we could compare any changes that might occur in a desegregated sample. These are shortcomings that limit the firmness with which we can draw conclusions about the effects of the Riverside desegregation program. Ideally we would have wanted a desegregated experimental treatment as well as a control treatment that remained segregated, with random assignment of pupils in each grade, sex, and ethnic group to each of the two treatments. The lack of a true experimental design introduces three

---

DAVID REDFEARN AND HAROLD B. GERARD • University of California, Los Angeles, California.

serious contaminants: history, regression, and attrition. We shall discuss these problems later.

Design and Sample

The basic design is a longitudinal study of an initial sample of 1731 Riverside, California, public school children who were in grades kindergarten through 6 in the 1965–66 school year. The sequence of events in Riverside made possible an approximation to a before–after experimental design. Most of the sample children were desegregated in the fall of 1966. For those children the study involves the comparison of one premeasure (1965–66) with multiple postmeasures (1966–67, 1967–68, 1968–69, and 1970–71). (Some postmeasures were also obtained in 1969–70.) Most measures were taken in the spring of each school year.

The original sample, broken down by ethnic group, grade, and sex, is shown in Table 3.1. This table also shows the actual timing of desegregation, which took place in three separate waves, and the number of children remaining in the sample through the 1970–71 school year. (An analysis of subject attrition will be presented later in this chapter.) After the arson burning of one of the minority schools in the summer of 1965, a group of 256 Mexican-American and Black children were desegregated that fall, which meant that these children, for whom we do not have premeasures, had already experienced nearly one year of desegregation at the time of our first measurements (Spring 1966). The early desegregation of the kindergarten children in this group provides us with a comparison group of children who experienced no segregated education whatsoever.

The school board planned to bus the remaining 712 minority pupils out of the three segregated schools in the fall of 1966. However, because of a later school board decision, approximately half of the pupils in one of the three minority schools (Casa Blanca) were not desegregated at that time. The second (and main) wave of desegregation took place in the fall of 1966 and involved 557 minority children. The final phase of desegregation was implemented in the fall of 1967, when the remaining 155 minority pupils (all but 6 were Mexican-American) in Casa Blanca School were bussed to majority schools. This one-year delay in the desegregation of these Casa Blanca pupils further complicates our analysis but provides us with a group that remained in a segregated situation against which to compare the desegregated children. This lucky circumstance involving the year's delay for half of the Casa Blanca pupils does represent a situation that approximates a true experiment.

In addition to these three distinct minority groups (children desegregated in fall 1965, fall 1966, and fall 1967), a small group of Black and Mexican-American children already attending predominantly Anglo schools in 1965–66 was included in the sample. After the main wave of desegregation in Fall 1966, these pupils experienced the impact of having a larger number of additional minority children in the school with them for the first time.

According to the vacancy patterns in the spring of 1966, there were 11 schools that were to receive the 712 minority children being reassigned from the segregated schools beginning in the fall of 1966. On the basis of known vacancies in classes, the school district staff had projected the number of minority children who were to be assigned to each grade in each receiving school. In order to study a comparable group of Anglo children, we randomly selected a number of children from each grade in each receiving school that was equal to the number of minority children who were to be assigned to that grade in that school. On this basis 711 Anglo children matched for grade and school with the minority children were selected for the study. As it eventually turned out, the minority children were assigned to a total of 20 receiving schools. In addition (as mentioned above), 155 of the minority pupils were not moved until the fall of 1967. These circumstances meant that the attempted matching procedure fell short of our ideal. As can be seen from Table 3.1, however, the match between the Anglo sample in the receiving schools and the minority children desegregated in fall of 1966 (the major comparison group) is still reasonably good.

The Classroom

In his reanalysis of some of the Coleman (1966) study data, McPartland (1969) reported that Black students who are in segregated classes in racially mixed schools receive no benefit in academic growth. It thus appears that an ethnic mix at the classroom level may be a

TABLE 3.1 Sample Frequencies for the Riverside School Study

	Total	Ethnic group			Grade in 1965–66							Sex	
		A	MA	B	K	1	2	3	4	5	6	M	F
Anglos in receiving schools													
Original sample	711	711	000	000	105	162	086	101	100	072	085	368	343
1965–66	652	652	000	000	094	150	078	094	094	063	079	343	309
1966–67	583	583	000	000	086	128	070	081	086	059	073	306	277
1968–69	500	500	000	000	073	112	061	067	070	049	068	267	233
1970–71[a]	150	150	000	000	059	089	002	000	000	000	000	082	068
Minority in receiving schools													
Original sample	052	000	038	014	008	010	009	006	008	008	003	024	028
1965–66	052	000	038	014	008	010	009	006	008	008	003	024	028
1966–67	052	000	038	014	008	010	009	006	008	008	003	024	028
1968–69	043	000	033	010	007	009	006	005	006	008	002	020	023
1970–71[a]	010	000	010	000	004	006	000	000	000	000	000	003	007
Minority desegregated fall 1965													
Original sample	256	000	109	147	100	061	048	041	005	001	000	120	136
1965–66	249	000	107	142	096	060	046	041	005	001	000	119	130
1966–67	230	000	104	126	087	059	041	037	005	001	000	113	117
1968–69	204	000	098	106	077	053	036	032	005	001	000	100	104
1970–71[a]	109	000	053	056	061	041	005	000	000	000	000	056	053

Minority desegregated fall 1966

Original sample	557	000	334	223	032	123	068	069	094	099	072	284	273
1965–66	548	000	331	217	032	121	066	068	094	096	071	278	270
1966–67	499	000	305	194	028	107	062	060	088	090	064	249	250
1968–69	425	000	277	148	025	085	052	051	080	081	051	213	212
1970–71[a]	102	000	066	036	024	073	005	000	000	000	000	049	053

Minority desegregated fall 1967

Original sample	155	000	149	006	035	029	032	024	019	016	000	084	071
1965–66	153	000	147	006	034	028	032	024	019	016	000	082	071
1966–67	153	000	147	006	034	028	032	024	019	016	000	082	071
1968–69	142	000	136	006	033	024	029	023	018	015	000	076	066
1970–71[a]	054	000	051	003	029	023	002	000	000	000	000	031	023

[a] Data were collected in 1970–71 only from those children still in elementary school.

critical factor in affecting minority academic performance. For this reason, it is important to examine the changes in classroom composition for our sample children.

Average class size increased significantly for the sample children across the school years 1965–66, 1966–67, 1968–69, and 1970–71, from 24.9 to 26.9 to 28.9 to 27.2 respectively. This increase in average class size is due primarily to the fact that classes tended to be smaller in the minority schools, averaging 22 pupils per class. As the segregated schools were phased out, minority pupils were moved into initially larger receiving school classes. Over the years the ethnic composition of classrooms also changed markedly for the minority children. In the 1965–66 school year—that is, prior to the main wave of desegregation—most of the minority children were in classes with virtually no Anglo children, whereas after desegregation they found themselves in classrooms that were, on the average, 80% Anglo. In 1965–66, prior to desegregation, there was an average of 2.1 minority pupils per class in the receiving schools. These minority children were those already in the receiving schools prior to desegregation and those who were desegregated after the burning of Lowell School. In 1966–67, after the main wave of desegregation had taken place, an average of 4.2 minority pupils (16%) were in each class. By 1968–69, when desegregation was complete, this figure had increased to an average of 5.9 minority pupils (20%) in each class. Minority students constituted 22% of the 1970–71 sample classes (6.0 pupils per class). Approximately 25% of Riverside's pupils belonged to ethnic minority groups (14% Mexican-American, 9% Black, 2% other). Thus it was not until the 1968–69 school year that our sample classes approximated the distribution of minority children in the district as a whole. The Anglo pupils had clearly remained as the majority group in their classrooms.

For our data analysis, two separate strategies of sample selection were employed. Where analyses are "static" and involve within-year comparisons only, the entire sample was used. This ensures the largest possible cell sizes for analyses involving several simultaneous categorizations. When comparisons were made across years in an effort to trace the effects of the desegregation experience, the sample selected included only the minority children desegregated in the fall of 1966 and the sample Anglo children in the receiving schools. For these groups of children it is possible to make clear pre- and postdesegregation comparisons.

Problems of Data Analysis

We will now consider some of the most critical problems faced in the data analysis. More detailed descriptions of these types of problems may be found in Campbell and Stanley (1963). The most tenable alternative explanation for any would-be pre- to postdesegregation change is that events other than desegregation affected the children of Riverside. The time period of our investigation, which followed in the wake of the Watts riots, witnessed much turmoil and social change at the national, state, and local levels. In addition, the Riverside schools moved toward decentralization, ungraded classes, and individualized instruction. A suitable control, which we mentioned earlier, would have been a comparable sample of Riverside minority and Anglo children who had not been desegregated. Another possible control, which was not feasible given the resources at our disposal, would have been a nearby city of comparable size that did not desegregate. The absence of a control group makes it difficult to isolate the extent to which changes in the children's behavior over time may have been a result of events extraneous to the school system and desegregation.

We are able to deal with special history effects in a number of ways. First, if we use built-in Casa Blanca comparison groups, it is possible to distinguish the amount of change resulting from the desegregation experience and the amount attributable to other events in the larger society. Unfortunately this comparison is possible only for Mexican-American children, since only six Black children were involved in the Fall 1967 desegregation of Casa Blanca School. The usefulness of such a comparison rests upon the prior equivalence of the desegregated and segregated subgroups of Mexican-American pupils. Although pupil selection at Casa Blanca for the two waves of desegregation was not explicitly random, the match between the two groups was fairly good when they are compared on a number of measurements taken in 1965–66. While the two samples did differ on standardized achievement test performance in 1965–66 (desegregated Fall 1966 = 94.30; desegregated Fall 1967 = 97.34; $F = 5.00$, $1/265$ df, $p < .05$), they did not differ significantly on Raven or Peabody IQ tests or on classroom grades in that year. In addition, the two groups of children were similar in predesegregation sociometric popularity, and there was no noticeable difference between them in terms of socioeconomic background and in the number of years of education of the head of the household. Thus, in terms of predesegregation characteristics, the two Casa Blanca Mexican-American groups were closely matched. The postdesegregation comparisons, however, must still be made with caution, for treatment differences (other than desegregation) may still have existed for the two groups in 1966–67.

Statistical Regression

A second potentially serious problem for the study concerns the effects of statistical regression. The mere fact of an imperfect test–retest correlation between two measurements implies that those children selected as most deviant on the first measurement will average nearer to the mean on the second. The operation of statistical regression may be viewed in terms of varying error of measurement. A child's score on a given measurement is assumed to reflect both the amount he possesses of the trait (or ability) the test is supposed to measure and error of measurement (other influences operating at the time of testing that might affect his performance other than the amount of the trait he possesses). Since errors are assumed to be independently and normally distributed around zero error, children with extreme scores on the first measurement will probably be less extreme on a second measurement (the error tends to be less the second time). When some experimental intervention (e.g., desegregation) separates the two measurements, an effect due to regression may be misinterpreted as having been caused by the intervention. In our case, for example, the regression artifact of successive testing can make the desegregation experience appear harmful to initially high-achieving pupils when, in fact, this is not the case. The drop in test scores may have been due entirely to measurement error. Regression effects are not confined solely to pre- and posttesting with the same or comparable forms of the same test. For example, children with the highest IQ scores will tend, because of measurement error, not to have the highest scores on school achievement tests, the highest grades in class, or the highest scores on any other variable positively, but imperfectly, correlated with IQ. This would also be true of a second IQ test.

A number of techniques are available for dealing with the regression problem. First, regression is less of a problem when the observed direction of change from pretest to posttest is opposite to that of any expected regression artifact. That is, if we find that high-achieving pupils increase their academic performance after desegregation, the change cannot be interpreted as being due to regression. In fact, the effect would be all the more impressive for its having overpowered any regression artifacts. On the other hand, the regression hypothesis would be a tenable explanation for any apparent postdesegregation improvement in academic performance by low-achieving pupils.

A technique is available in certain cases to estimate the magnitude of regression effects from pretest data and then to apply this correction to pretest–posttest comparisons. The test must be one made up of a number of separate items, such as an IQ test. The procedure is to divide the test into two equal and comparable parts, such as odd- versus even-numbered items, and from the correlation between the two parts to estimate the reliability of the total test by means of the Spearman–Brown formula (Ghiselli, 1964). This reliability coefficient may then be used to estimate the amount of regression likely to take place in any pretest–posttest comparison. For example, a test that has a reliability coefficient of 0.50 implies that if we look only at those subjects who have been poor scorers on the pretest, we would expect their scores on the posttest to have "regressed" halfway (0.50) back to the posttest mean.[1]

Attrition

A final major problem, unavoidable in all longitudinal studies, is attrition. Approximately 25% of families in southern California change residence every year. Such geographic mobility rapidly depletes the original sample of any longitudinal study extending over several years. Table 3.1 presents sample frequencies at each of the major measurement points in the study, from 1965–66 through 1970–71. Even before the premeasures were administered in the spring of 1966, 77 children (59 Anglo, 7 Mexican-American, and 11 Black) were lost from the original sample. Most of those children were withdrawn because their

---

[1] Note here that we are using internal reliability values as estimates of test–retest reliability. This substitution may slightly overestimate the true reliability value since the sources of error of measurement are not likely to vary as widely during a single administration as they would across several administrations separated by time (Crano & Brewer, 1973).

parents refused to give permission for their participation in the study. Between the 1965–66 and 1966–67 measurements 139 additional children (69 Anglo, 31 Mexican-American, and 39 Black) were lost from the sample, and 206 more children were lost between 1966–67 and 1968–69 (83 Anglo, 52 Mexican-American, and 71 Black). In 1970–71 data were collected only from those children still in elementary school.

A greater percentage of Mexican-American children remained in the study than did Anglos or Blacks. (The Mexican-American population of Riverside has had a stable history since before the turn of the century.) At the time of the Spring 1969 measurements we had lost 35% of the Anglo, 36% of the Black, and 19% of the Mexican-American sample. In the majority of cases sample losses after the first year of data collection were due to the families' having moved out of the school district. A very few children were moved to parochial schools. On the whole, attrition was evenly distributed across age and sex throughout the time span of the study.

Pretest scores on a variety of measures of achievement and adjustment were examined for those children dropping out of the study after the first year of data collection (1965–66) and for those dropping out subsequently. A differential loss of high- or low-achieving children from the three ethnic groups would confound any real achievement changes due to the desegregation experience. Fortunately we do not appear to have had this problem. There was a tendency for children who dropped out of the study subsequent to the 1965–66 measurement to have somewhat lower 1965–66 standardized achievement test scores, but this tendency was equivalent among all three ethnic groups. Even more reassuring is the fact that the in–out comparison reveals no significant differences in IQ or classroom grades as measured in 1965–66. Furthermore these three groups did not differ significantly on any of the large variety of personality measures administered prior to desegregation. Analysis of socioeconomic status data indicates that the children who dropped out of the study came from families slightly higher in socioeconomic status than those who remained. It was, however, only the minority children who left the study after 1965–66 that came from families of slightly higher socioeconomic status; the Anglo children did not differ in socioeconomic status for the in–out comparison. Economics was apparently the key to mobility for these minority families. It is important to note, however, that there were only 41 minority children involved, which had little biasing effect upon the total sample. Indeed, the mean ethnic group differences in socioeconomic status for those children who remained in the study hardly differed from those of the entire sample as measured in 1965–66.

In sum, we note a slight attrition bias favoring lower-achieving children of all three ethnic groups. This bias, however, does not appear serious enough to confound the analysis of achievement changes after desegregation. The magnitude of ethnic group differences in achievement varied only slightly between the whole sample and those children remaining in the study through 1968–69. The higher socioeconomic status of minorities leaving the study similarly introduced what is probably a negligible bias. On a variety of other cognitive and personality measures there were no significant in–out differences.

Procedure

The general set of measures utilized consisted of standardized achievement test scores, classroom grades, intellectual ability, peer group interaction, attitude toward the outgroup, feelings about self, emotional adjustment, achievement motivation, and level of aspiration. Characteristics of the home were also measured, since we assumed that the child's response to desegregation would be affected by his general family background. This wide-ranging set of variables was chosen since the general lack of previous research provided few guidelines as to what factors might moderate the effects of school desegregation. Our selection of measures was guided in part by the existing literature and in part by our intuition as to factors that might influence the minority child's adjustment to and achievement in the mixed classroom. In some cases we borrowed or adapted existing measures; in other cases we developed our own instruments.

Testing of Children

Each year, the children were tested individually in two one-hour sessions administered one month apart. The school released the sample children from class for the testing session during the spring semester of the 1965–66, 1966–67, 1968–69, and 1970–71[2] school years. In schools with a large number of sample children, testing trailers were used, whereas in schools with fewer sample children, testing was conducted in space provided by the school.

The staff hired to test the children received extensive training. The importance of maintaining a standard testing situation was stressed, as was the necessity of establishing rapport with the child. The staff all participated in role-playing practice sessions before beginning the actual testing program. A testing manual was prepared that gave detailed instructions and also outlined the purpose of the testing program. Spanish-speaking testers were employed for work in the Casa Blanca School, and Spanish-language forms of all the instruments were used whenever necessary.

The staff was drawn from the general Riverside city population. A few of the people hired were upper-division undergraduate or graduate students from the University of California at Riverside, but most were Anglo housewives from the Riverside community. Attempts to hire Blacks and Mexican-Americans were thwarted by university rules that required a certain minimum educational background for the workers doing such testing.

The fact that much of the testing was conducted by Anglos (83% of the Mexican-American children interviews, 91% of the Black children interviews, and 91% of the Anglo children interviews) poses a potentially serious problem since the ethnicity of the tester may have affected the child's performance. The magnitude and direction of such an effect, moreover, depends on a variety of factors, such as the type of task; the instructional set; the reinforcement conditions; subject variables of race, sex, age, and socioeconomic status; and the experimenter's attitudes and socioeconomic level (Sattler, 1970, 1973). The relatively small number of minority testers employed made impossible

[2] By the 1970–1971 year our youngest sample children were in the fifth grade. Since it was difficult to test children after they moved out of the elementary grades and many of our measures were not appropriate for older children, we decided not to continue testing a child beyond the sixth grade. Because of attrition, which was fairly rapid for Anglos and Blacks, and the fact that only fifth- and sixth-graders were available for testing in the final year of the study, cell sizes were in many cases quite small. The reader will therefore find that in a number of the chapters that follow analysis was carried out only through 1968–1969. This still allows us to estimate both short-term effects (after one year of desegregation) and long-term effects (after three years of desegregation).

any systematic analysis of the child ethnic-group by tester ethnic-group interaction. The tester's bias effects thus remain an alternative explanation for ethnic group differences on many of our measures. However, the experience of the minority child in the interview situation was not unlike the situation he constantly had to face in the "real world." American culture is dominantly White and middle class. In particular, most teachers and school officials are White. In this sense, the interview situation did not constitute a serious threat to validity.

Parent Interviews

Parents of the sample children were interviewed during the summers of 1966, 1967, and 1969. Manuals and instruction booklets were prepared and training sessions were held for all parent interviewers. Letters were mailed to the parents explaining the forthcoming interviewing, after which the interviewers contacted the parents to make appointments. Most of the parent interviews took place in the home, either during the evening or on a weekend. In 1966 both parents were interviewed separately. In 1967 only one parent was interviewed, usually the mother. Both parents were again interviewed in 1969. In families with more than one sample child, the family variables schedule and the mother and father's parent interview schedules were given once. Parents made separate behavioral ratings for each sample child in their family.

The staff hired to conduct the parent interview included some of the personnel who had conducted the child testing. Most parent interviewers, however, were teachers from the Riverside school district. Spanish-speaking interviewers were assigned to those Mexican-American homes in which English was not spoken. In most cases parents were interviewed by someone of their own ethnic group. Over the three years of parent interviews, 83% of the Black parent interviews were conducted by Blacks, 76% of the Mexican-American parent interviews were conducted by Mexican-Americans, and 94% of the Anglo parent interviews were conducted by Anglos.

Teacher Data

Each teacher was asked to complete behavior checklists on each sample child in her classroom in the spring of 1966, 1967, 1968, and

1969. Measures for this form, the teachers standardized behavior rating schedule, were taken from widely used checklists with the addition of a few new items. In special training sessions each teacher received a kit containing a list of the names of the sample children in her class, instructions for making the behavior ratings, and a set of rating scales for each sample child. Arrangements were made to reimburse teachers for the time spent in completing the ratings.

In the spring of 1968 a questionnaire was administered to the teachers to provide information for a study of the relationship between the teachers' characteristics and pupils' achievement. These questionnaires were filled out by 540 teachers at school meetings. A teacher code number was used so that the teachers could be identified and matched with the children in their classes.

Criterion Variables for Academic Achievement

Information concerning the academic performance of the sample children both pre- and postdesegregation was drawn from two main sources: the various state-mandated standardized achievement tests administered each year by the Riverside school district, and the class grades given to each child by his teachers. In order to have a standardized achievement test score for the maximum number of sample children, we were forced to combine scores from a number of different achievement tests. This was necessary since different standardized achievement tests were administered at one time or another to our sample children: Metropolitan Reading Readiness Test (kindergarten only), Stanford Achievement Test, School and College Cooperative Abilities Test (SCAT), and Sequential Test of Educational Progress (STEP).

In order to make the various individual achievement test scores comparable, so that we could assess the effects on achievement of the wide range of factors we examined, the raw test scores for our sample children were all standardized to the same mean and standard deviation, separately within each grade level, before being averaged together. These average achievement test scores were then restandardized to a mean of 100 and a standard deviation of 15. It is important to note that this procedure measured the performance of each sample child relative to the other sample children at his grade level, not to the Riverside school district children as a whole, nor to national norms. In examining longitudinal changes in achievement, as we do in the early part of Chapter 4, we assessed them against national norms. In Chapter 5 and following, standardized scores are used exclusively as the criterion variable.

Standardization within school years meant that we could not measure absolute changes in achievement test performance across years. However, we have managed to maximize the amount of achievement data available for analysis. In addition, the composite achievement scores are likely to be more reliable and accurate measures of achievement, since more than one test score per child entered the analysis. Also, the mean performance of the sample children as a whole (our basis of comparison) should be more consistent across grade levels than would be the national norms supplied with each individual achievement test. Finally, our average achievement variables are sensitive to any narrowing of the Anglo–minority group achievement gap in Riverside.

Classroom grade indexes were derived for the successive school years of the study. In each year, indexes reflecting both verbal and mathematical skills were constructed that reflect both class achievement and effort as rated by the teacher for a variety of subjects (arithmetic, reading, spelling, writing, composition and grammar, speech, etc.). The classroom grade indexes have not been standardized and thus reflect the actual grades given by the teachers.

Statistical Procedures

The specific analysis of variance procedures we employed deserve some mention. Because of missing data problems and unequal cell frequencies, we elected to employ an unweighted means analysis (Winer, 1962), which is considered appropriate if, as in our case, the number of observations in cells is not directly related to the experimental variables. This method considers each cell in the design as though it had an equal number of observations as all the other cells. Under the above assumptions, the number of observations per cell should still be approximately equal. In fact, this was not always the case, especially in the later years of the study. When the number of observations are not of the same magnitude, interpretation of the results becomes difficult. This is so because in the unweighted means procedure, main effect and interaction level means are computed as the mean of the appropriate cell means, not as the mean of all observations in the appropriate cells. These two methods of computing means differ when each cell does not have the same number of observations. Inspection of level means computed over all observations at each level do not always reveal why a particular main effect or interaction is or is not statistically significant. Cell frequencies must be taken into account when one interprets the analysis of variance results.

References

Campbell, D. T., & Stanley, J. C. Experimental and quasi-experimental designs for research in teaching. In N. L. Gage (Ed.), *Handbook of research on teaching.* Chicago: Rand McNally, 1963.

Coleman, J. S., Campbell, E. Q., & Hobson, C. *Equality of educational opportunity.* Washington, D.C.: U.S. Government Printing Office, 1966.

Crano, W. D., & Brewer, M. B. *Principles of research in social psychology.* New York: McGraw-Hill, 1973.

Ghiselli, E. E. *Theory of psychological measurement.* New York: McGraw-Hill, 1964.

McPartland, J. The relative influence of school and of classroom desegregation on the academic achievement of ninth grade Negro students. *Journal of Social Issues,* 1969, *25,* 93–102.

Sattler, J. M. Racial "experimenter effects" in experimentation, testing, interviewing, and psychotherapy. *Psychological Bulletin,* 1970, *73,* 137–160.

Sattler, J. M. Racial experimenter effects. In K. S. Miller & R. M. Dreger (Eds.), *Comparative studies of Blacks and Whites in the United States.* New York: Seminar Press, 1973.

Winer, B. J. *Statistical principles in experimental design.* New York: McGraw-Hill, 1962.

4

Achievement

Harry Singer, Harold B. Gerard, and David Redfearn

Desegregation in Riverside provided an excellent setting for testing the conclusion of the Equality of Educational Opportunity Survey (EEOS) (Coleman, 1966) that, with the exception of Orientals, the achievement of minority as compared with White pupils is more affected both by the educational background and aspirations of *other* pupils in the school and by the quality of the school. To quote the EEOS:

> If a White pupil from a home that is strongly and effectively supportive of education is put in a school where most pupils do not come from such homes, his achievement will be little different than if he were in a school composed of others like himself. But if a minority pupil from a home without much educational strength is put with schoolmates with strong educational backgrounds, his achievement is likely to increase. . . .
>
> The average White student's achievement seems to be less affected by the strength or weaknesses of his school's facilities, curriculums, and teachers than is the average minority pupil's. . . . the inference might then be made that improving the school of a minority pupil may increase his achievement more than would improving the school of a White child increase his. (p. 22)

Two of the processes suggested in Chapter 1 as possible mediators of such effects on the achievement of minority pupils are lateral transmission of peer group values and normalization of instruction. The

Harry Singer • University of California at Riverside, Riverside, California. Harold B. Gerard and David Redfearn • University of California, Los Angeles, California.

former mechanism implies that minority pupils in integrated schools, influenced through interaction with classmates from the majority group, would tend to acquire and act upon the values that underlie the achievement of majority pupils. *Normalization of instruction* refers to the tendency of teachers to adapt instruction to the average level of the class. Since the achievement of minority pupils from Riverside's three *de facto* segregated schools averaged lower than the achievement of Anglo children in the receiving schools, normalization of instruction in desegregated classes would, according to this argument, have tended to challenge and stimulate these minority pupils. Those pupils who were motivated and who could benefit from such stimulation would have tended to gain in achievement. If any adverse effects upon those minority pupils who could or would not benefit were insufficient to offset the gains, there would have been a net gain in the achievement of minority pupils in desegregated schools.

Since grading as well as instruction tends to be normalized in the classroom, desegregation tended to enhance the grades of Anglo pupils in the receiving school and lower the grades of minority pupils. This follows from the fact that the average performance in the receiving school classroom was lowered after desegregation since the performance of the minority children was generally below that of the Anglos. The higher-performing Anglo child thus showed a spurious improvement relative to the mean performance in the new classroom as compared with his predesegregated classroom. The poorer-performing minority child, by the same argument, found himself lower relative to the classroom mean after desegregation than he had been previously. Normalization of grading might be expected to produce effects opposite to those of normalization of instruction if we assume that grades act as rewards or punishments that enhance or depress motivation. Such motivational inducement would, in turn, tend to improve Anglo and depress minority achievement.

Since after desegregation in Riverside was complete, approximately 80% of the pupils in the receiving schools were Anglo, the ratio was high enough to allow the hypothetical mechanisms of lateral transmission of values and normalization of instruction to operate. Hence, we concluded that if the achievement of Anglo pupils were maintained and if, over time, there were a lessening of the gap in achievement between Anglo and minority pupils, we would have evidence supporting the EEOS conclusion.

Another opportunity afforded by the high-percentage Anglo class-rooms in Riverside was the possibility of also testing the conclusion reached in the U.S. Commission on Civil Rights report (1967) and by McPartland (1969), through additional analysis of the EEOS data, that the achievement of the Black child is positively related to the ratio of White pupils in his class. If the conclusion is tenable, we would expect the situation in Riverside to have a salutary effect on achievement because of the high proportion of Anglos in the typical classroom. We must keep in mind that most of the Black children studied by the EEOS had not been desegregated, as were the children in Riverside, but were, for the most part, especially at the elementary grades, attending neighborhood schools. This fact has been the basis of much of the criticism leveled at the EEOS and at those who have used those findings to argue in favor of desegregation.

The purpose of this chapter is to determine whether or not the con-clusions inferred from the EEOS data held under the conditions of desegregation as represented by the bussing program in Riverside. The criterion data available to reexamine those conclusions were the achieve-ment tests administered periodically to all pupils.

Review of Research

Only a paucity of evidence regarding the effects of desegregation on the scholastic achievement of Blacks, and less on Mexican-Americans, was available when Riverside desegregated (see Weinberg, 1968). Since then there have been some additional studies of minority group per-formance (e.g., Carrigan, 1969; Carter, 1970; St. John, 1970). Armor (1972), in his review of the effects of desegregation, has presented a quite pessimistic view, whereas Pettigrew, Useem, Normand, and Smith (1973), in their critique of Armor's review, are more positive. To put the present study into perspective, we will review the research that bears both on the original EEOS conclusions and on the U.S. Com-mission's conclusion regarding the effects of the percentage of Whites in the classroom.

The U.S. Commission on Civil Rights' (1967) reanalysis of the Coleman data indicated that at the ninth- and twelfth-grade levels the racial composition of the school to which a given minority child had been exposed during the previous year made a difference in verbal achievement over and above the effects of the social class of either the pupil or his fellow pupils or of teacher quality. St. John (1970) summarized three plausible interpretations of the relationship: (1) for those pupils tested in the ninth grade, the previous year's racial balance may reflect their experience with racial balance for all of their prior schooling; (2) ability grouping or tracking practices in desegregated schools may eventuate in placing brighter Black children in predominantly White classrooms, that is, ability influences the percentage of Whites in the class rather than vice versa; (3) the percentage of Whites in the classroom influences the Black child's achievement. This last interpretation is the one advanced in the Commission's report. McPartland (1968) argued, after some additional analyses of the EEOS data, that the relationship between achievement and the percentage of Whites in the classroom cannot be accounted for solely on the basis of tracking.

In an effort to explore the underlying dynamics of the effects of racial composition, Wilson (1967) attempted to control for hereditary differences and preschool home environment by partialing out variation associated with first-grade IQ scores. In a stratified random sample of 4000 junior and senior high school students, he found that the social class of the primary and intermediate schools had significant effects on sixth- and eighth-grade verbal scores, respectively. The racial composition of the school, however, had no effect on achievement scores over and above the effect of the social class of the school. But Pettigrew (1969) has argued that the data are not extensive enough to warrant this conclusion.

In an earlier study of residentially segregated schools in Berkeley, California, Wilson (1963) compared Black sixth-graders attending schools in the "Hills" (primarily middle- and upper-class Whites) with sixth-graders from the "Flats" (primarily low-social-class Blacks) on differentials in tested achievement and assigned grades. Children in the Hills tended to receive grades below their tested achievement, while children in the Flats tended to receive grades above their tested achievement. Wilson attributed the differential in grading practices to the tendency of teachers to normalize instruction and expectations, that is, to teach to the average level of achievement and to grade in reference to this norm. The higher relative grades received by Blacks may also be interpreted as having been caused by a "double standard," teachers assigning higher grades to Blacks than to Whites for the same performance. Since the mean level of tested achievement was higher in schools in the Hills than in the Flats, children from the Flats, when subsequently mixed in junior and senior high schools with children from the Hills, would tend to experience discontinuities in grades received if normalization continued and if the children were not tracked.

In the same study Wilson pointed to another factor that may tend to homogenize student achievement within schools. According to Wilson, peer group relationships in the ghetto schools may foster negative achievement values, while the more fragmented social structure of the peer group in the socioeconomically advantaged schools facilitates parents' and teachers' transmission of values for high educational aspirations and academic expectations.

Under the exceptional classroom conditions of UCLA's Fernald School, Feshbach and Adelman (1969) demonstrated that bussed-in Black and Mexican-American elementary and junior high school boys from low income areas who were of average intelligence but who were retarded at least one and a half years in achievement made slightly over one year placement gains in achievement in one year when mixed with tuition-paying Anglos of middle and upper socioeconomic status. A school enrichment group and another matched control group in regular school settings in the ghetto made only 0.68 and 0.75 years' placement gains, respectively, on achievement tests. The difference in results was attributed to the effects of integration, to behavior adaptation to changes in "school atmosphere" and norms (from low to middle class), to individualization of instruction, and to related attitudinal changes. Unlike most bussing studies, the Fernald study had an experimental design that made it possible to conclude that the treatment condition at the school was a significant factor in enhancing minority achievement. Unfortunately there is no way of determining whether the effect was due to desegregation per se, to the methods of instruction, to both, or to other influences that may have been operating (e.g., a "Hawthorne effect").

Despite the inconclusiveness of most of the evidence, St. John (1970) argued that "academic performance of minority group children will be higher in integrated than in equivalent segregated schools providing they are supported by staff and accepted by peers" (p. 128). This conclusion was based upon the Hartford Study, which found that bussed pupils who received "staff support" in integrated schools made the greatest gains (Mahan, 1968), and on the Civil Rights Commission's report (1967), which claimed that interracial friendships were conducive to achievement in integrated settings. St. John also noted that there is a "powerful" relationship between social class integration and achievement and a small effect of racial integration, per se, on achievement. The latter small effect could, however, be masked by a lack of control over school quality and home background factors.

Let us now turn to our own data, which are unusual in a number of respects, the major one being that they are based on a truly long-term longitudinal evaluation of a districtwide desegregation program with both pre- and postmeasures available. Another virtue of the study is that we were able, in an attempt to pinpoint mechanisms that might mediate the effects of desegregation on achievement, to collect a wealth of data on each child, some of which will be examined in the other chapters. Finally, as we shall see, the staggered bussing from one of the schools provided us with a built-in experiment.

All achievement data were derived from test batteries administered by the Riverside Unified School District. For 1966 the primary grade achievement battery was given in May and the intermediate grade battery in October, the times mandated by California for the administration of Stanford reading and arithmetic achievement tests (SAT) in grades 1, 2, 3, and 6. In 1967–70 California changed from using the Stanford achievement battery in grade 6 to the Comprehensive Test of Basic Skills. This change involved only one group of sample children, those who had been in first grade when the investigation began.

The remaining tests were adopted locally for districtwide testing. The Sequential Test of Educational Progress (STEP) and the School and College Achievement Test (SCAT) were administered in grades 4 and 5. Chart 4.1 summarizes the tests and the times they were administered.

Thus data on reading, arithmetic, and intellectual performance were collected, but we will report primarily on reading achievement data. Only the reading data were gathered systematically over all elementary grades, which makes them more amenable to treatment in our longitudinal design.

Pre- versus Postdesegregation Achievement

In order to assess the effects of desegregation, we compared each ethnic group's baseline predesegregation reading achievement for 1966

*CHART 4.1   Grade, Administration Time, and Type of Achievement Test
Used in the Evaluation*

Grade	Year	Test	Time of testing
1	1966–69	Stanford Achievement Test, Primary I, Form W	May
2	1966–69	Stanford Achievement Test, Primary II, Form W	May
3	1966–69	Stanford Achievement Test, Primary II, Form X	May
4	1966–69	Sequential Test of Educational Progress, Form 4B	October
5	1966–69	Sequential Test of Educational Progress, Form 4A	October
6	1966–69	Stanford Achievement Test, Intermediate II, Form W	October
7	1969–70	Comprehensive Test of Basic Skills, Form Q, Level II	October

with its longitudinal reading achievement for 1967–71 for those pupils
who were in first grade in the year prior to desegregation and who were
retested successively through sixth grade. The baseline data, which
consisted of the grade cross-sectional achievement test scores for grades
1–6 in 1966, were thus used as a predesegregation control for estimating
postdesegregation longitudinal effects on this group of children. Clearly
these data do not control for the influence of Riverside's history between
1967 and 1971, which might have affected achievement test scores.
Ideally we would have wanted for comparison two longitudinal samples
that were similar in all respects except for the desegregation experience.
But, as we shall see, our 1966 cross-sectional sample does appear to be
a fairly adequate control. Some children missed tests and others had
moved away sometime during the study. Consequently a "purified" longitudinal group was constructed. This group consisted of those students

who were first tested in 1966 in grade 1 and who were retested in grades 3 and 6.

In order to examine trends in the context of external national norms, we transformed the mean raw scores at each grade level into their respective grade equivalents as given in the manual for the particular tests used. At grades 1 and 3 the data for both the cross-sectional and the longitudinal groups were based on the SAT, but, as we noted earlier, at grade 6 the SAT was administered to the baseline groups while the longitudinal group took the Comprehensive Test of Basic Skills. Hence at grades 1 and 3 the grade equivalent scores were based upon the same test and norm group and are therefore directly comparable, whereas at grade 6 the longitudinal and cross-sectional grade equivalents are comparable to the extent that the norm groups came from the same population. All of the differences at the third- and sixth-grade levels between the baseline and the control groups, as shown in Figure 4.1, are not significant, although the difference for Blacks in the sixth grade approaches significance. The fact that the trends for the cross-sectional data resemble so closely those for the longitudinal sample does seem to justify the use of the 1966 data as a baseline control.

A trend analysis within both the cross-sectional and the longitudinal groups reveals that, in comparison with the norm group, Anglos gained in achievement. This upward surge shown by Anglos in the intermediate grades cannot, however, be attributed to desegregation, since the surge is also characteristic of the baseline, control group. As the figure indicates, Blacks and Mexican-Americans in both the longitudinal and the baseline groups lost ground relative to national norms from the first grade onward, so that by grade 6.2 they were about two grade equivalents behind the national norm, which coincides with the EEOS findings.

The Casa Blanca Experiment

The Casa Blanca School, whose predesegregation enrollment was 82% Mexican-American, was desegregated in two waves. The first group of 142 Mexican-American children entered the receiving schools in the fall of 1966, and the remaining 149 were desegregated in the following fall. As far as we can tell from questioning the school officials

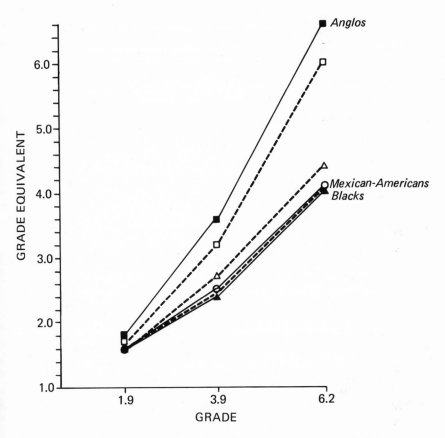

FIGURE 4.1. Mean reading achievement for the longitudinal (solid lines) and cross-sectional (dashed) samples of Anglos, Mexican-Americans, and Blacks.

involved, the assignment of children to each of the waves was made on a random basis. As we indicated in the previous chapter, close examination of our own extensive data on the children confirms the statement of the school principal; there were no discernible differences in background between the children in the two desegregation waves, save a small initial achievement test score advantage for those children who remained in Casa Blanca the additional year. The Casa Blanca situation thus provided us with the closest possible approximation to a true experiment. The second-wave children provide a control group against which to

TABLE 4.1   Pre- and Postdesegregated Achievement (in Standard Scores) for Mexican-Americans Desegregated from Casa Blanca School in 1966 and 1967

Year desegregated	1965–66	1966–67	1967–68	1968–69
1966	92.8 (113)	90.3 (77)	91.2 (75)	91.6 (53)
1967	97.4 (107)	94.6 (105)	95.2 (111)	93.9 (93)

evaluate those in the first wave who were exposed to one year of the experimental desegregation treatment, with the children from both groups being approximately comparable, randomly selected samples from the same population.

The reading achievement standard score data for both Casa Blanca Mexican-American samples are shown in Table 4.1 for predesegregation and successive years of postdesegregation achievement. For the "experimentals," the second-year data represent the first postdesegregation year, whereas the second-year data for the "controls" provide the segregated comparison mean. As is clearly evident, there was no apparent short-term effect of desegregation. Both groups showed approximately the same decline, which, as we saw in Figure 4.1 is characteristic of minority children. The two additional years, 1967–68 and 1968–69, also show no clear long-term effects of the initial desegregation year. Analysis of variance reveals a significant overall difference between the two groups, reflecting the initial difference, but no group by year interaction.[1] An interaction would have provided evidence that the additional year of desegregation experienced by the "experimentals" had a subsequent effect on their performance.

Overall Effects of Desegregation

Since years of desegregated education had no significant effect upon the Anglos, the Blacks, or the Mexican-Americans, data for all the groups were classified according to years of pre- and postdesegregated

---

[1] A repeated-measures analysis of variance using only those children who were tested in all years also yielded nonsignificant differences, as did a covariance analysis.

education. The two groups of Casa Blanca children, which both showed similar trends, were combined for the purposes of examining overall effects. The 1966–67 scores of the second-wave children were treated as predesegregation data, their 1967–68 scores as one year postdesegregation data, their 1968–69 scores as two years postdesegregation data, etc. A similar procedure was used for those children who were desegregated a year earlier in the fall of 1965. This redesignation according to time of desegregation rather than calendar year enabled us to include a maximum number of children for an overall assessment of desegregation effects. Table 4.2 presents standard score means, which enabled us to detect changes in the relative standing of the groups. If there had been a salutary effect of desegregation, the groups would have tended to converge. They clearly did not do so. With the exception of minor fluctuations, the Anglos maintained or increased their relative advantage through successive years.[2]

Effect of Quality of Receiving Schools on Minority Group Achievement

Assessing the overall impact of desegregation may obscure differential effects of local school conditions. Since the EEOS data revealed both school quality and White peer group socioeconomic status (SES) effects, we examined our data for similar trends. We performed two comparisons, one for the effect of academic performance of White peers and another for the effect of the White parent SES in the receiving school.

Achievement Level of Receiving Schools and Minority Achievement

Since teachers may tend to normalize instruction, schools with higher achievement may induce higher aspirations in the minority

---

[2] Purl (1971, 1973) has carried out additional analyses of the achievement test score data in Riverside. Her results, which indicate no overall tendency for the Anglo–minority achievement gap to lessen, are based on data from a much larger sample of children than our own. In addition to data from our sample of children, she included districtwide data on Anglo children who entered school after the 1965–66 year, as well as on a group of minority children who entered school sometime after the desegregation program was instituted. Her analysis, therefore, is not based upon the same longitudinal sample as the one studied here.

child, which, in turn, may lead to improved performance. To test this hypothesis, we rank-ordered the achievement levels of the receiving schools on the basis of their White students' predesegregation reading and arithmetic achievement scores. The schools were then categorized into three school achievement levels in such a way as to yield three approximately equal frequency groups of minority children attending the schools after desegregation. The effect of high-, middle-, and low-achieving schools on minority postdesegregation achievement was then assessed with a repeated-measures analysis of variance design. The data, which are shown in Table 4.3, revealed no effect of receiving-school achievement on minority performance. Furthermore, minority performance on all

TABLE 4.2 Pre- and Postdesegregation Reading Achievement Standardized Scores for the Three Ethnic Groups in Primary and Intermediate Grades[a]

	Prede-segregation	Post 1	Post 2	Post 3	Post 5
	Grades 1–3				
Anglo	107.8	113.0	108.3	115.1	—
	(300)	(184)	(186)	(64)	—
Mexican-American	94.4	93.0	92.8	93.4	—
	(271)	(191)	(131)	(78)	—
Black	91.6	92.9	94.0	93.9	—
	(108)	(149)	(99)	(72)	—
	Grades 4–6				
Anglo	109.6	108.5	109.4	106.6	108.7
	(204)	(206)	(193)	(206)	(97)
Mexican-American	94.0	93.0	92.1	90.2	92.7
	(225)	(188)	(165)	(96)	(77)
Black	93.6	94.5	93.5	94.9	93.5
	(92)	(79)	(79)	(79)	(43)

[a] Children were classified according to year of desegregation rather than calendar year. Ns are shown in parentheses.

TABLE 4.3   The Effect of Anglo Peer Group Achievement on Minority
Postdesegregation Reading Achievement Shown as Standard Scores

Achievement of peer group	Prede-segregation	Post 1	Post 2	Post 3
High	93.0	91.2	90.5	91.3
Medium	91.4	89.5	87.8	91.0
Low	96.5	91.2	95.0	93.5

three levels of initial receiving-school achievement was remarkably similar in the third year after desegregation.[3]

SES of Receiving Schools and Minority Achievement

The SES of the receiving schools was designated on the basis of an average of rankings on two criteria: the Duncan Scale Occupational Index of the father and the mean level of education of the head of the household. The schools were then grouped into categories of high, middle, and low socioeconomic status, which were adjusted in such a way as to yield near-equal frequency groups of minority children. These results, which are presented in Table 4.4, show little effect of type of receiving school. Initially, the minority children assigned to the low-SES schools were somewhat higher achieving than those assigned to the high- and middle-SES schools. In the first year following desegregation there was an effect that is in line with the EEOS conclusion, namely, that the children in the high-SES schools showed an *increase* in achievement, whereas those in the middle and low schools showed the typical decrease. The effect tended to wash out in the following two years, the groups becoming quite similar after three years of desegregation. The minority children in the low-SES schools maintained their initial superiority, although their edge diminished somewhat. Thus there appear to be no clear-cut effects of receiving school SES.

[3] In her analysis Purl (1973) did find a positive effect on minority achievement of the average achievement level of pupils in the receiving schools, but she did not examine these changes in a design that took account of changes over time from pre- to several years postdesegregation.

TABLE 4.4   *The Effect of Socioeconomic Status of Anglo Children in Receiving School on Minority Performance (Represented as Standard Scores)*

SES of receiving school	Prede-segregation	Post 1	Post 2
High	92.3	93.5	90.9
Medium	92.0	88.7	91.3
Low	96.5	91.1	93.5

Normalization of Grading

If teachers normalize the grades they assign in a given classroom, we would expect that in the predesegregation classrooms minority children would be overgraded relative to their scores on standardized achievement tests and that Anglo children would be undergraded. This is what Wilson (1963) found in his Berkeley study. With the mixing of higher-performing Anglos and lower-performing minority children in the same classrooms after desegregation, Anglos would tend to receive higher grades than before desegregation and minority children to receive lower grades than before, to the extent that the actual performance differential was sustained. If the differential increased, which it did (see Figure 4.1), we would expect the grading differential to be accentuated. This prediction assumes, of course, that teachers would continue to normalize their grades.

A reasonable method for determining whether or not normalization of grading occurred is to subtract each child's achievement in a given year from the grade he received in that year, comparing such differences successively, year after year. In order to derive a meaningful difference score, we used standard scores for both grades and achievement. In the data, which are presented in Table 4.5, a positive score signifies overgrading—i.e., that grade exceeded achievement test score—and a negative score signifies the reverse.

The data in the table, which are based on grades and achievement scores for those children desegregated in the fall of 1966, offer striking confirmation of both initial and postdesegregated grade normalization. Anglos were undergraded by their teachers in the predesegregation all-

Anglo classroom, where performance tended to be skewed away from the low end of the performance distribution, whereas both Mexican-Americans and Blacks were overgraded, exactly the situation grading normalization would create. After desegregation, with Anglo and minority children in the same classrooms and their being graded against the same performance standard, we see a progressive convergence of the difference score. By the third year after desegregation, the teachers' grading practices appeared to be completely normalized, as indicated by the negligible discrepancies between grades and achievement for all three groups. In the lower portion of the table we have presented the F ratios, which indicate the effective amount of the spread of grade–achievement discrepancy among the three groups each year. It is interesting that the teachers gradually eased into using the same grading standard for all children. One can, of course, only speculate as to why they did so. In the first year after desegregation the teachers may have acted to protect the minority children from discovering their poor relative standing but then gradually accommodated to the objective state of affairs. As time went on the teachers may have come to believe that, through social comparison, the minority children had become well aware of their low relative performance standing and therefore would be able to accept lower grades more easily.

All would have been well if academic performance as well as the grade-achievement discrepancy had converged in the years following desegregation. We know from our earlier discussion that the relative grade equivalent performance of the minority children progressively worsened. Given gradual grade normalization, this of course implies

TABLE 4.5 *Grade–Achievement Discrepancy for Anglos, Mexican-Americans, and Blacks Pre- and Postdesegregation*

	Prede-segregation	Post 1	Post 2	Post 3
Anglo	−3.2	−1.7	−0.7	−0.2
Mexican-American	4.8	3.1	1.2	0.8
Black	2.1	0.2	1.0	−0.5
F Ratio	23.10	9.27	1.31	0.26
P Value	0.001	0.01	ns	ns

that minority grades worsened. Anglo grades improved because of the lower performance anchor provided the teacher by the minority children.

The state of affairs presented above could well have had demoralizing effects on the minority children. Since grades signal success or failure, they may spur or reduce motivation. Anglos would then tend to be encouraged and Blacks and Mexican-Americans to be discouraged by the consequences of normalized grading, which, in turn, might affect performance and result in a widening of the achievement difference between the groups. Such a situation contains all the necessary ingredients for creating a vicious circle. The data in Figure 4.1, which compared a group of desegregated children with a cross-sectional control, hinted at a possible motivational increment for Anglos and a decrement for Blacks as a consequence of desegregation. One difficulty with those data is that the longitudinal sample was relatively small, being made up of those children who were in first grade in the year prior to desegregation and who participated in the testing in subsequent years.

Normalization of grading may provide a key, or one of the keys, to why desegregation did not have the effects that were hoped for. If minority achievement had normalized as Katz (1964) and others would have predicted, normalized grading would have had no untoward effects on minority achievement. The fact that achievement did not normalize placed the minority child at an invidious disadvantage that, we are suggesting, probably took its motivational toll. Grading makes it all too clear just where a child stands in his class. A child who is operating at a level well below others in the class faces an extraordinarily difficult task in attempting to pull himself up, a task that is fraught with the problems imposed by negative expectations both of his teacher about him (deriving from the stereotypes she holds) and of him about himself (deriving from his poor grades).

Minority students did not gain in achievement as a consequence of desegregation, nor did Anglos suffer. The absence of a salutary effect on minority children is at variance with the conclusion of the EEOS. In the EEOS the results were, as we recall, confounded by geographic variation and neighborhood school attendance. In Riverside Blacks and Mexican-Americans were bussed from ghetto areas into previously all-Anglo schools, that is, to a planned desegregation program. Since there were approximately 80% Whites in the typical desegregated classroom, lack of improvement in minority achievement does not support the U.S.

Commission on Civil Rights' (1967) conclusion, and that of McPartland (1969), that there should be a salutary effect on the achievement of minority children of a high percentage of majority group children in the classroom. Factors other than the percentage of Whites thus probably account for the relationship in the EEOS data.

Our results also do not support conclusions derived from the EEOS data that school quality, as represented in our data by White peer performance and White peer SES, affects the performance of the minority child. We found no effect of White peer achievement and only a hint of a short-term effect of school SES. In line with Wilson's (1963) findings, normalization of grading resulted in lower grades relative to achievement for Anglos and higher grades for minority pupils prior to desegregation. After desegregation, normalization of grading increased Anglo grades relative to achievement and lowered minority grades. The inevitable invidious comparison was likely to have had deleterious effects on the minority children. Some evaluation system other than grading seems more appropriate for the desegregation situation in which two groups of children in the same classroom are performing at different levels initially. Whatever salutary effects might have occurred as a result of achievement normalization—because of the teacher's teaching up to the level of the majority of Whites in the classroom—may have been nullified by the negative effects of normalized grading.

Riverside's desegregation, in and of itself, thus appears not to have enhanced the minority child's achievement. Additional ingredients are required to raise achievement up to par. Some educators assume that merely placing children in the same classroom affords each child the same opportunity to achieve. Educational inputs must be tailored to the needs of individual children if they are to realize their potential. In several of the following chapters certain moderating conditions are considered.

Special treatment conditions of minority students at UCLA's Fernald School (Feshbach & Adelman, 1969) did enhance achievement, which suggests that special programs are needed to fully realize the goal of equal opportunity. However, such treatment should begin at the preschool level since disparities in majority–minority achievement appear prior to formal schooling. For example, additional data collected in Riverside indicate that reading readiness scores at the end of kindergarten, even after desegregation, were still higher for Anglos than for both Blacks and Mexican-Americans (Purl & Kleinke, 1969).

In line with Katz's (1964) hypothesis, the aim of such preschool instruction should be to develop students who have the necessary motivational system of values, attitudes, and beliefs, as well as background experiences, for transforming capabilities into achievement prior to entering school in order to maximize their future learning.

Our study is unprecedented in the extent of follow-through achievement data examined. We analyzed the data in a number of ways, looking for salutary effects of the desegregation program, and found none. The analyses we did report seemed like the clearest way to present the findings. All of this work notwithstanding, we must remember that Riverside's program represents only one method of desegregation, namely, one-way bussing of minority children to previously all-Anglo schools. Other methods are possible, such as one-way bussing of Anglos into minority schools or two-way bussing. Perhaps these other methods might have yielded salutary effects. We feel, however, that given the weight of accumulating evidence around the country, effects of the kind policy makers and educators expected when nationwide desegregation efforts began are difficult indeed to realize.

References

Armor, D. J. The evidence on busing. *The Public Interest,* No. 28, Summer 1972, 90–126.

Armor, D. J. The double double standard: A reply. *The Public Interest,* No. 30, Winter 1973, 119–131.

Carrigan, P. M. *School desegregation via compulsory pupil transfer: Early effect on elementary school children.* Final Report, U.S. Office of Education, September 1969.

Carter, T. P. *Mexican-Americans in school: A history of educational neglect.* Princeton, N.J.: College Entrance Examination Board, 1970.

Coleman, J. *Equality of educational opportunity.* Washington, D.C.: U.S. Government Printing Office, 1966.

Feshbach, S., & Adelman, H. *A training, demonstration, and research program for the remediation of learning disorders in culturally disadvantaged youth.* Los Angeles: Department of Psychology, University of California, 1969.

Katz, I. Review of evidence relating to effects of desegregation on the intellectual performance of Negroes. *American Psychologist,* 1964, *19,* 381–399.

Katz, I. Academic motivation. *Harvard Educational Review,* 1968, *38,* 57–65.

Mahan, T. W. *Project concern: An interim report on an educational exploration.* Hartford, Conn.: Board of Education, 1968.

McPartland, J. *The segregated student in desegregated schools.* Final Report to the

Center for the Study of Social Organization Schools. Baltimore, Md.: Johns Hopkins University, 1968.

McPartland, J. The relative influence of school and of classroom desegregation on the academic achievement of ninth grade Negro students. *Journal of Social Issues,* 1969, *25,* No. 3, 93–102.

Pettigrew, T. F. The Negro and education: Problems and proposals. In F. Katz & P. Gurin (Eds.), *Race and the social sciences.* New York: Basic Books, 1969.

Pettigrew, T. F., Useem, E. L., Normand, C., & Smith, M. S. Bussing: A review of the evidence. *The Public Interest,* No. 30, Winter 1973, 88–118.

Purl, M. C. *The achievement of pupils in desegregated schools.* Riverside, Cal.: Riverside Unified School District, March 1971.

Purl, M. C. *The achievement of students in primary grades after seven years of desegregation.* Riverside, Cal.: Riverside Unified School District, February 1973.

Purl, M. C., & Kleinke, C. *Comparative data for the Lorge–Thorndike Intelligence and Stanford Reading Achievement Test.* Riverside Cal.: Department of Research and Evaluation, Riverside Unified School District, September 1969.

St. John, N. H. Desegregation and minority group performance. *Review of Educational Research,* 1970, *40,* 111–133.

U.S. Commission on Civil Rights. *Racial isolation in the public schools.* U.S. Department of Health, Education, and Welfare, Washington, D.C.: U.S. Government Printing Office, 1967.

Weinberg, M. *Desegregation research: An appraisal.* Bloomington, Ind.: Phi Delta Kappa, 1968.

Wilson, A. Social stratification and academic achievement. In A. Harry Passow (Ed.), *Education in depressed areas.* New York: Teachers College, Columbia University, 1963.

Wilson, A. Educational consequence of segregation in a California community. In *Racial isolation in the public schools,* Vol. II of a report by the U.S. Commission on Civil Rights. Washington, D.C.: Superintendent of Documents, 1967.

5

IQ

NORMAN MILLER AND MERLE LINDA ZABRACK

This chapter focuses on the measures of intelligence used in the Riverside School Study to assess the ethnic differences in measured intelligence that existed before desegregation and to explore whether desegregation affected these scores. In addition, this chapter examines the relation between IQ and other aspects of personality, academic achievement, and teacher attitudes. Before proceeding, however, we will present some of the past research so that our own findings can be viewed in perspective.

Studies examining racial differences in IQ scores reveal consistent differences, a finding that has aroused much controversy. The most persistent question raised revolves around the relative contribution of genetic and environmental factors to the obtained racial differences. Are they due to innate genetic structures (implying the unmodifiable nature of intelligence), or do they stem from differences in the cultural environments of various racial groups? Are differences in intelligence test scores attributable to factors associated with socioeconomic differences? Do personality variables such as anxiety and self-esteem affect test performance? Do such factors as parents' attitudes and expectations affect the child's performance on IQ tests? Do teachers' attitudes function similarly?

NORMAN MILLER AND MERLE LINDA ZABRACK • University of Southern California, Los Angeles, California.

Race and IQ

On the average, blacks obtain scores about one standard deviation or 15 IQ points below the average score of the White population. In a recent review, Shuey (1966) confirmed this frequent finding. Using the Wechsler Intelligence Scale for Children (WISC), she compared 719 southern Black children to a sample of 140 White children. The mean for Blacks on the WISC full scale was 84, well below the White mean of approximately 104. In addition, performance scale IQs (81) were found to be lower than verbal scale IQs (87) among the Black children.

Semler and Iscoe (1963), with samples of 115 Whites and 108 Blacks from Austin, Texas, found a difference of only 7 IQ points on the WISC full scale. In attempting to account for this smaller difference, they mentioned that the school attended by Black students was considered to be as good as that attended by White students, implying that environment contributes to the difference ordinarily found between races. In a subsequent study (Semler & Iscoe, 1966), they compared the performance levels of White and Black subjects both on the WISC and on Raven's Progressive Matrices. They hypothesized smaller racial differences on the latter because it is considered to be less "culturally loaded" than the WISC, that is, less susceptible to the influence of prior learning. Whereas comparison of 141 Whites and 134 Blacks, ranging in age from 5 to 9 years, showed a higher WISC full scale IQ for Whites at all ages ($p < .001$), the Raven Progressive Matrices (administered only to 7-, 8-, and 9-year-olds) indicated a significant Black–White IQ difference only for the 7-year-olds. This latter finding differs from that of Higgins and Sivers (1958), who found the difference in Raven IQ between 349 Blacks and 440 Whites aged 7–9 to be smaller than typical WISC comparisons between Blacks and Whites, yet nevertheless 10 points below that of the Whites ($p < .01$). Perhaps the inconsistency stems from differences in the average socioeconomic status of the children in the two studies. Whereas Tulkin and Newbrough (1968) found significant differences between approximately 200 lower-class Black and White children, comparisons of upper-class samples (of equivalent size) revealed no significant differences. To add further confusion, however, Jensen (1969) took an opposite stand and argued that Blacks obtain relatively lower scores on culture-free tests than on more "conventional" tests, such as the WISC.

Kagan (1969) noted two peaks in the distribution of urban Black children. Though a large proportion of children had IQ scores around 60, the scores of a larger group were normally distributed and similar to those found for a White population. He attributed the low scores to failure to understand certain problems, failure to know what to do, and failure to appreciate that a test was being administered (p. 128). Thus one interpretation is that lower-class Blacks are more likely than Whites to misunderstand aspects of IQ tests. Palmer (1968) provided support for this explanation among middle- and lower-class Black children from Harlem. The examiner was told not to begin testing unless the child was completely relaxed and understood what was required of him, entailing, as a result, five to seven hours of rapport sessions before any questions were administered. Test scores revealed few differences in ability between lower- and middle-class Black populations. Jensen (1969) confirmed this effect. However, the fact that scores can be boosted from 5 to 10 points from a first to second testing led him to "doubt that IQ gains up to this amount in young, disadvantaged children have much if anything to do with changes in ability" (p. 100). Rather, he interpreted them as a result of getting more accurate IQ scores by testing under optimal conditions. Yet at the same time he too pointed to residual differences between Blacks and Whites.

Jensen's main impact, however, stems from his discussion of genetic versus environmental contributions to IQ. Arguing that compensatory education programs (such as Project Head Start) fail to produce enduring gains in IQ achievement, he questioned whether IQ differences are largely the result of environmental influences and cultural biases of the tests, as is often claimed. In essence, based on studies of White American, British, and Danish twins, he rejected the notion of environmental and cultural bias and instead suggested that the proportion of variance in IQ measures due to genetic factors is .80, while the remaining .20 is due to nongenetic or environmental factors.

Several criticisms have been leveled at Jensen's discussion of IQ quite apart from the measurement problems mentioned above. Interestingly, using the same twin data but employing slightly different procedures or assumptions for generating path coefficients, Jencks (1972) estimates that heritability (genetic factors) controls approximately .45 of IQ variance. Jensen may also be criticized on the ground that he drew his conclusions from heritability studies that used Caucasian twins as subjects. Additionally, Kamin (1974) has seriously questioned the validity of much of the data upon which these estimates were based. Beyond this, the relative amounts of genetic and environmental variance may differ among racial and social class groups. Hirsch (1970) further pointed out various oft-ignored limitations of heritability estimates, specifically limitations due to population, situation, breeding generation, and developmental stage.

In arguing that environmental contributions to IQ scores are minimal, Jensen also pointed to Coleman's (1966) finding that environmental factors have little effect on school achievement. Since achievement scores are highly correlated with IQ, he took this as additional support for his position. However, as Deutsch noted (1969), there are several methodological problems with the Coleman report; consequently, one might question the basic appropriateness of these data for buttressing Jensen's position. Another specific type of problem posed for Jensen's argument stems from the equating of social class across caste lines. A middle-class Black may not have life experiences that are similar to those of a middle-class White, a criticism that applies to any study that tries to match racial groups on socioeconomic status (Dreger & Miller, 1960; Stinchcombe, 1969).

Since estimates of the genetic contribution to IQ scores derived from studies of White twins may not tell us as much as we would like about the genetic component in the IQ scores of other racial groups, data from both Black and White pairs of twins would clearly provide better information. Scarr-Salapatek (1971) collected data from 319 pairs of Black twins and 163 pairs of White twins. She compared the environmental disadvantage hypothesis (larger proportions of genetic variance will be found in advantaged groups than in disadvantaged groups) to the genetic differences hypothesis (equal amounts of genetic variance will occur across social classes and races). The major finding was that the proportion of variance in aptitude scores attributable to genetic factors differed markedly for advantaged and disadvantaged groups. Among the disadvantaged of both races, genetic factors were relatively unimportant, while for the relatively advantaged of the two races both genetic and environmental factors seemed to contribute to the similarity of scores obtained by opposite-sex twins. Since most Blacks are considerably more disadvantaged than Whites, the difference in IQ scores of two Black children is more likely to be due to environmental factors than would be the case for two White children. Another interesting aspect of Scarr-Salapatek's work is that when she applied Jensen's assumptions to her own data, her heritability estimates were substantially smaller than those suggested by Jensen and more in accord with those of Jencks (1972).

Socioeconomic Status (SES) and IQ

The preceding discussion suggests that some environmental factors do affect IQ scores and that socioeconomic status (SES) is a prime candidate in that it implies differences in the richness of the environment in which a child is raised.

Sperrazzo and Wilkins (1958, 1959) tested 480 children, aged 7–11, on the Raven Progressive Matrices test. One-third came from all-White schools, one-third from all-Black schools, and the remaining from schools that were 60% Black and 40% White. The children were divided into three socioeconomic status levels on the basis of parental occupations: (1) professional and semiprofessional; (2) skilled, semiskilled, and clerical; and (3) service, unskilled, and labor. Whereas the scores of Whites increased directly with level of SES, those of Blacks were the same at all levels of socioeconomic status; furthermore, at the lowest level of SES, the two races did not differ. This suggests that race itself will not suffice as a simple explanation of differences in IQ scores. The finding that both higher IQs and better emotional adjustment were related to superior SES (Wiener, Rider, & Oppel, 1963) as well as the previously cited data of Tulkin and Newbrough (1968) further supports this conclusion.

However, there has also been evidence that when gross SES is equated, the average difference between Blacks and Whites is merely reduced to 11 IQ points (Shuey, 1966); that is, differences do not disappear. Shuey also pointed out that in all studies that classify individuals by their SES (usually using matching procedures), high-status Black children average 2.6 IQ points below low-status Whites. Wilson (1967) also confirmed this residual difference when he took the mean IQs of a sample of Black and White children in a California school district and compared the two groups within four social class categories: (1) professional and managerial; (2) white-collar; (3) skilled and semiskilled manual; and (4) lower-class (unskilled, unemployed, and welfare). The mean IQ of Blacks highest in SES was 15.5 points below that of White children in the same category. Further, the mean for Blacks in this category was also 3.9 points below the mean of White children in the lowest SES category.

Scarr-Salapatek (1971) investigated social class and scholastic achievement. Within Black and White groups of twins from grades 2 to 12, the pairs were divided into three socioeconomic levels: below median for income and education (low SES); above in one dimension and below in the other (middle SES); above for both median income and education (high SES). Children were given the Iowa Tests of Basic Skills, a developmental test used to measure scholastic achievement. Similar to the difference typically found for IQ, Blacks' scores on these achievement tests were approximately one standard deviation below those of the Whites. The mean of low SES Whites equaled or exceeded the mean of high SES Blacks on verbal, nonverbal, and total scores. However, an overall comparison across races indicated that disadvantaged, low SES Whites scored in patterns similar to those of Blacks. In every test there were significant social class differences that interacted with race. The effect of social class differences was greater among Whites than Blacks, implying that socioeconomic status level is less important for Blacks. As previously suggested, although socioecomonic status levels have been externally and objectively imposed on the basis of income, education, etc., these data can nevertheless be taken as implying that the subjective experience of Blacks may not vary across SES levels as much as it does for Whites because of the caste differences that exist within the society.

Lesser, Fifer, and Clark (1965) took a different approach by focusing on patterns among abilities of children from different social classes and cultural backgrounds, rather than merely comparing mean scores. They administered the Hunter Aptitude Scales to Jewish, Negro, Puerto Rican, and Chinese first-grade children (80 from each cultural group). Each of the four groups was subdivided into middle and lower classes, and each child was tested by an examiner of his own cultural background. Scores were obtained for verbal, reasoning, numerical, and spatial factors. The Jewish group scored highest on the average, with those from the middle class scoring higher than those from the lower class. They scored highest on the verbal subtest, followed by the numerical, reasoning, and spatial subtests. The Black middle-class children scored the same as the lower-class Jewish children on verbal and numerical tests and scored higher than the midpoint between the middle- and lower-class Jewish children on the reasoning and spatial tests. The Black lower-class children scored next to lowest on the verbal test and lowest on the remaining three. They conclude that different ethnic groups do indeed have different patterns of abilities (see also, Stodolsky & Lesser, 1967) and further, that these patterns of ability are stable within each ethnic group and do not change across socioeconomic classes within the group. Therefore, it is not sufficient merely to equate ethnic groups on social class variables and expect differences in intellectual performance to disappear. Some of these ethnic group differences imply a differential importance or emphasis that might be attached to certain abilities within the different ethnic groups. Further, since abilities relate to each other in culturally determined ways, it is necessary to identify the strengths and weaknesses of different cultural groups as a prerequisite to making decisions on educational processes and aims. This notion receives support from certain linguists and psycholinguists (for example, Baratz & Baratz, 1971; Labov, 1972), who point out that although the Black dialect may be *different* from White standard English, it still constitutes a highly structured, well-developed language system. However, since it is White standard English that is used in school settings, on aptitude tests, etc., the Black child will necessarily have some difficulty.

Although it is obviously important to take socioeconomic status variables into account, as suggested above, problems emerge. Besides those pointed out by Lesser *et al.* concerning different patterns of abilities, there are methodological obstacles in equating social classes. For example, some investigators employ matching techniques while others attempt to make comparable divisions within the distribution of each of several ethnic groups. Whereas matching procedures create problems of differential regression effects, equivalent division of the distribution within each ethnic group (e.g., the upper 20%) leaves the comparison groups unequal in terms of absolute SES level. As indicated, caste differences may also underlie SES differences. Furthermore, as Stinchcombe (1969) argued, environments may be "cumulative." In other words, it is necessary to consider how many months a family has been middle class in comparison to how long that family was lower class, on welfare, etc. Therefore, if a family's status *has* changed, terming it middle class at one point in time does not account for the influences exerted when that family was at another socioeconomic status level. Since the majority of Blacks are in the lower class, many of those currently classified as middle class may have attained that status only recently, whereas this possibility seems less likely for White middle-class families.[1] Stinchcombe also notes that the existence of general or mean SES differences between Blacks and Whites, in combination with the fact that the society is highly segregated, might result in a greater likelihood that middle class Black children will have lower class Black children as playmates. Thus, even if families are equated on status, it is not certain that the children's environments will be equal.

To add still further to these issues, it is possible that SES level selects people on IQ. That is, SES may be a consequence rather than a cause of IQ. The point here is that matching or "controlling" SES cannot aid in isolating the genetic contribution of race to IQ scores, as has sometimes mistakenly been implied. The line of reasoning taken in such studies is that when one equates the SES levels of Black and White groups to be compared, environment has been made equivalent. Therefore if IQ differences between matched groups are smaller or negligible, it is because of the removal of differences in experience. The large differences ordinarily found when racial groups unmatched in SES are compared is thus interpreted not as genetic in origin but as due to the differences in richness of experience enjoyed by Blacks and Whites. If, however, SES is not simply an index of differences in experiences (and their attendant effects upon IQ) but rather a partial reflection of the genetic component of IQ, the preceding reasoning collapses. As argued effectively by Gallo and Dorfman (1970), it is hard to imagine that innate differences in ability make no contribution to the socioeconomic level one attains. To the extent that IQ has a genetic component, children will then exhibit IQ levels that reflect the SES of their parents. Gottesman (1968) eloquently makes this same point. In sum, the question of genetic differences between races and/or social classes cannot be easily solved at this time.

Personality Variables and IQ

Several investigators have suggested that personality variables such as self-concept, self-esteem, and anxiety may mediate intelligence and

[1] As Professor Thomas Pettigrew noted (personal communication), calculations from 1940 and 1970 census data indicate that up to 15 of every 16 "middle-income," "middle-status-employed" Black families today came from lower-class origins.

achievement (Dreger & Miller, 1968). Though few studies directly assess this relation, this section will present those that bear on it.

Ausubel (1958) found that Blacks in heterogeneous racial situations compete more and that their self-esteem increases. Henton and Johnson (1964) compared Black children to a sample of White children previously studied by Bledsoe and Garrison (1962). Though a low positive relation was found between self-concept and intelligence in both groups, nevertheless, a negative self-image was more characteristic of Black than of White children. Although they found no racial differences on an anxiety scale, other studies have found such a difference (e.g., Palermo, 1959). Yet Roen (1960) presented contradictory data for adults. Since adults may be more likely than children to be inclined toward favorable self-presentation on personality tests, perhaps disconfirmations in adult samples should be given less weight. Dreger and Miller (1968), summarizing studies on self-attitude, noted that Blacks consistently have more negative self-attitudes and implied that this affects their intelligence test scores (p. 47). Indeed, this position is a common one (Baughman & Dahlstrom, 1968; Christmas, 1973; Crain & Weisman, 1972; Hauser, 1971; Katz, 1967).

Teachers' Attitudes and IQ

Another variable that has most often been overlooked is the relation of IQ to the attitudes and expectations of teachers. Rosenthal and Jacobson (1968) found that teachers' expectations for a child's performance may act as a self-fulfilling prophecy. Elashoff and Snow (1971) severely criticized this study and impugned its conclusion. However, Baughman and Dahlstrom (1968) found that teachers' behavioral ratings of Black children were useful indicators or predictors of IQ change. A variety of traits basically reflecting "personal maturity" were positively correlated with IQ change. In addition, children who gained in IQ over the three-year period examined were better liked by teachers. It is quite plausible that shifts in IQ modify a teacher's perception of a child's personality. On the other hand, these results can be interpreted as essentially confirming Rosenthal's contention that teachers' expectations may influence changes in IQ scores. In an extensive and careful review of this literature, Brophy and Good (1974) concluded that teacher expectation effects clearly do occur.

Examining this kind of data from a slightly different perspective, Rubovits and Maehr (1971, 1973) found that differential treatment is accorded those children randomly labeled "gifted" (IQ between 130 and 135) and those labeled "nongifted" (IQ between 98 and 102). In addition, differences in the "quality of attention" given to the "gifted" and "nongifted" students interacted with race (Rubovits & Maehr, 1973). Not only were White students, as a group, given more attention, praised more, called on more, etc., than Black students, but, as might be expected, the White "gifted" students also received more attention. However, the "gifted" Black students received the least attention and were the most criticized, even in comparison to "nongifted" Black students. (This point receives confirmation in our own data as shown in Chapter 11. The achievement test performance of the most gifted Blacks showed the greatest relative decrement in the face of negative teacher expectations.)

In a similar vein, parents' attitudes and treatment of their children may reflect that child's IQ; that is, parents may grant more attention to brighter children and behave in a more favorable manner toward them. The implication of this differential treatment of children who have higher IQs is that the favorable attitudes and behaviors bestowed upon the "bright" child by both parents and teachers may increase confidence, motivation, and other personality variables and thereby lead to better performance in school settings on a variety of academic tests (IQ, achievement, etc.).

Scholastic Achievement and IQ

Intelligence has been fairly well accepted as a mediating variable that predicts an individual's academic performance and achievement. Generally the correlation between intelligence and academic achievement, as measured by standardized achievement tests (as opposed to teachers' grades), ranges from .50 to .70 (McCandless, 1970; Duncan, Featherman, & Duncan, 1972). Illustrative of the relationships typically found are those cited by Day (1968), who assessed the correlations between IQ scores and achievement among seventh- and eighth-grade Canadian students. The correlations obtained between IQ scores and test scores for various school subjects (English, math, science, etc.) ranged from .41 to .67. Furthermore, there were usually few differences between the correlations obtained for males and females, although Khan (1969) has suggested that measures of motivation in addition to measures of intelligence add more to the precision in predicting males' achievement scores than females' scores. Holtzman and Brown (1968) supported this latter finding but added that such additional information improves predictions for females as well.

There seems to be contradictory evidence regarding the accuracy of these predictions for disadvantaged children. Where McCandless (1970), in a review of some of the literature, suggested that the achievement of disadvantaged children is predicted with less accuracy by standard IQ tests than is the achievement of advantages or middle-class children (e.g., Schweiker, 1968), other investigators have stated that IQ tests have similar validity in their capacity to predict achievement for both disadvantaged and advantaged groups (e.g., Cleary, 1968; Stanley, 1971). Part of the inconsistency may be accounted for by the fact that the studies by Cleary (1968) and Stanley (1971) were conducted on college-level students. Thus a restricted range of scores was available in that they were collected from a portion of the population that would, expectedly, be brighter. As a result, it would not be surprising to find that differences in predictability had disappeared.

Finally, only recently has a study been conducted examining IQ scores, achievement test scores, and teachers' grades in relation to race, sex, and social class (McCandless, Roberts, & Starnes, 1972). The results indicated that IQ scores were generally good predictors of standardized achievement scores ($r = .45$) and of teachers' grades ($r = .56$). However, contrary to expectation, correlations between IQ scores and achievement were *higher* for disadvantaged than for advantaged children (.74 and .20, respectively), and higher for Blacks (.55) than for Whites (.19). A similar pattern obtained between IQ and grades, suggesting that predictions about relationships for subgroups cannot be made from those obtained from a general population. While subgroup differences might be interpreted as school-specific effects in that children of a particular race or SES level might tend to attend the same school, R. M. Hauser (1972) has convincingly shown that much too much weight has been given to so-called between-school effects.

Summary

To recapitulate, mean IQ scores for White children generally exceed by a standard deviation those obtained for Black children. When socioeconomic levels are examined and supposedly controlled, racial differences in IQ, though smaller in magnitude, generally remain. In interpreting these differences, one must first consider the definition of race. Although skin color is usually employed, there are obvious difficulties with so simple a criterion. Secondly, methodological issues involved in administering IQ tests to different racial groups also warrant consideration. Other problems may arise from the fact that the instruments have been standardized on American-born Whites.[2] A further problem stems from the likelihood that items of the tests are culturally loaded and therefore unfair to minority group children (Hunt, 1961). Additionally, samples of Whites and minorities matched on variables thought to affect IQ (such as socioeconomic status) have been difficult to obtain. Consequently it has not been easy to make an accurate assessment of the contribution of these variables to racial differences—quite apart from the substantial inferential problems that would remain after successful matching. Still another problem, often ignored, stems from the fact that the respective races of examiner and subject affect IQ achievement test scores (Dreger & Miller, 1968). Finally, the motivational problems and social expectancy sets that the minority child takes into the testing situation may lower his scores. These various factors must be considered in any appraisal of the studies conducted, and at this point it is unlikely that definite conclusions about the relative genetic and environmental contributions to IQ scores can be accurately assessed.

Personality variables, such as anxiety and self-esteem, do seem related to IQ; higher IQ scores are correlated with higher levels of self-esteem and lower anxiety. Teachers' attitudes and expectations may

---

[2] Given that the mean and the standard deviation have been arbitrarily set at 100 and 15 respectively, consider the interpretive problems that might arise for the educator who normally lacks technical psychometric training when he confronts the fact that underlying means and standard deviations of various racial-ethnic groups vary. For instance, if the distribution of raw intelligence test scores for Eskimos has a smaller standard deviation than the group on whom the test was standardized, the fact that they were omitted from the standardization would cause an Eskimo of above-average intelligence to obtain an IQ score that is lower than the one he would have obtained had Eskimos been included in the standardization.

either influence the child's performance (on IQ or other tests), and/or teachers' knowledge and perception of the child's IQ score may influence their attitude, expectation, and evaluation of the child. Finally, while IQ is positively related to measures of scholastic achievement, the relative strength of the relationship within racial, ethnic, or socioeconomic subgroups is not clear.

The Riverside Data

As indicated, the Riverside IQ data were analyzed to assess racial differences before desegregation in comparison to the data found in previous studies. Furthermore IQ scores were examined following desegregation so that changes could be assessed. Finally, differences and changes in IQ related to socioeconomic status, self-concept, parents' attitudes, and teachers' attitudes were explored.

Method

Three intelligence tests were administered to the Riverside School Study population: the Wechsler Intelligence Scale for Children (WISC), the Peabody Picture Vocabulary Test, and the Raven Progressive Matrices.

The WISC is designed for children aged 5–15 and consists of 12 subtests yielding three scores: verbal, performance, and total scores. The test was originally standardized on 2200 White children from various geographical locations. The WISC was administered only once to the Riverside School Study children, in 1967, after desegregation had occurred. Two highly trained White psychometrists administered the WISC in each child's school.

The Peabody and Raven tests were administered once prior to desegregation (1966) and then again in 1969 and 1971.[3] The Raven Progressive Matrices test consists of a series of designs with a piece missing from each one. The child is asked to choose the missing piece from among four alternatives. The Raven test is a test usually assumed to be more culture-free than most measures of intelligence. Both the Raven and the Peabody were administered as part of the children's test-

---

[3] In this chapter, only the postmeasures taken in 1969 will be used in the analyses.

ing schedule by the interviewers involved. Both intelligence measures were administered during the second of the two interviews with each child. Besides examining racial differences in intelligence, we will explore its relation to other psychological variables. These will be described more fully as the results pertaining to each are presented. Most analyses use the full Riverside sample of approximately 1800 Anglo, Black, and Mexican-American children.

Results

Intelligence before and after Desegregation

Racial differences in IQ before desegregation and changes after desegregation were assessed by analyses of variance. Even though there may be residual caste differences, nevertheless, gross differences in economic environment can be controlled in analyses that compare socioeconomic subgroups. The Duncan Socioeconomic Index (1961) defines SES in terms of position in the occupational structure. The mean SES levels are: Anglos = 55.01; Blacks = 28.9; and Mexican-Americans = 17.60 (maximum possible range: 1–96). Further analyses compared subsamples of Anglos similar to (the lower 20% of Anglos; mean SES = 20.04) and substantially below (the lower 5%; mean SES = 11.88) the mean SES of the minority groups. As can be seen, the mean of the lower 20% of Anglos fell below the mean SES level for the Blacks but slightly exceeded that of Mexican-Americans. Although it would have, of course, been possible to pick subsets of Anglos with means that exactly matched each of the minority groups, this exactitude would have been misleading in that the effects of regression would still have left the comparison groups unequal and, as mentioned previously, caste differences would still have existed. Thus these comparisons primarily serve an illustrative purpose. In terms of our procedure, even though the mean of the lower 20% of Anglos would have been higher if they had been measured again on SES (a consequence of regression), nevertheless, it is likely that the mean would still have been below that of Blacks. Obviously this is not true of the comparisons to the Mexican-Americans. For the comparison to the lower 5% of Anglos, it is clear that their mean SES level lay substantially below that of both minority groups. The mean IQ scores for these various subgroups are presented in Table 5.1.

TABLE 5.1 *IQ Comparisons among Blacks, Mexican-Americans, and Various Socioeconomic Groupings of Anglos before and after Desegregation*

	All Anglos	Anglos below lower 20% of SES distribution	Anglos below lower 5% of SES distribution	All Blacks	All Mexican-Americans
Predesegregation					
Peabody 1966	110.64	105.44	103.43	96.03	90.70
Raven 1966	107.33	106.14	102.64	92.97	95.47
Postdesegregation					
WISC total 1967	106.96	102.02	101.14	90.50	90.40
WISC performance 1967	107.98	104.59	104.04	91.85	96.64
WISC verbal 1967	104.80	99.41	98.21	90.84	86.38
Peabody 1969	111.30	108.29	109.57	95.88	90.96
Raven 1969	107.66	109.31	107.86	92.22	95.82

Predesegregation IQ Measures. First we will examine pre-desegregation differences in IQ. Only the Raven and the Peabody tests were administered to the children in 1966, prior to desegregation. On both measures, the Anglos scored higher than did either of the two minority groups (Peabody: $F = 382.82$; $df\ 2/1646$; $p < .01$; Raven: $F = 166.54$; $df\ 2/1660$; $p < .01$). For both tests, all means were significantly different from each other. It is also interesting to note that Blacks exceeded the Mexican-Americans on the Peabody test while the reverse was true on the Raven.

The IQ scores obtained by Anglos in the lower 20% of the SES distribution were slightly lower than those obtained by the full sample, but they were still significantly higher than those obtained by the minorities (Peabody: $F = 36.58$; $df\ 2/186$; $p < .01$; Raven: $F = 17.07$; $df\ 2/186$; $p < .01$). When Anglos in the lower 5% of the SES distribution were compared to the minority groups, they still performed somewhat better than the minorities on the Peabody ($F = 4.52$; $df\ 2/81$; $p < .05$), but there were no longer differences among the three groups on the Raven ($F = 2.21$; $df\ 2/81$; ns).

WISC Measures. As indicated in the method section, the WISC was given only in 1967, one year after desegregation. Again the Anglos obtained higher scores (WISC full scale: $F = 271.67$; $df\ 2/1510$; $p < .01$; WISC performance scale: $F = 186.72$; $df\ 2/1510$; $p < .01$; WISC verbal scale: $F = 264.23$; $df\ 2/1510$; $p < .01$). However, individual contrasts showed that Blacks and Mexican-Americans did not differ on the WISC full scale ($F = 0.02$; $df\ 2/1510$; ns). The two minorities did differ on the subscales, the Blacks scoring higher on the verbal scale ($F = 26.07$; $df\ 2/1510$; $p < .01$) but lower on the performance scale ($F = 28.64$; $df\ 2/1510$; $p < .01$). It should be noted that there were no language problems for the Mexican-American children on this test, so that the necessity of translating items was eliminated. Although this indicates that their comprehension of the English language may have been sufficient to understand test items, it does not necessarily mean that the scores obtained by these children are representative of their verbal ability. In fact, given that a second language is spoken in the homes of these children, thus decreasing the chances for practice of the English language, lower scores on tests tapping verbal ability would be expected in comparison to those tests that measure performance.

Examination of the scores obtained by Anglos in the lower 20%

and lower 5% of the SES distribution indicated that the differences between the races were substantially the same as those obtained with the full sample of Anglos (see Table 5.1).

Postdesegregation IQ Measures. When the Peabody and Raven were readministered, racial differences found in the premeasures remained intact (Peabody: $F = 314.61$; $df\ 2/1284$; $p < .01$; Raven: $F = 142.79$; $df\ 2/1320$; $p < .01$). Within each test, all means differed from one another.

Again, all differences were maintained when minority groups were compared to Anglos in the lower 20% of their SES distribution. Further, the IQ scores of the lower 5% of the Anglos still exceeded those of the minority children. The outcome of this latter comparison differed from the analyses of the predesegregation data. There, a difference between this lowest subgroup of Anglos and the minority groups appeared only for the Peabody and not the Raven.

Further analyses were performed to assess whether the attempt to equate the Anglos on SES level (that is, by looking at those in the lower 20% and the lower 5% of the SES distribution) with the minorities would significantly reduce the Anglo–minority difference in IQ. For example, the difference between the full Black sample's scores and the full Anglo sample's scores on an IQ measure was compared to the difference between the Blacks and those Anglos in the lower 20% (or 5%) of the SES distribution. This type of comparison was made for all the IQ measures. The differences between the minority groups and either the lower 5% or the lower 20% of the Anglo group were significantly smaller than those between the minority groups and the full Anglo sample for both the Peabody predesegregation data ($p < .01$) and the WISC total data ($p < .05$). These analyses show the important contribution of socioeconomic level to the IQ differences between races.

All the above results are fairly consistent with those obtained in previous studies. Prior to desegregation the difference between Anglos and minorities was approximately 15 IQ points on all measures used. When socioeconomic differences were either largely equalized or substantially overcorrected, the IQ differences did not disappear but were reduced to about 7–12 IQ points.

The differences in rank order of scores obtained by Blacks and Mexican-Americans remained consistent in terms of the relative performance of the two groups on the tests given here. That is, Mexican-Americans scored higher on the WISC performance scale and lower on the WISC verbal scale than Blacks. Furthermore, the Mexican-Americans scored higher on the Raven Progressive Matrices, which is less dependent on verbal ability than the Peabody test, and lower on the Peabody than the Blacks. Considering that Mexican-Americans can be seen as coming from a different linguistic background than Anglos or Blacks, these results are not surprising.

Repeated-measures analysis of variance confirmed the consistency in IQ scores from pre- to postdesegregation that is implied above. Separate analyses for both the Raven and the Peabody showed not only no changes as a function of time (i.e., grade or pre- to postdesegregation) but also no interactions between ethnic group and time. Thus the desegregation experience had no discernible effect on measured intelligence for any of the three ethnic groups, a result not totally unexpected since IQ scores are usually assumed to remain constant over time.

The Effects of "Environmental" Variables on IQ

As mentioned in the introduction, there is little doubt that the individual's environment has some effect on IQ scores. Thus a child's environment may influence his self-attitudes by reflecting how he perceives himself in relation to his peers. Other important individuals in the child's environment are his parents and his teachers. Their respective attitudes toward him may also have bearing on his intellectual performance. Therefore, analyses were performed on the IQ data in consideration of the possible mediating effects of several of these variables.

Self-Attitudes of the Children. As mentioned before, several investigators suggest that self-concept mediates IQ so that negative self-concepts lead to lower intellectual performance (Dreger & Miller, 1968) and poorer school performance (Coleman, 1966). High anxiety also lowers performance on tests (Katz, 1964; Spence, 1963; Taylor & Spence, 1952). In addition, Sarason, Davidson, Lighthall, Waite, and Ruebush (1960) suggested that low self-esteem goes hand in hand with school anxiety. Therefore, analyses were performed to examine the extent to which differences in these personality variables are associated with intelligence test performance.

All Anglos were compared to a subsample of the minorities that consisted of Blacks and Mexican-Americans who were high in self-

TABLE 5.2 Mean IQ Scores of All Anglos and Those Blacks and Mexican-Americans Who Were High in Self-Attitude and Low in General Anxiety

	Anglos	Blacks	Mexican-Americans
Peabody 1966	110.64	99.29 (96.03)[a]	95.58 (90.70)
Peabody 1969	111.30	100.87 (95.88)	95.17 (90.96)
Raven 1966	107.33	94.99 (92.97)	96.86 (95.47)
Raven 1969	107.66	93.12 (92.22)	96.39 (95.82)

[a] Bracketed scores are those obtained by the full sample of Blacks and Mexican-Americans, as in Table 5.1.

attitude (above the 67th percentile) and low in general anxiety (below the 33rd percentile). Each of these measures consisted of 15 direct questions to which children could answer "yes" or "no." For example, a question representative of general anxiety was "Do some of the stories on television scare you?" and one representative of self-attitude was "Do you ever wish you were someone else?" Separate analyses of variance compared the three groups on the Peabody and Raven IQ scores both before (1966) and after (1969) desegregation.[4] Table 5.2 summarizes the means.

For all measures, the Anglos still scored significantly higher than the Blacks and Mexican-Americans (Peabody 1966: $F = 40.84$; df $2/742$; $p < .01$; Peabody 1969: $F = 41.31$; df $2/569$; $p < .01$; Raven 1966: $F = 25.55$; df $2/754$; $p < .01$; Raven 1969: $F = 30.39$; df $2/584$; $p < .01$). Comparison of the means shows that the subsample of minorities obtained IQ scores that exceeded the full minority sample by 5 IQ points on the Peabody ($p < .05$). This

[4] First of all, it should be noted that the IQ scores reported in 1966 were for those minority children who were high in self-attitude and low in anxiety in 1966. Similarly the IQ scores reported in 1969 reflect the personality ratings obtained in 1969 for the children. Thus it is possible and even likely that the subsamples of minority children did not include all the identical individuals in 1966 and 1969. Further, since the WISC was administered only in 1967 but personality ratings were obtained in 1966 and 1969, as indicated above, the WISC IQ scores were not included in this analysis. However, given that our other analyses, using all three IQ measures, indicated consistent outcomes among the tests, we might safely assume that similar results would have been obtained had the WISC scores been analyzed as well.

amounts to approximately one-third of the gap between Anglos and minority groups. However, the 1–2 point increase on the Raven was not significant. Although these results suggest that a more positive self-concept and a lower anxiety level may lead to somewhat better intellectual performance, the causal direction is by no means unambiguous. A higher IQ score may be the *source* of better scores on these adjustment measures.

Attitudes of Parents. The preceding section considered the relation between high self-esteem or positive self-attitudes and IQ scores. Another approach to this same issue focuses on the parent data. Children whose parents have favorable attitudes toward them may, as a consequence, perform better on intelligence tests. However, whereas favorable parent attitudes might exert a causal influence in raising IQ scores, it should be apparent here too that an opposite causal direction is equally likely. That is, parents may be more favorable toward or display more positive, affectionate feelings toward children with higher IQs. Alternatively, and perhaps most likely, we might expect both of these causal processes to operate in the normal home.

The parent interview schedule provided information on feelings of "favorability" toward their children from a factor analysis of ratings of the children on 21 personality trait dimensions.[5] Those Black and Mexican-Americans who had been rated favorably by their mothers, by their fathers, and by both parents jointly (highest 20% of the distribution) were compared to the total sample of Anglo children. Interestingly the results indicated little to no difference between the mean scores obtained by the full sample of minority children and this subsample of children. For example, the largest difference was obtained between the full-sample Mexican-American mean on the Peabody 1966 (mean = 90.70) and the mean obtained by Mexican-Americans rated favorably by their fathers (mean = 93.2). The Anglos still scored significantly higher than either of the minority groups and the same pattern of scores attained by the minorities persisted (Blacks scoring higher than Mexican-Americans on all measures except the Raven and the WISC performance subscale). Thus parents' attitudes of "favorability" toward their children, as reflected in personality trait ratings, are not associated with IQ scores.

Teachers' Attitudes Toward Children. Research by Rosenthal

[5] This factor analysis parallels that described in Chapter 11.

TABLE 5.3   Mean IQ Scores of All Anglos and Those Blacks and Mexican-Americans Rated Favorably by Teachers on Ability–Motivation Dimension

	A	B	MA
Peabody 1966	110.64	101.33 (96.03)[a]	96.67 (90.70)
Peabody 1969	111.30	102.47 (95.88)	95.93 (90.96)
Raven 1966	107.33	99.81 (92.97)	100.97 (95.47)
Raven 1969	107.66	103.28 (92.22)	100.58 (95.82)
WISC total	106.96	99.66 (90.50)	97.76 (90.40)
WISC performance	107.98	98.84 (91.85)	101.99 (96.64)
WISC verbal	104.80	100.36 (90.84)	94.34 (86.38)

[a] Full-sample IQ in parentheses.

and Jacobson (1968) and Baughman and Dahlstrom (1968) suggests that teachers' expectations may influence changes in IQ scores. Teachers who anticipate poor performance from minority children entering their class may, perhaps inadvertently, create the circumstances that confirm their expectations by being overly critical, prematurely assigning them to lower reading groups, ignoring them, etc. Further, Rubovits and Maehr (1971, 1973) suggested that teachers' knowledge and/or accurate perceptions of children's mental abilities and IQ scores may lead to more positive and favorable attitudes toward those children.

Among the data collected from teachers were their ratings of children in their classes on several personality traits. Factor analysis of these adjectives yielded an "intellectual competence–motivation" factor (including adjectives such as *intelligent, good memory, persevering*), and a "passivity–compliance" factor (including adjectives such as *obedient, cooperative, patient*). Analysis of summary scores compiled from the adjectives contributing to each factor compared the IQ scores of all the Anglos with those minority students who had been rated favorably by their teachers.[6] Table 5.3 presents the data for the intellectual competence–motivation factor. For all intellectual measures, the Anglos

[6] Teachers' favorability ratings and the IQ scores that are reported were obtained in a manner similar to that used in obtaining personality ratings and IQ scores (as described in footnote 4). That is, the IQ scores of the subsample of children reported in any particular year correspond to favorability ratings obtained in the same year (for example, IQ scores in 1966 are based on favorability ratings made in 1966, etc.)

still scored significantly higher than the minorities and the rank order of scores for the minorities remained the same. However, when a comparison was made between this subsample of minority children and the full sample, there were obvious differences. Minority students rated favorably by their teachers on an ability–motivation dimension had IQ scores 5–10 points higher than other minority children ($p < .01$). These differences decreased to only 2 IQ points (ns) for those minority children rated favorably by their teachers on the Passivity–Compliance dimension.

Consistent with results obtained by others (Baughman & Dahlstrom, 1968; Rubovits & Maehr, 1971, 1973), those minority children rated more favorably on the ability–motivation dimension did possess higher IQ scores. Yet, interestingly, there was no relation between IQ and the favorability of ratings on the passivity–compliance dimension. It is also interesting to note, although not totally unexpected, that whereas a child's IQ might have been an important contributor to teachers' favorable attitudes and ratings, IQ scores were less influential in determining parents' attitudes and ratings; that is, the parents were more apt to have favorable and loving attitudes toward their children based on a variety of attributes of which IQ was only one, and probably one of minimal importance at that.

IQ Scores and Their Relation to Achievement and Educational Aspirations

Although IQ, achievement, and educational aspirations are commonly assumed to be related, few studies have gathered information on all three variables. The following section assesses their relation in the Riverside School Study data.

Correlations of IQ and Achievement Scores. Correlations between the seven IQ measures and the several achievement scores are summarized in Table 5.4 for each ethnic group as well as low SES Anglos. Three of these achievement scores were based on a composite of several standardized achievement test scores (math, verbal, etc.). One summary score was compiled for each child in 1965–66, one in 1966–67, and one in 1968–69. All were standardized within grades and across races. The other eight achievement scores used consisted of classroom grades for mathematical and verbal ability between the years 1965 and 1969. These, too, were standardized within grades.

*TABLE 5.4   Mean   Correlations   between   Achievement   Scores   and
IQ Measures*

	Anglos	Anglos in lower 20% of SES distribution	Blacks	Mexican-Americans
Standardized achievement tests and IQ[a]	.45	.34	.43	.42
Classroom grade scores and IQ[b]	.29	.26	.18	.17

[a] Each correlation represents the mean correlation obtained among the 3 standardized achievement scores and 7 IQ measures (21 scores) for each group.
[b] Each correlation represents the mean correlation among 8 classroom achievement scores and 7 IQ scores (56 scores) for each group.

Generally, and for all groups, the IQ measures correlated higher with the three standardized achievement scores than with the classroom grade scores. In addition, t-tests were performed (with the correlations themselves used as scores) to assess which mean correlations might be significantly different among the three ethnic groups.[7] Analyses of the mean correlations between the standardized achievement scores and IQ measures (row 1 in Table 5.4) indicated that there were no significant differences between the full sample of Anglos and both minority groups. However, mean correlations obtained by the Blacks and the Mexican-Americans were significantly higher than that obtained by the lower 20% subsample of Anglos ($p < .05$ and $p < .10$, Black and Mexican-American comparisons, respectively). These data appear consistent with those of Cleary (1968) and Stanley (1971), who found that IQ tests predict achievement equally well for advantaged and disadvantaged individuals. However, these data are somewhat inconsistent with the findings of McCandless *et al.* (1972), which indicated higher correlations between IQ and achievement among disadvantaged as opposed to ad-

[7] Although t-tests are not entirely appropriate, in that the data examined are not independent, there did not seem to be any statistic that was sufficiently suitable or better suited, for that matter, to give order and meaning to the large number of correlations.

vantaged children and among Blacks versus Anglos. Only when SES is grossly adjusted do we find the stronger relation for minorities reported by McCandless *et al.* (1972).

The mean correlations between classroom grade scores and IQ measures (row 2 of Table 5.4) show a different picture. For both the full-sample Anglos *and* the Anglos in the lower 20% of the SES distribution, the mean correlations were significantly higher than those obtained by the minorities ($p < .001$, for all comparisons). The reasons for this difference are not totally clear. However, two possibilities come to mind.

First, the three types of tests probably differ in terms of the extent to which they measure "fluid ability" versus "crystallized ability" (Cattell, 1963, 1971). According to Cattell's distinction, fluid intelligence is largely nonverbal, abstract, culture-free mental ability, and efficiency, whereas crystallized intelligence primarily consists of knowledge, skill, and abilities acquired through cultural experience. Fluid intelligence would presumably be tapped most strongly by tests measuring recall of number of letter series, figure classification, and recognition of figure analogies. Tests measuring vocabulary, general knowledge, word analogies, and knowledge of the mechanics of language structure primarily tap crystallized intelligence. (Other tests, such as verbal reasoning, arithmetic reasoning, and syllogistic reasoning, are thought to tap these two abilities fairly evenly). If this distinction is applied to the data above, the IQ tests are probably loaded highest in fluid ability, the standardized achievement summary scores intermediate, and the classroom grade scores lowest in fluid ability and highest in crystallized ability. If so, higher correlations between IQ and standardized acheivement measures would be expected since these types of tests are more similar in terms of what they measure than are the IQ scores and classroom grade scores. This would account for the fact that the correlations between IQ scores and standardized achievement scores were higher for all ethnic groups.

A second possibility focuses on teacher bias. If teachers had expectations of poorer performance among minority children, these expectations and their subsequent reflections in biased evaluations would appear in classroom grade scores, which are vulnerable to a teacher's subjectivity. It would be much more difficult for such bias to enter the standardized achievement test scores. Such bias would occlude the true differences in the classroom performance of minority children and thereby lower the measured relation between IQ and classroom performance.

These results also bear some discussion in terms of Jensen's (1969) hypotheses regarding Level I ability (associative learning) and Level II ability (conceptual learning, abstract problem solving).[8] Jensen argued that although Level I ability seems to be distributed equally among all socioeconomic groups, Level II ability is distributed "differently in lower and middle SES groups" (p. 114). Furthermore, since it is Level II ability that is being tapped by IQ tests (Jensen cited the Raven Progressive Matrices and Stanford–Binet tests as examples), these tests are unfair to disadvantaged children. In addition, Level II ability "has been most important for scholastic performance" (Jensen, 1969, p. 114). If so, higher correlations between achievement scores (scholastic performance) and IQ scores might be obtained by the Anglos than by the minorities, since the latter predominantly occupy the lower social class whereas Level II ability is more predominant in the higher social classes.

Our analyses pooling all three IQ measures indicated that correlations were of equal magnitude for Anglos and minorities when standardized achievement scores were used, apparently disconfirming Jensen's contention. The magnitude of these mean correlations (0.45, 0.43, and 0.42 for Anglos, Blacks, and Mexican-Americans, respectively) in combination with our large sample sizes suggests that it is unlikely that we simply failed to detect true differences.

It could be argued, however, that among the three IQ measures the Raven constitutes the best measure of what Jensen terms Level II ability, whereas among the three, the Peabody comes closer to reflecting Level I ability (associative ability) than the total score of the other two. Consequently the correlations of these measures with achievement were examined separately. Among the Anglos, the Raven predesegregation IQ scores (1966) correlated more highly with both standardized achievement scores ($p < .05$) and classroom grade scores ($p < .05$) than do the Peabody IQ scores. The 1969 data for both minorities present a contrasting picture in that the Peabody IQ scores correlated more highly

[8] To some extent these terms parallel Cattell's distinction. However, whereas the overlap between Jensen's "Level II ability" and Cattell's "fluid intelligence" seems quite substantial, there do seem to be some discrepancies between Jensen's "Level I ability" and Cattell's concept of "crystallized intelligence."

than the Raven with the standardized achievement scores ($p < .01$). Curiously, however, these differences did not exist for the Anglos in the postdesegregation data, nor did they appear for the minorities in the predesegregation data.

These differences that emerge in correlations of individual IQ measures with achievement do seem somewhat supportive of Jensen's notion that Level II ability appears in the higher social classes (that is, among the full-sample Anglos in comparison to the minorities). However, there are two major inconsistencies. First, as mentioned, the differences in correlations observed among the Anglos in 1966 no longer existed in 1969. Changes in Level II ability over the years could conceivably account for this weakened relation. Yet Jensen has suggested that innate neural structures underlie Level II ability and furthermore that these differ from those that underlie Level I ability (Jensen, 1969, p. 114). From this standpoint, the decreased correlation can be taken as pointing to the role of environment. It probably reflects an increase in the importance of social factors that influence achievement test scores. Similarly, the appearance in the minorities of a difference in correlations between achievement and Level I versus Level II ability in 1969 but not in 1966 also points to a modifying effect of environment upon the relation between genetic structures and performance on standardized achievement tests.

Secondly, the correlations obtained by the Anglos in the lower 20% of the SES distribution should reflect the same respective differences as those expected for the minorities. Specifically, the Peabody correlations should be higher than the Raven correlations for these lower-class Anglos. Instead, our analyses indicated that there were no significant differences, either before or after desegregation. Therefore, in taking all the above analyses into consideration, we are left with some support but also some major discrepancies regarding Jensen's hypotheses about Level I and II abilities.

IQ and Educational Aspirations. Analyses of variance were performed to determine how IQ related to educational aspirations. There were three levels of educational aspiration examined as part of the interview data: desire to attend high school and college; desire to attend high school only; and desire to attend neither.

On all measures, racial differences remained intact and were significant. However, there was only a main effect for aspiration on two of the seven IQ measures. On two measures (Peabody in 1966 and Raven in 1969) those children who had higher educational aspirations also had higher IQ scores. The fact that this was not a consistent finding is interesting. It suggests that perhaps there was an element of realism versus idealism being tapped here as well. That is, for the minority groups, it might be more realistic *not* to aspire too high, no matter how "intelligent" one might be. A cursory examination of the data indicates that this may be the case. For the Blacks, on most measures, the highest mean IQ scores occurred for those who said they planned to attend high school only (for example, WISC total IQ means: desire to attend high school and college = 90.21; desire to attend high school only = 100.00; desire to attend neither = 85.80). For the Mexican-Americans, although the highest scores were attained by those with the highest educational aspirations, there was a tendency for those desiring to attend neither high school nor college to have higher or equal IQs to those desiring to attend high school only (for example, Peabody 1969 scores: desire to attend high school and college = 90.56; desire to attend high school only = 84.36; desire to attend neither = 88.67). In both cases, the scores may reflect a realistic attitude on the part of these groups.

Discussion

We can now review the answers to several questions posed at the outset. First, our data show that the IQ differences among ethnic groups prior to desegregation were similar to differences found in previous studies. For all measures used, the minority children attained scores approximately 15 points below the Anglos. Additionally, results from the WISC subtests also conformed to those previously found for Blacks; verbal scores exceeded performance scores. However, our results do not support Jensen's contention that Blacks obtain higher scores on tests such as the WISC than on culture-free tests. Blacks scored significantly higher on the Peabody than on the WISC or the Raven ($p < .05$). From Jensen's view, we might have expected them to be lower on the Raven than on either of the other two measures. The Mexican-Americans scored significantly higher on the Raven than on the other two IQ measures ($p < .05$), again contrary to Jensen's notion that those of lower SES perform more poorly on culture-free tests. Additionally, there seems to be some confirmation of Lesser *et al.*'s (1965) suggestion that different types of abilities may be differentially reinforced for each ethnic group. Our data showed that Blacks seemed to perform better on tests tapping verbal ability, while Mexican-Americans obtained higher scores on tests of performance. Although linguistic differences between the two groups could partially account for this, these abilities may also have received differing amounts of emphasis in the home.

A second question concerned what kinds of change, if any, would occur in IQ scores after desegregation. That changes were negligible should not be surprising, since IQ scores typically do not vary to any great extent unless children are involved in intensive enrichment programs or extremely special care is taken in testing situations.

The Riverside School Study did not systematically collect any information on twins, or genetically related children, and therefore cannot speak on the genetic contribution to racial differences in IQ. However, data were obtained on factors other than race that might influence IQ. Even with full realization of the problems involved in trying to match ethnic groups on socioeconomic status, analyses comparing socioeconomic subgroups were performed. Our results were again consistent with those found previously: differences in IQ reduced to about 11 IQ points when SES level was grossly equated. Nevertheless, the differences between Anglos and minorities still remained significant. Yet the fact that the differences between Anglos and minorities *did* significantly decrease when SES was grossly equated indicates the importance of social class as a factor to be dealt with. However, as we indicated in the introduction, the effect of social class cannot be interpreted as only reflecting the role of experimental or environmental factors (as routinely assumed in prior research). We must still entertain the possibility that socioeconomic differences are at least partially due to familial genetic differences.

There is some suggestion from previous research and from ours that certain personality variables such as self-concept and anxiety may mediate IQ. While our analyses cannot separate this hypothesis from one stressing the reverse causal sequence, our data can be interpreted as providing some support for it. Those minority children with a comparatively high self-concept and low anxiety level did have higher IQ scores than the full sample of minority children (although the differences between these subgroups of minority children and the Anglos were still significant). Given that the minorities have generally been found to have lower self-concepts and higher anxiety levels than the Anglos, in our study as well as in others, these results are suggestive.

Although parents' attitudes did not seem to be reflected in children's IQ scores, teachers' attitudes were. Minority children rated highly by teachers in terms of intellectual ability and competence did, in fact, have higher IQs than the full minority sample. Although it seems more reasonable to interpret this relation as indicating the effect of IQ on teacher's trait ratings rather than vice versa, both causal sequences may be operating. Since racial differences did decrease to some extent when each of the above environmental influences was assessed individually, if a comprehensive index of environmental effects had been available, racial differences might have been even more substantially reduced.

Finally, our data show a fairly strong relation between IQ and achievement, an outcome consistent with other recent studies (McCandless *et al.,* 1972; Scarr-Salapatek, 1971; Tulkin, 1968). This relation receives further support from the fact that those minority students who had attained fairly high achievement scores also had higher IQs than did the other minority students. Additionally, minority children seemed to express a more realistic attitude toward educational aspirations than that reported by Coleman (1966) and others.

References

Ausubel, D. P. Ego development among segregated Negro children. *Mental Hygiene,* 1958, *42,* 362–369.

Ausubel, D. P., & Ausubel, P. Ego development among segregated Negro children. In A. H. Passow (Ed.), *Education in depressed areas.* New York: Columbia University, Teacher's College, 1963.

Baratz, S. S., & Baratz, J. C. Early childhood intervention: The social science base of institutional racism. *Harvard Educational Review,* 1971, *41,* 111–132.

Baughman, E. E., & Dahlstrom, W. G. *Negro and White children.* New York: Academic Press, 1968.

Bledsoe, J. D., & Garrison, K. C. Relationships between self-concepts of Negro elementary school children and their academic achievement, intelligence, interests and manifest anxiety. *Comparative Research Project No. 1008,* 1962, U.S. Office of Education.

Brophy, J. E., & Good, T. L. *Teacher–student relationships: Causes and consequences.* New York: Holt, Rinehart, & Winston, 1974.

Cattell, R. B. Theory of fluid and crystallized intelligence: A critical experiment. *Journal of Educational Psychology,* 1963, *54,* 1–22.

Cattell, R. B. *Abilities: Their structure growth and action.* Boston: Houghton Mifflin, 1971.

Christmas, J. J. Self-concept and attitudes. In K. S. Miller & R. M. Dreger (Eds.), *Comparative studies of Blacks and Whites in the United States.* New York: Seminar Press, 1973.

Cleary, T. A. Test bias: Prediction of grades of Negro and White students in integrated colleges. *Journal of Educational Measures,* 1968, *5,* 115–124.

Coleman, J. S., & staff. *Equality of educational opportunity.* U.S. Department of Health, Education, and Welfare. Washington, D. C.: U.S. Government Printing Office, 1966.

Crain, R. L., & Weisman, C. S. *Discrimination, personality and achievement: A survey of northern Blacks.* New York: Seminar Press, 1972.

Day, H. Role of specific curiosity in school achievement. *Journal of Educational Psychology,* 1968, *59,* 37–43.

Deutsch, M. Happenings on the way back to the forum: Social science, IQ and race differences revisited. *Harvard Educational Review,* 1969, *39,* 63–97.

Dreger, R. M. Intellectual functioning. In K. S. Miller & R. M. Dreger (Eds.), *Comparative studies of Blacks and Whites in the United States.* New York: Seminar Press, 1973.

Dreger, R. M., & Miller, K. S. Comparative psychological studies of Negroes and Whites in the U.S. *Psychological Bulletin,* 1960, *57,* 361–402.

Dreger, R. M., & Miller, K. S. Comparative psychological studies of Negroes and Whites in the U.S. *Psychological Bulletin,* Monograph Supplement 70, 1968.

Duncan, O. D. A socioeconomic index for all occupations. In A. J. Reiss *et al., Occupations and social status.* New York: Free Press, 1961, pp. 109–138.

Duncan, O. D., Featherman, D. L., & Duncan, B. *Socioeconomic background and achievement.* New York: Seminar Press, 1972.

Elashoff, J. D., & Snow, R. E. *Pygmalion reconsidered.* Worthington, Ohio: Charles A. Jones, 1971.

Gallo, P. S., & Dorfman, D. E. Racial differences in intelligence: Comment on Tulkin. *Representative Research in Social Psychology,* 1970, *1,* 24–28.

Gottesman, I. I. Biogenetics of race and class. In M. Deutsch, I. Katz, & A. R. Jensen (Eds.), *Social class, race and psychological development.* New York: Holt, Rinehart, & Winston, 1968.

Hauser, R. M. Socioeconomic background and educational performance. Arnold & Caroline Rose Monograph Series in Sociology, American Sociological Association, 1972.

Hauser, S. T. *Black and White identity formation.* New York: John Wiley, 1971.

Henton, C. L., & Johnson, E. E. Relationships between self-concepts of Negro elementary school children and their academic achievement, intelligence, interests and manifest anxiety. *Comparative Research Project No. 1592,* U.S. Office of Education, 1964.

Higgins, C., & Sivers, C. H. A comparison of Stanford–Binet and Colored Raven Progressive Matrices IQs for children in low socioeconomic status. *Journal of Consulting Psychology,* 1958, *22,* 465–568.

Hirsch, J. Behavior–genetic analysis and its biosocial consequences. *Seminars in Psychiatry*, 1970, *2*, 89–105.

Holtzman, W. H., & Brown, W. F. Evaluating the study habits and attitudes of high school students. *Journal of Educational Psychology*, 1968, *59*, 404–409.

Hunt, J. M. *Intelligence and experience*. New York: Ronald Press, 1961.

Jencks, C., *Inequality: A reassessment of the effects of family and schooling in America*. New York: Basic Books, 1972.

Jensen, A. R. How much can we boost IQ and scholastic achievement? *Harvard Educational Review*, 1969, *39*, 1.

Kagan, J. Inadequate evidence and illogical conclusions. *Harvard Educational Review*, 1969, *39*, 2.

Kamin, L. J. Heredity, intelligence, politics and psychology. Unpublished paper, received from author, 1974.

Katz, I. Review of evidence relating to effects of desegregation on the intellectual performance of Negroes. *American Psychologist*, 1964, *75*, 1045–1050.

Katz, I. The socialization of academic motivation in minority children. In D. Levine (Ed.), *Nebraska Symposium on Motivation*, Lincoln, Nebraska: Nebraska University Press, 1967.

Khan, S. B. Affective correlates of academic achievement. *Journal of Educational Psychology*, 1969, *60*, 216–221.

Labov, W. Academic ignorance and Black intelligence. *The Atlantic*, June 1972, *221*, 59–67.

Lesser, G. S., Fifer, G., & Clark, D. H. Mental abilities of children from social class and cultural groups. *Monograph Social Research Child Development*, 1965, *30*, 4.

McCandless, B. R. *Adolescents: Behavior and development*. Illinois: The Dryden Press, 1970.

McCandless, B. R., Roberts, A., & Starnes, T. Teachers' marks, achievement test scores and aptitude relations with respect to social class, race and sex. *Journal of Educational Psychology*, 1972, *63*, 153–159.

McClelland, D. C. *The achieving society*. Princeton: Van Nostrand, 1961.

McPartland, J. As reported in I. Katz, Factors influencing Negro performance in the desegregated school. In M. Deutsch, I. Katz, & A. R. Jensen (Eds.), *Social class, race, and psychological development*. New York: Holt, Rinehart, & Winston, 1968.

Palermo, D. S. Racial comparisons and additional normative data on the Children's Manifest Anxiety Scale. *Child Development*, 1959, *30*, 53–57.

Palmer, F. Unpublished research reported at colloquium at Harvard University, November 1968. As reported in J. Kagan, Inadequate evidence and illogical conclusions. *Harvard Educational Review*, 1969, *39*, 126–129.

Roen, S. R. Personality and Negro-White intelligence. *Journal of Abnormal and Social Psychology*, 1960, *61*, 148–150.

Rosenthal, R., & Jacobson, L. *Pygmalion in the classroom*. New York: Holt, Rinehart, & Winston, 1968.

Rubovits, P. C., & Maehr, M. L. Pygmalion analysed: Toward an explanation of the Rosenthal–Jacobson findings. *Journal of Personality and Social Psychology*, 1971, *19*, 197–203.

Rubovits, P. C., & Maehr, M. L. Pygmalion Black and White. *Journal of Personality and Social Psychology,* 1973, *25,* 210–219.

Sarason, S. B., Davidson, K. S., Lighthall, F. F., Waite, R. R., & Ruebush, B. K. *Anxiety in elementary school children.* New York: Wiley, 1960.

Scarr-Salapatek, S. Race, social class and IQ. *Science,* 1971, *174,* 1285–1295.

Schweiker, R. Discard the semantic confusion related to "intelligence": A Comment of "Social class, race and genetics: Implications for educations." *American Educational Research Journal,* 1968, *5,* 717–721.

Semler, I. J., & Iscoe, I. Comparative and developmental study of the learning abilities of Negro and White children under four conditions. *Journal of Educational Psychology,* 1963, *54,* 38–44.

Semler, I. J., & Iscoe, I. Structure of intelligence in Negro and White children. *Journal of Educational Psychology,* 1966, *57,* 327–336.

Shuey, A. M. *The testing of Negro intelligence.* New York: Social Science Press, 1966.

Spence, J. T. Learning theory and personality. In J. M. Wepman & R. W. Heine (Eds.), *Concepts of personality.* Chicago: Aldine Publishing, 1963.

Sperrazzo, G., & Wilkins, W. L. Further normative data on the Progressive Matrices. *Journal of Consulting Psychology,* 1958, *22,* 35–37.

Sperrazzo, G., & Wilkins, W. L. Racial differences on the Progressive Matrices. *Journal of Consulting Psychology,* 1959, *23,* 273–274.

Stanley, J. C. Predicting college success of the educationally disadvantaged. *Science,* 1971, *171,* 640–647.

Stinchcombe, A. L. Environment: The cumulation of events. *Harvard Educational Review,* 1969, *39,* 511–522.

Stodolsky, S. S., & Lesser, G. Learning patterns in the disadvantaged. *Harvard Educational Review,* 1967, *37* (4), 546–593.

Taylor, J. A., & Spence, K. W. The relationship of anxiety level to performance on serial learning. *Journal of Experimental Psychology,* 1952, *44,* 61–64.

Tulkin, S. R. Race, class, family, and school achievement. *Journal of Personality and Social Psychology,* 1968, *9,* 31–37.

Tulkin, S. R., & Newbrough, J. R. Social class, race and sex differences on the Raven (1956) Standard Progressive Matrices. *Journal of Consulting and Clinical Psychology,* 1968, *32,* 400–407.

Wiener, G., Rider, R., & Oppel, W. Some correlates of IQ changes in children. *Child Development,* 1963, *34,* 61–67.

Wilson, A. B. Educational consequences of segregation in a California community. In *Racial isolation in the public schools,* Appendices, Vol. 2, U.S. Commission on Civil Rights, 1967.

6

Effects of Desegregation on Achievement-Relevant Motivation

Lois Biener and Harold B. Gerard

In spite of public acceptance of the democratic ideals of school desegregation, many citizens have expressed serious reservations about bussing. The one advantage that could possibly outweigh the costs, in the eyes of some critics, would be a significant improvement in the academic performance of the desegregated minority children. As indicated in Chapter 1 underlying the expectation of such an improvement has been the belief that through interracial contact minority children will develop the motivations and values that are presumed to be the necessary mediators of academic achievement. Included in the battery of instruments administered to our sample children were several measures designed to assess achievement motivation. These measures were included in order to provide data for detecting if, in fact, a change in values occurred and further to examine the relationships between change in values and change in achievement. In the initial sections of this chapter we will review the framework of reasoning and research that bears on our notions about motivation and school achievement and that underlies the expectation that desegregation can have a beneficial

Lois Biener • University of Massachusetts, Boston, Massachusetts. Harold B. Gerard • University of California, Los Angeles, California.

impact on minority children. The latter sections will discuss the measures in some detail and present a summary of our findings.

Some Views of the Causes of Deficiencies of the Achievement Motivation of Minority Children

It is widely held that the root of an individual's motivation to achieve can be traced to a particular pattern of early childhood experiences. Need achievement (*n* ach) (McClelland, Atkinson, Clark, & Lowell, 1953), one of the most commonly used indicators of achievement motivation, has been found to be positively related to parental behaviors such as early demands for accomplishment, intense physical and verbal rewards for success, and the expression of interest in and favorable evaluations of the child's efforts (Smith, 1969). This pattern of behaviors is most commonly found in middle-class White families. Many researchers conclude that lower-income Black families do not provide their children with the experiences crucial for developing the need to achieve. There is some dispute, however, about the exact locus of the problem in the low-income family. Ausubel (1963) cites parental authoritarianism and early withdrawal of supervision as the two characteristics that preclude the development of a strong desire to succeed, whereas McClelland (1961) believes that the absence of a strong father figure in most Black families is the root of the problem. Hunt (1968) sees early experiences of success as the prime source of achievement motivation. He argues that the impoverished environment of low-income families handicaps the child's cognitive development and hence reduces the frequency of success experiences.

There are theorists who feel that the racial prejudice in White society as a whole is an important contributor to the lower achievement motivation in ethnic minorities. According to Allport (1954), continuous disparagement from others evokes responses of self-hatred, withdrawal, and passivity on the part of the victim. These defensive mechanisms are incompatible with the active, self-assertive responses that characterize an individual who is striving to master his environment. Hence White expectation of minority failure is seen as an important contributor to the inferior performance of Blacks. The process is reminiscent of Merton's (1948) "self-fulfilling prophecy," which describes the now-familiar dynamics by which people tend to adopt and live out the expectations others hold for them—be they positive expectations or negative ones.

While we will not attempt to evaluate these various theories in this chapter, it is important to point out that, according to one's point of view about the determinants of achievement motivation and the causes of deficiencies in motivation and performance among minorities, one will look with more or less optimism at the various programs aimed at improving minority achievement. Those with a psychoanalytic orientation, who feel that adult personality is irrevocably shaped in the preschool years, would not expect a change in the racial composition of the classroom to alter effectively the motives of ethnic minorities (*cf.* Bettelheim, 1964). A similar conclusion would be reached by theorists who believe there are early critical periods in the development of cognitive abilities that mediate motivation. There do exist several orientations that entertain the possibility that a child's school experience can have an impact on his motivation. In examining our data, we used these more optimistic points of view as a guide to the conditions that may bring about a change in achievement-related behaviors.

Allport's beliefs about the deleterious effects of prejudice led to his "contact theory" (Allport, 1954), which Armor (1972) feels was partly responsible for the promotion of school desegregation as a social policy. Using results of studies of interracial contact (Deutsch & Collins, 1951; Stouffer, 1949), Allport concluded that, "prejudice . . . may be reduced by equal status contact between majority and minority groups in the pursuit of common goals" (Allport, 1954, p. 267). Eliminating prejudice would break the chain in the vicious circle in which disparagement by Whites leads to feelings of inferiority among minorities. Such feelings understandably erode the person's ability to succeed, having as a consequence the reinforcement of White prejudice.

The "lateral transmission of peer group values" is another process that provides a basis for expecting that social contact between minority and White children will have a beneficial effect on the motivation of the minority children. Research on small-group processes has repeatedly demonstrated that the norms and values of a group are usually assimilated by individuals who identify themselves as group members or who simply aspire to membership (Kelley, 1952; Newcomb, 1952; Siegel & Siegel, 1957). In an experimental study of social influence processes, Gerard (1954) found that members of a majority exerted more influence on a minority subgroup than vice versa. Generalizing from these findings, we should expect that if the norms of the White group to which a minority child is introduced stress high motivation for school achievement, and if the minority child either identifies himself as a member of that group or aspires to membership, then he should take on the values of the White peer group and become similarly motivated to achieve in school.

The work of Irwin Katz provides an additional basis for expecting school experience to have an impact on achievement motivation. Katz (1967) believes that the essence of motivation is the acquisition of self-regulatory behaviors. Unlike McClelland, Katz rejects the assumption that Black children have not internalized standards of excellence. He argues, on the contrary, that they have internalized dysfunctionally rigid standards. He cites experimental evidence indicating that low-achieving Black children are highly self-critical.

> The Black child, in a sense, has been socialized to impose failure upon himself. . . . I believe what is involved is not merely a lack of prior rewards for achieving efforts, but also a history of punitive reactions by socializing agents to such efforts. (p. 164)

Katz saw self-reinforcement (which he likened to a process of internal self-praise for one's efforts) as one of the central mediating behaviors that enables a child to sustain effort on tasks that are not consistently interesting and attractive and that offer no immediate extrinsic payoff. Self-mediated reinforcement strengthens the tendency to engage in achievement-related tasks. If a child internalizes this self-regulating behavior, one would expect his motivation to be affected.

According to Katz, self-reinforcement as well as self-discouragement are consequences of social learning—a process mediated by social reinforcement and modeling. This theory gives us reason to expect that under certain conditions desegregation can have a beneficial effect on the motivation of minority children. There is some reason to believe that teachers in predominantly Black schools are more punitive and rejecting of pupils regardless of their academic performance (Clark, 1965; Davidson & Lang, 1968; Gottlieb, 1966). It is possible that positive reinforcement of minority children is more frequent when most of the class is composed of middle-class White children. Even if this is not the case, we might expect that in the desegregated school there would be a greater opportunity for minority students to learn self-reinforcement by modeling the behavior of the White students, who, according to Katz, have internalized this response more adequately.

In summary, there are at least three theoretical positions that predict increased achievement motivation among minority children as a consequence of desegregation:

1. Given equal-status cooperative interaction between minority

and White groups, Allport's contact theory would predict improvement.

2.   To the extent that the desegregated minority child sees himself as a member of the White peer group or aspires to membership in that group, improvement would be expected because of lateral transmission of norms and values.

3.   If teachers in the receiving schools are supportive and encouraging of achievement efforts of the minority child and/or self-reinforcing behavior is displayed by his White classmates, the child will learn internal self-reinforcement and should, in turn, display achievement-oriented behavior.

Existing Evidence for the Impact of Schooling on Motivation

The existing literature does not provide much information about the effect of school desegregation on the achievement motivation of minority children. Motivation is often not considered important enough to study—most reports of research concentrate exclusively on achievement scores. Furthermore, when motivation is examined it is usually measured with direct questions about how hard the children work (Coleman, 1966) and what they want to be when they grow up (*cf.* Armor, 1972; Carrigan, 1969). This type of measure is beset with problems. Responses are easily distorted by situational demands and consequent overcompliance to the assumed wishes of the interviewer—a problem that is especially relevant to minority children (see Proshansky & Newton, 1968, and Veroff & Peele, 1969, for a discussion of this problem). Coleman's data indicate that Black children reported spending more time on their homework than White children. When asked about their aspirations as students, Black children more than any other group indicated that they wanted to be best in their class. Neither of these responses, however, bore any relationship to actual achievement scores. Since the children in Coleman's sample were interviewed by their teachers, it is possible that their responses reflected a desire to give what they considered was the "right" answer. With these cautions in mind, we take note of two reports of negative results. Carrigan (1969) reports a lack of effect of desegregation on the aspirations of a sample of minority children in the Midwest. Armor (1972), discussing the results of a desegregation study in a northern city, reports no significant effect of bussing on Black children's self-report of aspirations for college or future occupations. It is interesting to note that a follow-up interview of some of these same students revealed that bussed students were, in fact, more likely to go to college than their segregated siblings. Although Armor tempers this report of a positive impact by citing a higher drop-out rate for the bussed students, Pettigrew *et al.* (1973), in a critical analysis of the Armor paper, notes that the drop-out rate is actually slightly lower than the national rate for White students. The lack of comparable results for self-report of college plans and actual college attendance underscores the need for caution in interpreting self-report data.

Veroff and Peele (1969), using children from the school district studied by Carrigan, report the results of one of the few attempts to measure achievement motivation in a field study by a method more subtle than self-report of aspirations. They used two measures of risk taking: one assessed the child's responsiveness to his own past behavior (autonomous achievement motivation) and the other measured his choice of a level of risk when the past performance of the other children was the standard (social comparison achievement motivation). Although Carrigan's self-report measure on a similar sample of children showed no effect of desegregation, Veroff and Peele's results indicated that Black males who were bussed to White schools increased in autonomous achievement motivation significantly more than boys who remained in ghetto schools. The difference was not significant for the social comparison measure, but the trend was in the same direction.

In addition to self-report of effort and aspirations, the Coleman (1966) study included several questions that tapped the children's sense of control over their environment. This measure was found to be significantly related to the actual achievement scores of Black children and furthermore to be significantly related to the percentage of White children in the school. Coleman also reported that the achievement scores of Black children were directly related to the proportion of Whites in the school. The U.S. Commission on Civil Rights undertook some further analyses of the Coleman data and found that the relationship between Black pupil achievement and percentage of Whites in the school persisted even when the quality of school facilities, the family background of the Black children, and the characteristics of the teachers were held constant. Although the Coleman study was not concerned with effects of desegregation, these two results are generally taken to be evidence for the positive effects of interracial contact on motivation (Pettigrew, 1969).

The Riverside study included in its battery of instruments several measures that have been theoretically related to achievement motivation. In addition to the advantage of being more covert than self-report of motivation and aspiration, these variables were selected because they have been the object of a good deal of independent research into the nature of achievement motivation. In the next section each of the measures will be described and the literature relevant to minority performance will be reviewed.

Indexes of Achievement Motivation Used in the Riverside Study

Responsiveness to Success and Failure

Atkinson (1966) postulates that when an individual's motivation to achieve success (M_S) is greater than his motivation to avoid failure (M_{AF}), he will tend to set goals for himself that are of intermediate difficulty. When a person's desire to avoid failure predominates, however, it is precisely those intermediate level tasks that he will avoid. A person motivated by fear of failure $(M_{AF} > M_S)$ is more likely, says Atkinson, to set goals that are either very easy (so that success is guaranteed) or very difficult (so that failure can be attributed to external causes). Based on Atkinson's theory, Smith (1969), using measures of fantasy n ach and test anxiety, predicted that children who were designated $M_{AF} > M_S$ would set goals either considerably above or considerably below the level of their past performance on a puzzle task, while those in the $M_S > M_{AF}$ group would choose a goal slightly higher than their past outcomes. His predictions were borne out by results of a sample of White middle-class boys.

There is some evidence in the literature that as compared with Whites, Black children respond more erratically to their past performance and set less realistic future goals. Boyd (1952) found that on a motor performance task Black children had higher expectations about their outcomes than did Whites. Strickland (1971) reported more "unusual shifts"—setting a goal higher after failure and lower after success—among Black than among White adolescents.

In each of three years of data collection, the children in our sample performed a ring-toss task that allowed us to examine goal-setting behavior. The child's task on each of 11 trials was to try to toss nine rope rings onto a peg. On 7 of the trials the child was asked to decide how far from the peg he wished to stand by choosing among nine lines that varied in distance from the peg. On the other 4 trials the distances were standardized within age group. Before the start of a trial, the child was asked how many of the nine rings he expected to get on the peg. Two scores were computed for the present set of analyses: goal discrepancy and unusual shifts.[1]

1. *Goal discrepancy*. Each child was given a goal discrepancy score based on the sum of the absolute differences between his expected performance on each trial and his actual performance on the preceding comparable trial. The lower the score, the more realistic were the child's expectations based on his own past performance.

2. *Number of unusual shifts*. "Number of unusual shifts" is a somewhat different score. Its presumed relationship to achievement motivation is based on the expectation that if a child sets a goal for himself and fails, he should set his next goal lower. Likewise, if he meets his goal, he should set his next one either at the same level or higher. An unusual shift is recorded whenever the child's behavior does not conform to this pattern—when he lowers his expectations after success and raises them after failure. Thus "number of unusual shifts" is not necessarily correlated with goal discrepancy. If a child set his expectations at a high level and performed at a low level but never changed his expectations, he received a high score for goal discrepancy and a low score for "number of unusual shifts."

Sense of Control over the Environment

The importance of a person's sense of control over his environment as a factor contributing to his motivation and achievement has received a great deal of discussion in the literature. It is intuitively reasonable

---

[1] Although it may seem appropriate to assess the tendency to choose distances of intermediate difficulty, we have omitted consideration of that variable. Since the level of difficulty was not announced to the child by the tester, we would have to rely on a distance choice that was intermediate relative to the abilities of the child—a difficult decision to make *a priori* since ability on this task varies with age, sex, and ethnic group and seems to change over time.

that a child will strive to master his environment only if he sees it as malleable and responsive to his efforts. Sense of control takes on special importance when one considers ethnic minorities whose real-life options are, in fact, more limited than those of the Anglo majority. If a child's everyday experience consistently teaches him that he is unable to change the things that happen to him, it makes little sense to strive to achieve high grades. The concept of sense of control has become particularly salient for investigators of minority achievement since Coleman found it to be an important predictor of school performance among Blacks.

Sense of internal control has been measured in several different ways, most measures being derived from Rotter's work (Rotter, Seeman, & Liverant, 1962). Examining Rotter's items, one sees that they generally deal with the extent to which the person believes that "fate" controls his life. "Can you do anything about what is going to happen tomorrow?" is a prototypical question. The items used by Coleman fit into this category. They are quite general and seem to tap an almost ideological fatalism. A second type is represented by Crandall's (Crandall, Katkovsky, & Preston, 1962) Intellectual Achievement Responsibility scale (IAR), which was specifically designed for children. A series of specific outcomes is described to the child and he must choose between attributing them to his own efforts or to uncontrollable factors such as luck or the capriciousness of some external authority. As Katz (1967) points out, internality on one of these scales does not necessarily imply internality on the other. It is quite possible for a child to believe that he received a bad grade in math because he did not study and still maintain that even if he were a great mathematician he would not be able to get a job. It thus appears that internality may not be a unitary trait. Furthermore there is reason to believe that internality is not always positively associated with achievement motivation.

Weiner and Kukla (1970) present a rather explicit rationale for rejecting the notion that internality *per se* is a mediator of achievement motivation. They note that attributions to internal causes are more likely to produce feelings of pride or shame than are attributions to external causes. Furthermore they maintain that the tendency to engage in achievement-related behaviors is a function of a person's past history of positive or negative affect in similar situations. The greatest net amount of positive affect would be produced if a person attributed his success to his own effort or ability but blamed his failure on external causes. Thus the relationship between achievement motivation and responses to internal–external questions cannot be predicted without consideration of the type of outcome being described. It is essential to take account of whether the outcome is seen as a success or as a failure.

Two types of questions, which we shall refer to as fate control and IAR, respectively, were included in the RSS battery.

Fate Control

The fate control scale was composed of the following eight questions:

1. Do you really believe that a child can become whatever he or she wants to become?
2. Can you do anything about what is going to happen to you tomorrow?
3. When people are good to you, is it usually because you have been nice?
4. If another child was going to hit you, could you do anything about it?
*5. Do you often feel you get punished when you don't deserve it?
6. When someone gets mad at you, can you usually do something to make him your friend again?
7. When you get into an argument, is it sometimes your fault?
*8. When bad things happen to you, is it usually someone else's fault?

These items were taken from Bialer's scale (1961), an adaption for children of Rotter's I–E scale. A child was scored as internal for each question to which he answered "yes" except for starred items, which were scored internal if the child answered "no."

IAR Scale

The IAR scale consisted of the following six items, which were modified from Crandall's instrument.[2]

Negative outcome—lack of effort versus external
1. When you have trouble understanding something at school, is it usually
   a. because the teacher didn't explain it clearly, or
   b. because you didn't listen carefully?

---

[2] Although three additional items were administered in 1967, they are not included in this discussion because time requirements led them to be dropped from the 1969 inventory.

2. When you find it hard to work arithmetic problems or math problems at school, is it
   a. because the teacher gave problems that were too hard, or
   b. because you didn't study well enough before you tried them?
3. When you forget something in class, is it
   a. because the teacher didn't explain it well, or
   b. because you didn't try very hard to remember?

Negative outcome—lack of ability versus external

1. When you play a game with someone and lose, is it usually
   a. because the other player is good at the game, or
   b. because you don't play well?
2. When a boy or girl tells you that you are dumb, is it
   a. because they are mad at you, or
   b. because you really did something dumb?
3. Suppose you are showing a friend how to play a game and he has trouble with it. Would that happen
   a. because he wasn't able to understand how to play, or
   b. because you couldn't explain it well?

The six items fall into two categories. Although they all describe negative outcomes, the first three offer internal attributions to lack of effort. The second three offer internal attributions to lack of ability. Attributing an outcome to either of these internal deficiencies leads to negative affect. If the child sees his failure as due to a lack of ability, however, it implies that he expects continued failure in the future, whereas a lack of effort can be corrected if the child wishes to try harder. Two scores were computed for each child, reflecting his tendency to attribute failure (1) to a lack of effort and (2) to a lack of ability rather than an external cause.

Tendency to Delay Gratification[3]

Interest in the person's ability to delay gratification stems in part from the observation that most socially desirable goals require prolonged effort and the concurrent inconvenience of forgoing many immediate rewards. In school settings the self-control required to delay gratification would seem to be an essential prerequisite for completing the numerous and sometimes tedious tasks that are part of the learning process. For example, such activities as television viewing and play must be curtailed to make time for studies. On these grounds it would be ex-

---

[3] Thanks are due to Jerry Zadny for the literature review in this section.

pected that a preference for valuable delayed rewards rather than less valuable but immediately available ones should be associated with sound academic achievement. There are surprisingly few studies bearing on this point.

Older children are typically more likely than younger ones to forgo small immediate rewards for larger rewards in the future (Mischel, 1968; Mischel & Metzner, 1962). There is some evidence that delay preferences are more likely to be inculcated in middle-class children than in children of lower-class families (Maitland, 1967). The evidence for ethnic differences in this behavior is mixed. On the one hand, Jessor, Graves, Hanson, and Jessor (1968) found that, counter to expectations, Mexican-American high school students were often *more* likely than Whites to prefer delayed rewards. On the other hand, a more recent study by Zytkoskee, Strickland, and Watson (1971) predicted and found that Black ninth-graders were more likely than their White classmates to prefer an immediate reward in a hypothetical situation.

There is some evidence that delay preferences are associated with achievement-related factors, but no evidence exists that ties delay preferences to academic achievement per se. Mischel (1961) reported a moderate correlation between fantasy n ach and delay of gratification ($r = 0.27$) for a sample of Trinidadian children. Other studies by Mischel and Metzner (1962) and Mischel (1968) indicated a positive relationship between IQ and choosing to wait for larger delayed rewards. These results led us to expect that academic achievement would be positively related to preferences for delayed rewards.

Most research into the antecedents of delay preference has focused on situational factors (*cf.* Mischel, 1966) and is relevant to the present study insofar as it suggests that changes in the school environment associated with desegregation might alter delay preference. For example, Bandura and Mischel (1965) performed an experiment in which elementary school children with strong preferences of either immediate or delayed rewards were exposed to an adult model who displayed opposite choice patterns. Subsequent measures of delay preference immediately after exposure to the model and a month later showed marked changes toward the preference pattern exhibited by the model. Though generalization from these results is tenuous, it is possible that interethnic and interclass contacts established after desegregation may have provided opportunities for the minority child to witness delay patterns divergent from his own and to mimic those pat-

terns. Indeed, if Katz's theory regarding the importance of self-reinforcement is tenable, one would expect a change in that behavior to be
reflected most clearly in an increased ability to delay gratification.

As part of the test battery used during the first year of our data
collection, the child was offered a choice between a small candy bar that
he could eat immediately or a larger candy bar that he could have when
the testing session was over. The results of the candy bar choice indicated that practically all children delayed gratification. The evidence
that their friends had in fact received the large candy bar probably
contributed to their choice to delay. This measure of the ability to delay
gratification was not used in subsequent years because of complaints
from teachers about children disrupting the class when they returned
with candy bars and from parents who did not want their children eat-
ing candy during the day. In order to meet the problems of the candy
bar choice, the second and third data collections included the following
two items describing hypothetical choice situations. Responses to these
items are included in the present analyses.

> Suppose a friend of yours gets fifty cents a week for doing some extra
> work around the house. Do you think he should spend the money right
> after he gets it on things he wants a lot like candy and soda pop, or should
> he save the money and buy something else that he wants but that costs a lot
> of money, like a toy or a game? If he spends the money now, he can have
> the candy and soda pop right away, but he will have to wait a long time,
> perhaps two months or more, if he saves up for a game. What should he
> do?
>
> Suppose you have money to buy a particular toy or game you've been
> wanting for a long time, and you go to the only store in town that sells it,
> and you find that they're all sold out. They haven't got any more left, but
> they will have some more next week. While you're there you see another
> toy you like that costs the same amount but isn't quite as nice as the toy
> you want. Would you wait till next week for the toy you want, or would
> you buy the other nice toy so you could have something to play with now?

The remainder of this paper will discuss the analyses of the following measures of achievement motivation:

1. Absolute goal discrepancy
2. Number of unusual shifts
3. Fate control
4. Attributions to lack of effort as a cause of failure
5. Attributions to lack of ability as a cause of failure
6. Tendency to delay gratification

Design of the Analyses

The analyses of the Riverside School Study data were designed with three questions in mind:

1. Do the measures show the expected differences for age and ethnic group? Since each of the variables was theoretically related to achievement motivation, the assumption of a deficit in the two minority populations would lead one to expect ethnic differences. Also, since most of the measures were assumed to be indicators of cognitive development, one would expect age differences in performance.

2. Do the measures predict school performance? The relationship of some of our variables to measures of achievement motivation—typically to n ach—has been previously examined. Evidence of their association with achievement *behavior*, however, was sparse and, when one searches for examples of relationships to minority achievement, practically nonexistent. The Riverside School Study data provided an opportunity to investigate the relationships within each of the three ethnic groups in our sample.

3. Is there any indication that desegregation has an impact on achievement-related behaviors?

The Sample

Unless otherwise specified, the sample of minority children whose data are included in these analyses was limited to the minority children who, until the spring of 1966, attended *de facto* segregated schools and were then bussed in the fall of 1966 to the Anglo receiving schools. The Anglo children included in the analyses were enrolled in the receiving schools. The approximate number of children in the various ethnic and age groups is indicated in Table 6.1. These ns are based on the children for whom we had data in the spring of 1966. The exact n for any particular analysis varies somewhat because of missing data on individual variables and gradual attrition of the sample from year to year.

Ethnic and Age Group Differences

The six variables were analyzed with grade, sex, and ethnic group as independent variables. The two indexes of goal-setting represent the scores obtained in the spring of 1966 prior to desegregation. The rest of the measures were not introduced until the spring of 1967 and hence

TABLE 6.1   Number   of   Children   Included   in
Analyses

	Grade		
	K & 1	2 & 3	4–6
Anglo	230	165	225
Mexican-American	80	80	155
Black	65	45	85

represent scores collected after the minority children had experienced one year of desegregated schooling. A summary of the results of our analyses appear in Table 6.2.

Goal Setting

Both goal-setting measures showed the expected age differences. The main effect of grade on goal discrepancy indicates that the older children tended to expect outcomes more in line with their past performance than did the younger children. The main effect for ethnic group in both of these analyses indicates that as compared with Anglos, the Mexican-American and Black children seemed to be less realistic in reporting their future expectations in the ring-toss game and were more erratic in setting goals in relation to their past performance. That is, in general, a minority child was more likely than an Anglo child to set lower goals after success and higher goals after failure. Internal analyses suggest that the grade by ethnic group interaction in unusual shifts was due to the lack of difference between the scores of the youngest Anglo and Black children. Although the Anglos made significantly fewer unusual shifts than did both minorities in grades 2 through 6, in kindergarten and first grade there was no difference between the Anglo and the Black children, whereas the Mexican-American children showed a relatively high level of unusual shifts.

Fate Control

Belief in fate control shows the same pattern of results as goal setting. The grade effect reveals that older children responded to these questions in a manner indicating more perceived control over their environment. Anglos were significantly more internal than either of the

TABLE 6.2   *Probability Values[a] for the Effects of Grade, Sex, and Ethnic Group on Six Measures of Achievement Motivation*

Variable	p value of main effects			Interactions
	Grade	Sex	E.G.	
Absolute goal discrepancy	.001	—	.001	—
Number of unusual shifts	.001	—	.01	Grade × sex ($p < .01$); Grade × ethnic group ($p < .01$)
Fate control	.001	—	.001	—
IAR-attributions to lack of effort	.001	.05	—	—
IAR-attributions to lack of ability	—	—	.01	—
Tendency to delay gratification	.001	—	.001	Grade × sex × ethnic group ($p < .01$)

[a] p values, which indicate the likelihood that the observed differences could have occurred by chance, are based on an unequal n, weighted means analysis of variance (Winer, 1971). The direction of mean differences is discussed in the text.

minority groups, while Black and Mexican-American children did not differ significantly from each other.

Intellectual Achievement Responsibilities (IAR)

Analysis of the IAR items indicates that the tendency to attribute failure to a lack of effort rather than to an external cause increased significantly with age. Girls were generally more likely than boys to see failure as having been due to external causes. The effect of ethnic group was not significant, nor were any of the interactions. The results for the set of three ability items were quite different, yielding only a significant ethnic effect. Given a choice of attributing failure to an external agent or to their own lack of ability, minority children were more likely than Anglos to blame their ability. Contrasts indicated that Mexican-American children were significantly more likely than Anglos to make internal attributions on these items, but the difference between Anglos and Blacks was not statistically significant.

Delay of Gratification

The tendency to delay gratification, as indicated by responses to the two hypothetical situations, demonstrated the now familiar pattern of results. As expected, older children were more likely than younger children to delay gratification, and Anglos were more likely to delay than either of the two minority groups.

Relationship between Achievement Motivation Variables and Score on Standardized Achievement Tests

Our variables, which link theoretically to achievement motivation, yielded relationships that generally conform to expectations regarding developmental and ethnic group differences. If our measures reflect underlying achievement motivation, and if this general motivation is an important mediator of school performance, then we should find a relationship within each ethnic group. As we mentioned earlier, there is little prior evidence, pro or con, linking motivation to the performance of minority children. A simple correlation between our motivational indexes and achievement scores would seem to be the most direct way to assess the degree of relationship. It is possible, however, that an overall analysis might mask the relationship within minority groups while reflecting the presence of a relationship among Anglos. We chose analysis of variance over correlation in order to simplify comparison of the relationships among the various age, sex, and ethnic groups. In our analysis, level of performance on standardized achievement tests was included as a fourth independent variable along with grade, sex, and ethnic group.[4]

[4] The standardized total achievement score was used for these analyses. This score is based on a variety of state-mandated standardized tests administered by the schools. (See Chapter 4 for a more complete description of the achievement score.) For the present analyses, the score was trichotomized within each sex and ethnic group. Since we were interested in the relationship between motivational variables and performance *within* each ethnic group, we were able, using this procedure, to compare scores on the dependent measure of minority children who did well or poorly relative to each other. The child's achievement score for the 1965–66 school year was used for analyses of the goal-setting variables. The 1966–67 score was used for the rest of the variables since they were administered for the first time during that year.

Goal Setting

The analysis, which is summarized in Table 6.3, demonstrated very little if any association between goal-setting behavior and scores on standardized achievement tests. The only significant effect for goal discrepancy was an achievement × sex × ethnic group interaction. Inspection of the means indicated that the interaction was due to a linear relationship between goal discrepancy and achievement for young Anglo and Black girls, a finding that is difficult to interpret. The analysis of "number of unusual shifts" by level of achievement yielded no main effect for achievement nor any interactions between achievement and the other variables. The obvious conclusion seems to be that ring-toss goal-setting behavior does not predict school achievement.

Fate Control

The analysis of fate control did show a significant negative relationship with achievement. Inspection of the means revealed, however, that this pattern did not hold for the Black children.

TABLE 6.3   Probability Values for the Relationship between Scores on Standardized Achievement Tests and Six Measures of Achievement Motivation[a]

Variable	Main effect of level of achievement (p value)	Interactions with level of achievement
Absolute goal discrepancy	—	Achievement × sex × ethnic group ($p < .05$)
Number of unusual shifts	—	—
Fate control	$< .05$	—
IAR-attributions to lack of effort	—	—
IAR-attributions to lack of ability	$< .05$	Achievement × sex ($p < .05$)
Tendency to delay gratification	—	Achievement × grade × sex ($p < .05$)

[a] See footnote to Table 6.2.

IAR

Analysis of the two IAR variables indicated that internal attributions to a lack of effort had no consistent relationship with scores on standardized achievement tests for any of the three ethnic groups. Derogating one's *ability* in the face of failure, however, *was* significantly associated with poor performance. Here is a case where externality was predictive of achievement. The significant interaction between level of achievement and sex was investigated by means of contrasts and indicated that the positive relationship between externality and achievement was significant for girls only.

Delay of Gratification

The relationship between achievement and the tendency to choose the delayed alternative is quite complex. Comparing means for high and low achievers in each grade indicated that delay was significantly related to achievement only for third- and fourth-grade boys, with a linear relationship for minority boys only. The small differences in means for Anglos suggested, if anything, an inverse relationship, that is, an association between the tendency to delay gratification and *poor* performance. Given these complex findings, it is difficult to draw any general inferences about the effects of impulse control on achievement. In summary, our analysis demonstrates that only a miniscule proportion of the variance in achievement can be accounted for by achievement motivation or at least by our measures of it. We obtained a moderate relationship for fate control and for self-attributions of ability, but the other four variables appeared to be virtually unrelated to achievement scores. The lack of relationship may have stemmed from one or more causes.

One possibility is that the instruments may not have been administered with sufficient care, introducing a large amount of error variance. The children's scores therefore may not have reflected the tendencies we set out to measure. The fact that the scores demonstrated highly consistent developmental and ethnic trends would, however, argue that our data were sufficiently reliable. Furthermore, by 1967 our psychometrists were well trained.

The lack of a strong relationship between our variables and achievement suggests that it is untenable to assume that there is a general unitary trait called *achievement motivation*. Mischel (1968), after a careful review of attempts to find stable cross-situational traits, concludes that the evidence is much stronger that human behavior is situationally determined rather than trait-specific. He believes that much more attention must be paid to the particular rewards and punishments associated with each individual activity. To the extent that the reinforcements are similar across activities, we would expect consistency of behavior. Moss and Kagan (1961), for example, reported the results of a study in which observers rated the amount of striving displayed by children in intellectual, mechanical, and athletic tasks. There were substantial correlations between motivation on the intellectual and mechanical tasks, but neither of the two scores was related to striving in athletics. Mischel's caution is clearly applicable to our use of behavior in the ring-toss game as a predictor of motivation in academic tasks since there were obviously vast reinforcement contingency differences between the two contexts.

One of the reinforcement contingencies that may have influenced the child's responses on some of the other measures involves his perception that it was "correct" to give socially desirable answers. Children may learn as they grow older that it is more acceptable to say that their failures were due to not having tried hard enough than to blame the environment. Likewise it is more acceptable for the person to say that he will save money than that he prefers to spend it right away for candy and soda pop. The age and ethnic group differences we obtained on these variables may simply be an indication of the extent to which the various groups of children had acquired a sense of the socially desirable response.

The Impact of Desegregation

In spite of the fact that most of the variables we have been discussing seemed to be unrelated to performance on achievement tests, the behaviors that they measured are interesting in their own right. The two scores derived from the ring-toss game were indicators of the child's responsiveness to his own past outcomes. The better a child scored on these variables, the better he understood the probability-related process of predicting his score on the next trial on the basis of his score on the previous one. This process engages memory and reasoning skills. Thus, even though an improvement in goal discrepancy and "unusual shifts" scores as a consequence of desegregation may not predict the child's achievement test scores, it would imply an improvement in the particular reasoning skills involved. Similarly changes in responses to the fate control, IAR, and delay of gratification items, even if they were a function of social desirability pressures, would suggest that desegregation had an impact on the minority child's concept of the social norms.

In order to investigate the effect of desegregation on the minority child's responses to our measures, we performed cross-sectional analyses to compare the scores of children who had attended desegregated schools for varying lengths of time. Most of these measures were introduced for the first time during the second year of data collection—when the minority children in our sample had been desegregated for one year. For those items the scores of children who had attended desegregated schools for one year were compared with those of children who had experienced three years of desegregated schooling. Since the ring-toss game was administered during each of the three years of data collection, it was also possible to compare the scores obtained from children before desegregation was implemented with the scores of children of the same age who had attended desegregated schools for a year.

So that we could compare predesegregation with one-year post-desegregation performance, a sample was selected of children who were in the first, third, and fifth grades in the spring of 1966 and children who were in the first, third, and fifth grades in the spring of 1967. Any children who either repeated or skipped a grade, and would therefore be members of both samples, were dropped from the analysis. A comparison of one with three years of desegregated experience was accomplished by the comparison of children in the third, fourth, and seventh grades in 1967 with children in those same grades in 1969. These grades were chosen because they allowed construction of independent matched samples. The analysis was structured as a four-way factorial design with time, grade, sex, and ethnic group as the four independent variables. Table 6.4 summarizes the results of the cross-sectional analysis.

Goal Setting

Spending one year in a desegregated school seems to have had a significant effect on the goal-setting behaviors of the children in this sample. Since both analyses resulted in desegregation by grade interactions, contrasts were performed that compared pre- and postdesegregation scores for children in each of the three grades. These analyses indi-

TABLE 6.4   Probability Values for the Effect of Desegregation on Six Measures of Achievement Motivation[a]

I.   Predesegregation *versus* One Year Postdesegregation

Variable	Main effect of desegregation (*p* value)	Interactions with desegregation
Absolute goal discrepancy	< .01	Desegregation × grade (*p* < .01)
Number of unusual shifts	—	Desegregation × grade (*p* < .01)

II.   One Year *versus* Three Years of Desegregation

Variable	Main effect of length of desegregation (*p* value)	Interactions with length of desegregation
Absolute goal discrepancy	< .05	Length of desegregation × sex (*p* < .05)
Number of unusual shifts	—	—
Fate control	—	—
IAR-attributions to lack of effort	—	—
IAR-attributions to lack of ability	—	—
Tendency to delay gratification	< .001	Length of desegregation × sex × ethnic group (*p* < .05)

[a] See footnote to Table 6.2.

cated that desegregation had no significant effect on goal-setting scores of third- and fifth-graders but that desegregated first-graders were performing at a significantly better level than segregated first-graders. Examination of the mean scores (Table 6.5) for these children indicated that the effect was due to improvement by the minority children. The performance of Anglo first-graders actually showed a slight nonsignificant decrement.

The pattern of these results was precisely what we would have expected. Since for the Anglo children the ethnic composition of the classroom in 1967 was much the same as it was for their predecessors in 1966, we did not expect much difference in their performance. For the minority children, on the other hand, there was a striking difference. In 1966 they were attending neighborhood schools, where virtually all of their classmates were minority children from relatively poor families, whereas in 1967 the majority of their classmates were middle-class Whites. One might expect any changes in goal setting to be most apparent for the younger children since they are presumably more impressionable. This is what Table 6.5 reveals. We must, however, interpret these results with some caution. The mean for the Black first-graders in 1967 was strikingly low, implying that they were even more realistic in their goal setting than fifth-grade Anglos. The fact that the mean for first-grade Blacks in 1967 was based on only 10 children leads us to suspect that this sample may not have been comparable to the

TABLE 6.5   Mean Absolute Goal Discrepancy Pre- and Postdesegregation for Each Ethnic Group at Three Grade Levels[a] *(the Lower the Score the More Accurate the Performance Estimate)*

			Grade		
			1st	3rd	5th
Anglos	Predesegregation (1966)	X (*n*)	11.26 (102)	8.34 (89)	7.68 (63)
	Postdesegregation (1967)	X (*n*)	11.53 (73)	9.00 (57)	7.69 (74)
Mexican-Americans	Predesegregation (1966)	X (*n*)	16.83 (52)	10.15 (41)	9.40 (65)
	Postdesegregation (1967)	X (*n*)	11.12 (16)	11.24 (25)	7.73 (45)
Blacks	Predesegregation (1966)	X (*n*)	15.23 (47)	11.08 (24)	9.65 (24)
	Postdesegregation (1967)	X (*n*)	5.60 (10)	11.00 (18)	10.00 (33)

[a] Averaged over sex.

1966 sample. The scores for the Mexican-American children were more in line with what we would expect from first-graders and were based on a larger sample. We can therefore have more confidence that desegregation did have an impact on these children.

A comparison of the performance of children who had one year of experience in desegregated schools with those having had three years of experience continued to show the beneficial impact of desegregation on goal setting. The significant interaction effect between sex and amount of desegregated experience on goal discrepancy scores was due to the improvement of the Black and Mexican-American girls, who also improved on "number of unusual shifts."

Fate Control–IAR

Our cross-sectional analysis indicated that after three years of desegregated schooling, the children did not respond to the fate control or IAR questions any differently than did an age-matched group after one year of desegregation. Whether these items tap an internal versus external orientation or simply reflect conformity to social desirability norms, scores were not influenced significantly by three years of desegregated schooling.

Delay of Gratification

The delay of gratification measure (hypothetical items) yielded strikingly different results. Three years after desegregation, all children were much *less* likely to delay gratification than were their age mates two years earlier. The Anglos were more consistent in becoming oriented toward immediate rewards than were the minority children. This change may reflect a general and rapid shift in cultural norms toward immediate gratification.

Summary

We now turn to a review of the questions posed at the outset. We found differences among the three ethnic groups on all measures except for the tendency to attribute failure to a lack of effort. The measures indicated that as compared with minority children, Anglos showed higher achievement motivation; at least the differences were consistent with what current theories of achievement motivation would predict. During the ring-toss game, the goal setting of the average Anglo child demonstrated a more sensitive awareness of his own performance. He was also more likely to report having control over his environment and more likely to choose a more valuable deferred reward rather than a small immediate one when presented with a hypothetical choice. The Anglo child was less likely than the minority child to derogate his ability in the face of hypothetical failure and more likely to attribute failure to an external cause.

In examining the relationship between these motivational measures and school achievement, we found much less confirmation of the theoretical models. Goal-setting behavior and the tendency to delay gratification showed no consistent relationship with actual school performance for any of the three ethnic groups. Fate control and self-attribution of ability showed some association with achievement, but the effects were anything but uniform. Fate control predicted achievement only for the Anglo and the Mexican-American children, and self-attribution of ability predicted achievement for girls but not for boys.

In the absence of any clear relationship among our six variables and indexes of actual academic achievement, we are unable to use the results of the cross-sectional analyses to draw conclusions about the effect of desegregation on achievement motivation. We can, however, draw some conclusions about changes in the particular behaviors involved. Our cross-sectional analysis suggested that goal setting by the youngest minority children improved as a consequence of desegregation. Desegregation, however, had no effect on internal–external control and appeared to reduce impulse control (delay) for all groups.

These effects and the absence of effects are interesting in their own right. However, given the weak evidence regarding the relationship between our motivational measures and academic achievement, the logic of using the results in attempting to draw conclusions about the effects of desegregation on the achievement of minority children is tenuous, at best.

Mediators of the Impact of Desegregation

Our attempt to assess the impact of desegregation has thus far been modeled after the tradition of longitudinal studies. We selected samples of children who had in common a single dimension of experience: the length of time spent in schools where the majority of students were White. Our statistical design enabled us to examine differences between samples of minority children at different points along this experience dimension—zero years in the receiving schools, versus one year, versus three years—controlling for variations in response due to age and sex within each group. Considering the large amount of uncontrolled variability in the children's actual school experience, it is surprising that we found any differences at all. We stated at the outset that existing psychological and educational theories would lead us to predict that desegregation could have beneficial effects on the motivation of minority children if certain conditions were met, such as equal-status interracial contact, the perception of the minority child that he was accepted by his Anglo peer group, and supportive attitudes of his teacher. By comparing responses of children at different points in time without regard to the nature of their individual classroom experiences, we have assumed, as desegregation studies typically do, that for the most part these conditions were met in the desegregated classroom. Other data we collected reveal that, on the contrary, there were wide differences in teacher attitude toward minority pupils and in degree of Anglo peer acceptance. A careful evaluation of the effects of desegregation on motivation must take into account the extent to which important moderating conditions are met. In the final section of this chapter we will describe an attempt to control for the effect of teacher attitude.

Effects of Teacher Discrimination on Changes in Goal-Setting Behavior

Using the teacher's ratings of the students in her class during the first year of desegregation (see Chapter 11 for the details of deriving this measure), we created a discrimination index measuring the extent to which the teacher perceived a greater difference between the intellectual ability of the Anglo and the minority children in her class than actually existed (as measured by their performance on standardized achievement tests). The children in our sample were categorized into three equal frequency groups on the basis of teacher's score on this index. The children in the "low discrimination" group were those whose teacher tended to have a relatively accurate appraisal of the difference between the intellectual ability of the Anglo and the minority children. Children in the "moderate" and "high discrimination" categories had teachers who tended to overestimate, either moderately or highly, the relative achievement inferiority of the minority children in their classes.

Absolute goal discrepancy was analyzed in a repeated-measures analysis of variance design with level of teacher discrimination, grade level, and ethnic group as factors. Each child's goal-setting score during the first year of data collection (predesegregation) was compared with the score he received in the second year (one year postdesegregation). An interaction between the effect of years and level of teacher discrimination would indicate that the change from pre- to postdesegregation varied as a function of teacher discrimination. Results of this analysis suggest that this is precisely what happened ($p < .01$ for the triple interaction among years, teacher discrimination, and ethnic group). Contrasts between scores received by children who had low versus those who had moderate and high discrimination teachers revealed that while the level of their teacher's discrimination had no effect on the goal setting of the Anglo children, it appeared to influence the goal setting of minority children. The Mexican-American and Black children in the third and fourth grades who were assigned to teachers low in discrimination improved their goal setting more than did their counterparts who were assigned to teachers moderate or high in discrimination.[5]

These findings suggest some of the consequences of Riverside's desegregation program. It seems likely that variation from classroom to classroom within a desegregated school in factors that may influence school performance is at least as great as the variation between segregated and desegregated schools. We believe that it is unreasonable to expect desegregation to have overall effects given the wide variation in the classroom situation facing individual children, and we find no overall effects. We do not interpret our results as an indication that placing a minority child from a ghetto school into an integrated classroom will fail to have an important impact on achievement-relevant motivation. The observed interaction between years in a desegregated school and teacher discrimination reinforces our belief that there will be no understanding of the effects of desegregation unless researchers take account of the social

[5] A previous analysis had demonstrated that there was no systematic relationship between the predesegregation goal-setting scores and the level of discrimination of the teacher to whom the children were assigned postdesegregation. Hence the significant interaction cannot be attributed to regression effects.

setting that the child confronts in the classroom. A more detailed look at events occurring in the classroom must necessarily be the direction of future research.

References

Allport, G. W. *The nature of prejudice.* Cambridge, Mass.: Addison-Wesley, 1954.

Armor, D. J. The evidence on bussing. *The Public Interest,* 1972, *28,* 90–126.

Atkinson, J. W., & Feather, N. T. (Eds.), *A theory of achievement motivation.* New York: John Wiley, 1966.

Ausubel, D. P., & Ausubel, P. Ego development among segregated Negro children. In A. H. Passow (Ed.), *Education in depressed areas.* New York: Teachers College, 1963.

Bandura, A., & Mischel, W. Modification of self-imposed delay of reward through exposure to live and symbolic models. *Journal of Personality and Social Psychology,* 1965, *2,* 698–705.

Bettleheim, B. Review of B. S. Bloom's *Stability and change in human characteristics. New York Review of Books,* September 10, 1964, *3,* 1–4.

Bialer, I. Conceptualization of success and failure in mentally retarded and normal children. *Journal of Personality,* 1961, *29,* 303–320.

Boyd, G. F. The levels of aspiration of White and Negro children in a non-segregated school. *Journal of Social Psychology,* 1952, *36,* 191–196.

Carrigan, P. M. School desegregation via compulsory pupil transfer: Early effects on elementary school children. Unpublished mimeo. Ann Arbor Public Schools, Ann Arbor, Mich., 1969.

Clark, K. B. *Dark ghetto.* New York: Harper & Row, 1965.

Coleman, J. S., & staff. *Equality of educational opportunity.* U.S. Department of Health, Education, and Welfare. Washington, D.C.: U.S. Government Printing Office, 1966.

Crandall, V. J., Katkovsky, W., & Preston, A. Motivation and ability determinants of young children's intellectual achievement behaviors. *Child Development,* 1962, *33,* 643–661.

Davidson, J. J., & Lang, G. Children's perceptions of their teachers' feelings toward them related to self-perception, school achievement, and behavior. *Journal of Experimental Education,* 1968, *29,* 107–118.

Deutsch, M., & Collins, M. *Interracial housing: A psychological evaluation of a social experiment.* Minneapolis: University of Minnesota Press, 1951.

Gerard, H. B. The anchorage of opinions in face-to-face groups. *Human Relations,* 1954, *7,* 313–326.

Gottlieb, D. Teaching and students: The view of Negro and White teachers. In S. W. Webster (Ed.), *The disadvantaged learner.* San Francisco: Chandler, 1966.

Hunt, J. McV. The psychological basis for preschool cultural enrichment programs. In M. Deutsch, I. Katz, & A. Jensen (Eds.), *Social class, race, and psychological development.* New York: Holt, Rinehart and Winston, 1968.

Jessor, R., Graves, T. D., Hanson, R. D., & Jessor, S. R. *Society, personality, and deviant behavior.* New York: Holt, Rinehart and Winston, 1968.

Katz, I. Socialization of academic motivation. In D. Levine (Ed.), *Nebraska symposium on motivation.* Lincoln: University of Nebraska Press, 1967.

Kelley, H. H. Two functions of reference groups. In G. E. Swanson, T. M. Newcomb, & Hartley (Eds.), *Reading in social psychology,* New York: Holt, Rinehart and Winston, 1952.

Maitland, S. D. Time perspective, frustration–failure and delay of gratification in middle-class and lower-class children from organized and disorganized families. *Dissertation Abstracts,* 1967, *27* (10), 3676–3677.

McClelland, D. C. *The achieving society.* Princeton, N.J.: Van Nostrand, 1961.

McClelland, D. C., Atkinson, J. W., Clark, R. A., & Lowell, E. L. *The achievement motive.* New York: Appleton-Century-Crofts, 1953.

Merton, R. K. The self-fulfilling prophecy. *The Antioch Review,* 1948, *8,* 193–210.

Mischel, W. Delay of gratification, need for achievement, and acquiescence in another culture. *Journal of Abnormal Social Psychology,* 1961, *62,* 543–552.

Mischel, W. Theory and research on the antecedents of self-imposed delay of reward. In B. A. Maher (Ed.), *Progress in experimental personality research,* Vol. 3. New York: Academic Press, 1966.

Mischel, W. *Personality and assessment.* New York: Wiley, 1968.

Mischel, W., & Metzner, R. Preference for delayed reward as a function of age, intelligence, and length of delay interval. *Journal of Abnormal Social Psychology,* 1962, *64,* 425–431.

Moss, H. A., & Kagan, J. Stability of achievement and recognition seeking behaviors from early childhood through adulthood. *Journal of Abnormal Social Psychology,* 1961, *62,* 504–518.

Newcomb, T. M. Attitude development as a function of reference groups: The Bennington study. In G. E. Swanson, T. M. Newcomb, & Hartley (Eds.), *Reading in social psychology.* New York: Holt, Rinehart, and Winston, 1952.

Pettigrew, T. F. The Negro and education. In I. Katz & P. Gurin (Eds.), *Social science and race relations.* New York: Basic Books, 1969.

Pettigrew, T. F., Unseem, E. L., Normand, C. and Smith, M. S. Busing: A review of "The Evidence." *The Public Interest,* 1973, *30,* 88–115.

Proshansky, H., & Newton, P. The nature and meaning of Negro self-identity. In M. Deutsch, I. Katz & A. Jensen (Eds.), *Social class, race, and psychological development.* New York: Holt, Rinehart and Winston, 1968.

Rotter, J. B., Seeman, M., & Liverant, S. Internal vs. external control of reinforcement: A major variable in behavior theory. In N. F. Washburne (Ed.), *Decisions, values, and groups,* Vol. 2. London: Pergamon Press, 1962.

Siegel, A. E., & Siegel, S. Reference groups, membership groups, and attitude change. *Journal of Abnormal and Social Psychology,* 1957, *55,* 360–364.

Smith, C. P. The origin and expression of achievement-related motives in children. In C. P. Smith (Ed.), *Achievement-related motives in children.* New York: Russel Sage Foundation, 1969.

Stouffer, S. A., *The American soldier.* Princeton, N.J.: Princeton University Press, 1949.

Strickland, B. R. Aspiration responses among Negro and White adolescents. *Journal of Personality and Social Psychology*, 1971, *19*, 315–320.

Veroff, J., & Peele, S. Initial effects of desegregation on the achievement motivation of Negro elementary school children. *Journal of Social Issues*, 1969, *25*, 71–92.

Weiner, B., & Kukla, A. An attributional analysis of achievement. *Journal of Personality and Social Psychology*, 1970, *15*, 1–20.

Winer, B. J. *Statistical principles in experimental design* (2nd ed.). New York: McGraw-Hill, 1971.

Zytkoskee, A., Strickland, B. R., & Watson, J. Delay of gratification and internal versus external control among adolescents of low socioeconomic status. *Developmental Psychology*, 1971, *4*, 93–98.

7

The School Experience and Adjustment

Jacqueline D. Goodchilds, James A. Green, and Tora Kay Bikson

We were interested in determining the effect of the desegregation experience on the child's emotional adjustment to the new setting on the assumption that adjustment would be one of the mediators of achievement. One of the bases for the Supreme Court's rejecting the "separate but equal" doctrine in the historic *Brown vs. Board of Education* decision was the contention by social scientists that segregation in the schools has devastating consequences for the psychological well-being of the Black child (Clark & Clark, 1947, 1950; Kardiner & Ovesey, 1951). However, it has been suggested (Katz, 1968; Proshansky & Newton, 1968) that the desegregation process too—as generally implemented during the 1960s—may well have been psychologically debilitating for minority children. There is a need for research into questions of adjustment, both of minority and majority children, as affected by school experiences—particularly the desegregation of school systems.

It is not the intent of this chapter to develop a general construct of healthy adjustment that would be applicable interethnically to children of various ages, nor to suggest that such a task is feasible. The difficulty of distinguishing pathological from normal or adaptive styles among

Jacqueline D. Goodchilds and Tora Kay Bikson • University of California, Los Angeles, California. James A. Green • Los Angeles County Mental Health Services, Los Angeles, California.

minority persons in a racially discriminative social system is well known (Parker & Kleiner, 1965). Moreover, Dohrenwend and Dohrenwend (1969) provided impressive evidence that diverse ethnic groups do adopt different styles of expressing psychological distress; they concluded from an extensive review of previous research as well as from their own work, that measured between-group differences in psychological impairment and adjustment are explained methodologically as often as substantively. Lacking any single validated construct, then, we propose to examine a number of different measures of the sort that have been used to index adjustment and that have some *prima facie* relevance to the question of adjustment in the desegregation situation, noting any between-group differences and/or changes in such differences and what they might imply. Our investigation includes measures of behavior during the testing session as rated by the interviewer, as well as measures ostensibly indicative of responsiveness to others (pressure by peers and involvement in the school setting), of self-attitude, and of ethnic identification. These measures are described, in turn, below; results are then presented for each class of measures, with, finally, a report of relationships among the adjustment variables and between these variables and estimates of school achievement.

Description of Measures

All the measures were taken during the twice-yearly testing sessions conducted with each child in the sample. Our first area of interest concerns the one standard setting in which each child's behavior could be observed, that of the testing session itself. At the close of each session the interviewer rated the subject on a set of scales adapted from Meyers, Dingman, Orpet, Sitkei, and Watts (1964), tapping dimensions of physical health and activity level, reaction to the interviewer and to the assigned tasks, apparent anxiety, self-confidence, and the like. Scores on the 18 items (15 nine-point, 2 four-point, and 1 three-point scale) from the first sessions for the first year (N of usable sets $= 1683$) were subjected to factor analytic procedures (varimax rotation solution), yielding three evidently meaningful factor dimensions. Of the original 18 items, 5 showed no loadings on these factors; 3 (anxiety, initiative, and self-confidence) loaded positively on two of the factors and negatively on the third—suggesting that for our raters these concepts were unclear and/or multidimensional. Of the 10 remaining items, a cluster of 5 (average intercorrelation = .49) constituted Factor I, termed *evaluation*: (1) cooperation given to examiner, (2) interest in tasks, (3) effort displayed, (4) attention, and (5) lovability. Factor II, termed *activity*, consisted of 3 items whose average intercorrelation was .44: (1) amount of motor activity, (2) amount of speech, and (3) impulsivity (rated from "extreme restraint" to "no inhibition"). The final 2 items, Factor III, with a Pearson r of .42, referred to personal appearance, specifically *grooming*: (1) cleanliness (from "well-scrubbed, hair combed" to "very dirty, long-term neglect of personal cleanliness") and (2) clothedness (from "completely" to "incompletely clothed: obvious holes or tears"). The behavior ratings thus yielded three adjustment variables, each a simply summed score across a set of correlated items, each representing a relatively distinct dimension of interviewer response to the subject. An average correlation of .40 between the scores on these variables for the first and for the second interview session (Year I) indicated considerable stability in these response patterns. This estimate, it should be noted, represents a confounding of two sources of instability—one child seen by two people, one person's interaction with the same child at two different points in time—because the two sessions in any year were not conducted systematically by either the same or a different person. For this reason also we have limited our substantive analysis of the interviewer ratings to the data gathered on the first of the two testing sessions scheduled in each measurement year.

Responsiveness to Others

There were two measures, one obtained early in the first, the other late in the second of the yearly interviews, which dealt with the subject's responsiveness to or involvement with other people. During the first session the child was shown a sequence of four line drawings illustrative of schoolroom and school playground scenes. For three of the pictures, in a task modeled on the early work of Horowitz (1943) and of Hartwell, Hutt, Andrew, and Walton (1951), the subject was asked to indicate which of the actors was "most like" him and which he would "most like to be." Responses to these pictures, scored along a dimension of active–involvement versus passive–isolation, gave an unclear and inconclusive pattern of results and will not be further reported. The remaining picture, actually the first in the set, was of a teacher standing at the head of a row of six unoccupied desks. The child's identification of the seat he "would like to sit in" represented a numerically linear expression of desired distance from the teacher (or from the front of the schoolroom).

A second attempt to assess responsiveness to other people, adapted from the Asch (1952) paradigm for measuring vulnerability to peer pressures, was administered during the second interview. Devised especially for this study, it consisted of a set of 12 cards, each picturing three silhouettes—one blue, one orange, one yellow—of a familiar object (cat, airplane, house, etc.). The silhouettes on a card differed slightly in size from one another; as each was presented the interviewer commented, "Most children pick the [blue flower, for example] as the biggest." The child's task was then to indicate (by pointing or by color-naming) which he thought was the biggest. For 9 of the 12 instances, the peer suggestion was incorrect.[1]

Self-Attitude

The final task assigned the child in the second interview sessions differed for the group of younger (initially kindergarteners through third-graders, thus 6 to 9 years old) as compared to older children (fourth through sixth grade, 10–12 years of age). The two tests (Bower & Lambert, 1962a,b) were designed to assess the emotional health of the school-age child and to assist elementary school personnel in detecting the emotionally handicapped among the school population (Bower, 1960). These instruments were used as rough indices of a child's attitude toward himself—his self-confidence perhaps, or his self-esteem.

For the young group the appropriate Bower–Lambert test (1962a) involves a deck of 54 cards depicting a child in various daily-life situations, which the subject is required to sort into two stacks, one representing "happy" pictures and the other "sad" pictures. The number of pic-

[1] A suspicion that the judgment task was not sufficiently ambiguous led to a change in procedure in the second year's testing: the stimulus material, originally placed 4 feet from the subject, was removed to an 8-foot distance. In testing subsequent to the second year, the original distance was restored.

tures called happy, a reflection of the relative optimism with which the child views the world of childhood (his world), is the major index derivable from the test. In addition we examined the relative "happiness" of three subsets of the stimulus cards, each clearly representing a specific area of activity: (1) *play*—8 cards, 4 showing the child playing alone, 4 showing peer-group play; (2) *school*—10 scenes in the schoolroom, 5 of the child and teacher alone together, 3 of the child, other children, and the teacher, 1 of the child with other children, 1 of the child alone; and (3) *home*—10 indoor home scenes, 2 each of the child with father, with mother, and with both parents, and 4 of the child at home alone. For these subsets the pictures are identical for boys and girls except for the sex of the protagonist child figure; for the overall card set the stimuli are not comparable across the sexes.

The Bower–Lambert measure used with our older sample (Bower & Lambert, 1962*b*) is a partially self-administered paper-and-pencil test in two sections, one of which was completed near the start of the testing session, the second at the close. With the interviewer's guidance the subject read 40 short phrases describing an imaginary child and marked on a 4-point scale the degree to which he *would or would not* "like to be him/her" (section I—ideal) and *is or is not* "like him/her" (section II—self). A self–ideal discrepancy score calculated as a Pearson correlation between the two sets of responses to the 40 items is the measure of most interest here. A second discrepancy score was also obtained, this one a correlation between each subject's individual "self" responses and a standard "ideal" derived from the summing of the ideal response patterns for the entire sample.

Unlike the self-attitude measure used with the young children, the 40-phrases measure employs items comparable across the sexes. Also unlike the younger child's measure, however, the items cannot be subsorted to provide area-specific estimates. There is, finally, cause for concern that this test contains a large dose of social desirability—or at least "school desirability"—in the responses. A rank ordering of the items in terms of overall amount of endorsement on the "ideal" scoring yields as the five highest rated items, in order, the following: "is very good in arithmetic," "gets to school on time," "getting good grades is very important to him/her," "is very smart," and "studies hard at home." Among the least favorably ranked items were such things as "does not have to go to school," "plays when should be studying," and "is going to quit school as soon as possible." Clearly the "ideal" pattern from which the self-discrepancy scores are estimated is an ideal exceedingly well-disposed toward school and schooling.

Ethnic Identification

The question of ethnic attitudes—toward one's own and toward other groups—is of particular importance with a subject population that is multiethnic and involved in an enforced change in interethnic contact. The medium chosen to explore this area with the Riverside children was the color photograph. A set of six head-and-shoulders close-up snapshots of third-grade schoolboys and another of schoolgirls were presented (in that order) to the subjects during the first testing sessions; in each sex-set of six there were two Anglo, two Mexican-American, and two Black children. A description of these materials, the questions asked about them, and the results of data generated thereby are reported in detail elsewhere (Green & Gerard, 1974). Here we are concerned only with the item that tapped racial identity: The child was asked to pick from the same-sex pictures "the one who is most like you." Scored in terms of whether or not a subject chose each of the three ethnic groups, this response provided three nonindependent but separately interesting measures of ethnic identification.

Presentation of Results

General methodological and design considerations are presented elsewhere in this book, as is an overall description of the Riverside sample, the population from which it was drawn, and the community and school-system events involving that population at the time the data were being collected. Obviously there are difficulties in dealing with material of this type, only some of which can be adequately resolved with available statistical techniques. For the particular measures we discuss here, analysis of variance (ANOVA) was used, specifically the "unweighted means" analysis described in Chapter 3. The constant independent sources of variance were sex, ethnic membership (as categorized by school personnel), and age group (operationally, the group of children who were in grades kindergarten through third grade in the first year of the study compared to those in grades 4 through 6).

For each dependent variable measure we performed four analyses of variance: (1) a static or base-line analysis, (2) an attrition estimate, (3) an estimate of socioeconomic influence, and (4) a repeated-measures longitudinal analysis. The first employs the full sample as obtained with the first yearly testing in the spring of 1966—approximately 1700 children,[2] one-half male, two-thirds in our primary-grade "young group," with approximately 650 Anglo, 650 Mexican-American, and 400 Black.

The second and third analyses attempted to control for possibly confounding sources of variance. Included in the base-line sample were roughly 100 Mexican-American and 150 Black children who had already been moved to the receiving schools prior to our initial testing (see Table 3.1). This plus the delay past the scheduled fall of 1966 "desegregation date" in moving some minority children (mostly Mexican-American) and the expectable attrition of any sample over time necessitated our second analysis of variance, one that would estimate "attrition" effects. For each measure, a fourth variance source was added to the design, comparing all subjects for whom data were available across the three test years of the study and who—if minority children—also were desegregated in the fall of 1966 (the *retained* sample) versus all minority children desegregated before or after the target date, and all children, minority or White, who for whatever reasons were not tested in all three test years. The third analysis employed the original base-line minority sample but restricted the Anglo sample to a socioeconomically similar subset—children from the 20% of Anglo households scoring lowest on a status estimate based on measures of education and occupational level of the family head ($N = 120$)—making possible cross-ethnic comparisons in which status was roughly equated.

We were gratified to find that these two sources—attrition and socioeconomic status—did not account for any significant amount of the variance on most of our measures. The only exceptions occurred with respect to interviewer ratings. For attrition, an F value significant at $p < .05$ for interviewer judgments on the *grooming* dimension suggests that the children retained in our sample were the slightly cleaner and

---

[2] These numbers are approximate because missing data on any particular measure altered the exact number of available cases.

better-clothed group. Comparisons employing the Anglo subsample that approximated minority socioeconomic status gave between-group *F* values below statistical significance levels on *evaluation* and *activity*; interviewer-rated ethnic differences on these dimensions were small among lower-status subjects and increased in magnitude with increasing socioeconomic status. Because attrition and status affected only these results, our second and third analyses are not mentioned further, here.

The fourth analysis employed was the one of most interest, a repeated-measure longitudinal analysis of three years of data from the *retained* sample defined above (*N* equals approximately 825: 450 Anglos, 250 Mexican-Americans, and 125 Blacks). To the three constant sources (sex, ethnicity, and age group) the repeated measure added a fourth, namely, "year," a three-level factor: Year I = Spring 1966; Year II = Spring 1967; and Year III = Spring 1969. Between 1966 and 1967 most of the minority children were moved from segregated to desegregated schools; between 1967 and 1969, the children had experienced an additional two years of desegregation. Our focus here was on ethnicity and, more importantly, any evidence for significant interaction between the factors of ethnicity and year. In what follows we limit our report to such findings; the reader is reminded that differences associated with the sex and age group of the children have been systematically accounted for in these four-way analyses, even though attention focuses on the other two factors.

Interviewer Ratings

The mean values by ethnic group for the base-line (Year I) analysis and by ethnic group per year for the repeated-measure analysis for the three sets of scores derived from the interviewer ratings are presented in Table 7.1. For each measure there was a statistically significant (*p* values < .05) main effect for ethnicity in the first (full-sample) ANOVA and an interaction of ethnicity by year in the second. *Evaluation* is a 5-item score with a possible range from 5 to 45 and a mid-point of 25; *activity* contains 3 items with a 3-27 range and a mid-point of 15; *grooming* (which was scored in the reverse direction low = good) has but two items with a 2-7 range and a mid-point of 4.5.

The summary data reported in Table 7.1 reflect the individual perceptions of the interviewer, whose viewpoint was typically that of the

TABLE 7.1   Interviewer Rating Scores for Riverside Children[a]

Measure	Ethnic group	Base line	Repeated		
			I	II	III
Evaluation	A	29.3	29.1	29.0	31.2
	M	28.3	28.3	28.1	29.3
	B	28.8	28.8	26.5	28.6
(*F* value, *df*)		(3.65, 2/1612)	(5.22, 4/1644)		
Activity	A	14.9	14.8	14.9	14.7
	M	14.2	14.3	13.1	13.5
	B	14.7	14.6	13.7	13.8
(*F* value, *df*)		(4.28, 2/1671)	(3.85, 4/1720)		
Grooming	A	2.5	2.5	2.2	2.2
	M	3.0	3.0	2.7	2.5
	B	3.1	3.2	2.8	2.6
(*F* value, *df*)		(55.74, 2/1671)	(3.20, 4/1722)		

[a] For evaluation and activity high scores are good; low is good for grooming. A = Anglo, M = Mexican-American, B = Black. *F* value cited for repeated-measure ANOVA is that for the interaction term, ethnicity X year.

adult, Anglo, middle-class "establishment." The situation in which the testing took place was also structured along generally mainstream-America middle-class lines—a question-and-answer, paper-and-pencil, table-and-chair mini-world (not unlike the school situation itself). In that setting and seen through those eyes, the Anglo child was clearly a superior performer. At the start he scored more favorably than the minority children on *evaluation,* increasing his advantage over time, particularly improving from Year II to Year III; he was consistently more *active* (talkative, uninhibited, moving about) on all testings and consistently better *groomed.*

The two minority groups differed initially only on the *activity* dimension, with the Mexican-American child being seen as less active than the Black. This difference in relative standing persisted across the test years, along with an activity drop for both groups from Year I to Year II, a drop from which they had not fully recovered by Year III. On the *grooming* dimension all subjects improved over the years, reflecting a general age trend; however, the minority children improved slightly more than did the Anglos. It was only on the *evaluation* factor that the two minority groups appeared to differ across the years. Mexican-Americans showed no change at first and an improvement later, whereas Blacks showed a quite startling slump in Year II, and their better Year III scores still left them below original levels. Evidently Black children were seen as more "cooperative," "attentive," "lovable," etc., in the test-session context after their first years of the desegregated experience or else the expectations of the study's testing personnel shifted noticeably for these children—or perhaps both occurred.

Responsiveness to Others

The modal classroom seating choice for our sample—fully 60% of the first year's answers—was the very front seat. Nevertheless there were stable differences among subject groups in the extent of their commitment to that position. Choosing to sit closest—expressed as ordinal distance in number of seats from the front—were girls ($F = 8.86$, *df* $1/1672$, $p < .01$), younger children ($F = 4.84$, *df* $1/1672$, $p < .05$), and minority children ($F = 7.09$, *df* $2/1672$, $p < .01$). The ethnic difference did not show any change over time.

A significant ethnicity × year interaction ($p < .01$) did appear on the Asch-paradigm measure of responsiveness to suggestions about peer judgments; it is presented in Table 7.2. Scores per subject were averaged across nine trials, in each of which the subject chose the actually correct stimulus ($= 3$), the peer-suggested stimulus ($= 1$), or the "other" ($= 2$). Theoretically scores could range from 9 to 27 with a mid-point of 18, a high score indicating a perceptually accurate series, low reflecting considerable responsiveness to pressure, and a compromise selection of the neutral figures producing middle-range scores.

On this task girls and older children were generally more accurate in their perceptual responses (thus more resistant to suggestions of peer pressure); there was no evidence of differential ethnic-group response. Because scores were approaching 100% accuracy even in our first testings ($\bar{X}$ of 24.6 for older girls), the measure was administered across the three time-testings only for the original kindergarten through third-grade group. And it is for this group only that we report a shifting ethnic-group pattern (Table 7.2): an initially low score by Blacks, made

TABLE 7.2 *Perceptual Accuracy/Resistance to Pressure (among Younger Riverside Children Only)*[a]

Ethnic Group	Year		
	I	II	III
A	22.3	23.2	24.4
M	22.3	23.3	23.8
B	20.8	23.6	23.7
(F value, df)	(4.33, 4/952)		

[a] N of subjects = 482; high score = accurate response.

up by Year II; a continued rise in scores for Anglos through Year III that is not visible in the minority-group scores. It is not clear whether these data represent increasing involvement in perception tasks, on the one hand, or rather represent decreasing dependence on peer group suggestion; nor are these explanations mutually exclusive (Ausubel & Ausubel, 1963; Berenda, 1950; Katz, 1968).

Self-Attitude

Our younger group of children (N of approximately 1100), it will be recalled, was required to describe a set of pictures as "happy" or "sad," yielding four scores per child: relative "happiness" perceived generally and in the specific settings of play, of school, and of home. The results were unequivocal. For the overall and for the play and home settings, Anglo as compared to Mexican-American and Black children express a happier viewpoint (p values < .01); for the school setting there was no apparent difference in perception. At Year II these findings were exactly the same. The card sort was administered to the original kindergarten sample alone at Year III; with a sample size of barely 100, although the relative ordering of the means was unchanged, only the sort for play was statistically stable (p < .05), replicating again the ethnic difference.

Our self-attitude measure for older children similarly suffered from the reduction in sample size over time. As the children moved into the junior high schools they were less accessible to us for study purposes. The Bower–Lambert "Thinking About Yourself" test (1962*b*) was not administered in Year III. Furthermore, the base-line sample contained only slightly more than 500 children and dropped to under 400 for Year II. Despite these restrictions the data are provocative. There were no stable findings associated with the discrepancy scores calculated from a standardized "ideal," but there was a significant ($p < .01$) interaction between sex and ethnicity for the discrepancy scores calculated from individual "ideal" responses, and it was exactly repeated in Year II (see Table 7.3). It seems as if—at least for children aged 10 and up—the Black male child may have an unusually high and the Black female child an unusually low satisfaction-with-self attitude.

Ethnic Identification

Self-attitude, involvement with peers, responsiveness to an interviewer-researcher aside, it is preeminently ethnic identification that would seem to touch the core of the adjustment question for the Riverside sample during the study period. The data concerning this aspect deserve, and have received (Green & Gerard, 1974), extended analysis and report; here we focus on the simple choice of one same-sex picture as "most like me." Each child's single choice was scored three times, once for each ethnic group—1 if the chosen picture was of that

TABLE 7.3 Self–Ideal Discrepancy Scores (Older Riverside Children Only) [a]

	Sex	
Ethnic group	Male	Female
A	.580	.632
M	.600	.595
B	.670	.551
(*F* value, *df*)	(5.68, 2/518)	

[a] Scores are averaged Pearson *r*s; data are from year I; N of subjects = 524.

group, 2 if it was not—and the three sets of scores were then separately analyzed. The results are presented in Table 7.4. The main effect for ethnicity of subject was significant for each analysis, as was the interaction, ethnic group × year, for choice of Anglo and choice of Mexican-American pictures (all p values < .01). One must keep in mind of course that these analyses were not independent; choice of one ethnic group precluded choice of either of the other two.

The major determinant of choice was the chooser's own ethnicity: those who identified themselves with Anglos were Anglos, with Mexican-Americans were Mexican-Americans, with Blacks were Blacks. The two stable time-trends principally reflected a strengthening of this "reality choice" among Mexican-Americans; they identified less with Anglos and more with their own group across Years II and III.[3] While Blacks similarly showed a decreasing identification with the majority group, the change was equally to Mexican-American as to Black pictures for these subjects.

Of necessity in our analyses we grouped together all children called "Black." To do this without regard for the wide variation in features and skin coloring among these children no doubt introduced for them considerable error in this picture-judging task. For the Mexican-American group too the physiognomic cues to ethnicity were unclear. In truth, the distinction between the two minority groups itself is a blurred one when made solely on the basis of physical appearance. Thus in interpreting these results we must allow for some unavoidable slippage between the operation, "choose a picture," and the concept, "ethnic identification."

Interrelationships

In all, we described and reported measures derived from six different test-tasks administered to our children. What of the relationships among these items? The two self-ideal discrepancy scores showed a not unexpected correlation of +.87; the three subsorts of the "happy–sad" cards had an average intercorrelation of +.51 and an average correlation with the total sort of +.76; the two interviewer ratings, *evaluation*

---

[3] Age differences in the base-line analyses suggest that this is a naturally occurring developmental change for Mexican-Americans.

TABLE 7.4 *Ethnic Identity: Picture Chosen as Most Like the Chooser*[a]

Picture	Ethnic group	Base line	Repeated		
			I	II	III
Anglo	A	1.20	1.20	1.22	1.22
	M	1.56	1.55	1.66	1.76
	B	1.75	1.74	1.82	1.86
(*F* value)		(187.89)		(3.67)	
Mexican-American	A	1.88	1.89	1.86	1.86
	M	1.48	1.49	1.37	1.27
	B	1.82	1.82	1.78	1.76
(*F* value)		(139.40)		(5.12)	
Black	A	1.90	1.90	1.91	1.91
	M	1.96	1.96	1.96	1.97
	B	1.42	1.43	1.40	1.37
(*F* value)		(409.51)		(1.22)	

[a] Low score = choice; *df*s for base line are 2/1671, for repeated-measure interaction, 4/1710.

and *activity* (which it will be recalled were based on but not actually calculated as factor-analytic scores), were correlated +.28; the three ethnic-identification scores were naturally negatively tied. But except for these within-task associations, our measures were essentially unrelated one to another.

How and what sort of relationships obtained between our adjustment measures and available indices of school achievement is a subject at once more involved and less easily determined. Working with our base-line Year I sample, we examined—overall and separately by ethnic group—the correlations for each adjustment item (Year I) with the standardized school achievement test scores (Year I). As a check on the effects, if any, of the school-system change between Years I and II, we compared these same adjustment estimates (Year I) to the Year II achievement scores. In addition, we made these same sets of comparisons using verbal and math school grades (standardized by grade) in place of achievement test scores. The matrix of Pearson *r*s generated by this effort clustered closely around zero, rarely reaching past ±.10.

High *evaluation* had a low positive relationship to achievement test scores for both years; good *grooming* showed some association both with achievement tests and with school grades across years, particularly for Black children; among Anglos—the young ones—there was a suggestion of a relation between good grades and a "happy" *home* sort; and, finally, a favorable self-attitude (low self-ideal discrepancy) might for Black (older) children accompany higher test achievement and better school grades. In fairness, however, one cannot assign more than heuristic value to these findings because the zero-order outcomes far outnumbered these cited few.

Conclusion

Children apparently respond in complex ways both to the tasks we researchers set for them and to the changes society imposes on the social situations in which they must function. There are regularities in these ways of responding that are associated with a child's sex, age, and developmental pattern. Depending on ethnic membership, moreover, children view the researcher, the world, and themselves quite differently.

If we can accept the measures here reported as indicators, however crude, of some vague valued thing called *adjustment* then it appears that the average Anglo child has more of it than the average minority child. And the introduction of a scattering of minority children into his school situation leaves the Anglo child's adjustment relatively undisturbed. The analyses above suggest, though, that the changed school experience does disturb the adjustment situation of the minority child, but not for long. In fact within the time span covering the data we analyzed the minority children seemed well recovered.

References

Asch, S. *Social psychology*. New York: Prentice-Hall, 1952.

Ausubel, D., & Ausubel, P. Ego development among segregated Negro children. In A. Passow (Ed.), *Education in depressed areas*. New York: Teachers College, Columbia University Bureau of Publications, 1963.

Berenda, R. W. *The influence of the group on the judgments of children*. New York: King's Crown, 1950.

Bower, E. M. *Early identification of emotionally handicapped children in school.* Springfield, Ill.: Charles C. Thomas, 1960.

Bower, E. M., & Lambert, N. M. *A picture game.* Princeton, N. J.: Educational Testing Service, 1962. (*a*)

Bower, E. M., & Lambert, N. M. *Thinking about yourself.* Princeton, N.J.: Educational Testing Service, 1962. (*b*)

Clark, K. B., & Clark, M. P. Racial identification and preference in Negro children. In T. M. Newcomb & E. L. Hartley (Eds.), *Readings in social psychology.* New York: Holt, Rinehart, and Winston, 1947.

Clark, K. B., & Clark, M. P. Emotional factors in racial identification and preference in Negro children. *Journal of Negro Education,* 1950, *19,* 341–350.

Dohrenwend, B. P., & Dohrenwend, B. S. *Social status and psychological disorder: A causal inquiry.* New York: Wiley, 1969.

Green, J. A., & Gerard, H. B. School desegregation and ethnic attitudes. In H. Fromkin & J. Sherwood (Eds.), *Integrating the organization.* New York: Free Press, 1974.

Hartwell, S. W., Hutt, M. L., Andrew, G., & Walton, R. E. The Michigan picture test: Diagnostic and therapeutic possibilities of a new projective test for children. *American Journal of Orthopsychiatry,* 1951, *21,* 124–137.

Horowitz, R. A pictorial method for the study of self-identification in preschool children. *Journal of Genetic Psychology,* 1943, *62,* 135–148.

Kardiner, A., & Ovesey, L. *The mark of oppression.* Gloucester, Mass.: Peter Smith, 1951.

Katz, I. Factors influencing Negro performance in the desegregated school. In M. Deutsch, I. Katz, & A. Jensen (Eds.), *Social class, race, and psychological development.* New York: Holt, Rinehart, and Winston, 1968.

Meyers, C. E., Dingman, H. F., Orpet, R. E., Sitkei, E. G., & Watts, C. A. Four ability-factor hypotheses. *Monographs of the Society for Research in Child Development,* 1964, Serial No. 96, *29* (5).

Parker, S., & Kleiner, R. *Mental illness in the urban Negro community.* New York: Free Press, 1965.

Proshansky, H., & Newton, P. The nature and meaning of Negro self-identity. In M. Deutsch, I. Katz, & A. Jensen (Eds.), *Social class, race, and psychological development.* New York: Holt, Rinehart, and Winston, 1968.

Winer, B. J. *Statistical principles in experimental design* (2nd ed.). New York: McGraw-Hill, 1971.

8

Personality Traits and Adjustment

DUANE GREEN, NORMAN MILLER,
AND DESY S. GERARD

A central assumption behind the expectation that the desegregation program in Riverside would improve the academic performance of minority children was that contact with the majority Anglo children in the desegregated classroom would strengthen certain motives and values believed to be important mediators of academic achievement. Both the Coleman report (1966) itself and reanalyses of its data (e.g., Mosteller & Moynihan, 1972) have strongly suggested as much. This chapter examines personality factors that might mediate the child's adjustment to the desegregation experience. It has been shown, for example, that anxiety partially mediates performance on intellectual tasks (Katz, 1964; Spence, 1963). Likewise, numerous other personality traits might also be expected to predict the child's response to desegregation, and to the extent that such traits mediate adjustment, they are of particular interest to us.

The inclusion of measures reflecting the child's self-esteem seemed essential. The relations between self-esteem and school performance (Coleman, 1966), occupational aspirations (Klausner, 1953), general anxiety level (Thorne, 1954), ego defenses (Stotland & Hillmer, 1962),

DUANE GREEN AND DESY S. GERARD • University of California, Los Angeles, California.
NORMAN MILLER • University of Southern California, Los Angeles, California.

feelings of accomplishment (Coopersmith, 1967), and satisfaction with decisions (Gerard, Blevans, & Malcolm, 1964) argue strongly that a feeling of self-worth is an important key to emotional and, therefore, school adjustment. Consequently two measures of self-esteem were employed, one for assessing the child's self-attitudes and one for assessing how the child perceived others' attitudes toward him.

At its onset, one might expect that desegregation would be disruptive and threatening to minority group members. One potential cause of this disruption was the objective fact that there were large academic performance differences in the direction of Black and Mexican-American inferiority relative to the Anglo children that might have been expected to have a negative effect on the minority child's self-esteem. Furthermore, since the minority child was separated from his peer group, he found himself not only in a more competitive situation but also in an unfamiliar setting, one lacking the kind of social support he had been used to receiving. Bettelheim and Janowitz (1964) suggested that self-rejection may be increased by the transferal of Black children from one school to another in an attempt to achieve racial balance. Studying a desegregated situation, Hauser (1971) found large between-race differences in self-image, with Blacks exhibiting greater self-rejection and depressive images over a four-year period even when socioeconomic status was controlled. There is no reason to assume that, in this sense, the self-image of the Mexican-American child would be affected any differently by desegregation than that of the Black child.

Coopersmith's (1967) findings suggested that children with low self-esteem are more likely than high-esteem children to show anxiety and are less able to deal with threats as they arise. Given Coopersmith's findings and the fact that the new experience would tend to be somewhat traumatic for the minority child, we would expect that his initial self-esteem and emotional well-being would, in part, condition the degree to which he would successfully adjust to the new classroom. To the extent that desegregation lowered the minority child's self-image, the child's adjustment to his new situation would be negatively affected. In addition, initial level of self-esteem should partially mediate the desegregation effect; minority children with relatively high initial self-esteem should respond more favorably, or at least less negatively, than those with relatively low initial self-esteem. Also, assuming that the child's self-esteem is based, at least in part, on his acceptance by others, the child's perception of others' attitudes toward him should be highly correlated with his self-attitudes.

Presumably both general anxiety and specific anxiety about school reflect emotional adjustment. Sarason, Davidson, Lighthall, Waite, and Ruebush (1960) found that children high in test anxiety are most often dependent and self-derogatory in test situations. They suggest that since children are cognitively less complex in self-perceptions than are adults, low self-esteem tends to generalize to other situations, including the child's anticipation of the approval or disapproval of significant others, like his teacher. This in turn will further affect his feelings of adequacy and security. Proshansky and Newton (1968) found much greater anxiety in Black than in White schoolchildren. They suggested that Blacks in the desegregated classroom accept the higher prestige of Whites and increasingly withdraw into their own group in response to White rejection, the result being increased anxiety, lowered self-esteem, and lowered "others' attitudes." Consequently measures of adjustment as reflected by both general and specific anxiety about school should be expected to show a relationship similar to those anticipated for the measures of self-attitudes and others' attitudes. That is, to the relative extent that the minority child is initially low in anxiety, he tends to "adjust" successfully to the desegregated classroom. At the same time, however, the new classroom tends to raise his anxiety level because of its strangeness and competitiveness.

One would expect that a child's adjustment to the school setting would also be reflected in his motivation to succeed in school. Presumably the child with past experience of success expects success in the future and his need for school achievement should mirror this expectation. On the other hand, if he has experienced repeated failure, the child begins to downgrade himself and, among other things, begins to derogate the school and the teachers who make public the evidence of his failures (Silberman, 1964).

The fact that minority children as a group are less successful in school than their White contemporaries is more than adequately documented in Chapter 4 and in other work as well (e.g., California State Advisory Committee to the U.S. Commission on Civil Rights, 1968; Coleman, 1966; Schwartz, 1971). That this lower success rate is reflected in lower achievement motivation as compared with that of Whites is, however, far from unequivocal. Proshansky and Newton (1968), after reviewing the voluminous literature on educational and occupational aspirations of Black and White children and their parents, concluded that the two groups do not differ significantly in achievement motivation. Coleman (1966) reached a similar conclusion, suggesting that the major difference appears to be not in aspirations but in expectations of attaining them; low-income students and parents expect to achieve lower goals. Thus, since there are minority–White socioeconomic status differences, we should also expect to find attainment expectancy differences as well.

One possible reason that previous research has not found minority–White achievement motivation differences may be that the techniques employed attempted to assess what could be termed "idealized," long-term goals. For example, Coleman's (1966) measures included items assessing such "idealized" goals as how far the child wanted to go in school, how the child would feel if something happened that would require him to stop school, and whether the child wanted to be a good student. Most research using such general measures has found no ethnic differences in "idealized" achievement motivation (e.g., Schwartz, 1971). The need-for-school-achievement items used in our measure were concrete and specific, assessing school achievement in a realistic, present-oriented situation. For example, items were included assessing the child's reaction to obtaining a low grade in spelling and to obtaining all C's on his report card. If the lack of White–minority differences in achievement motivation reported in previous research is indeed an artifact of the kinds of measures used, more concrete items may detect a difference.

The various personality traits we were assessing were expected both to mediate and to be affected by the desegregation experience. In general we expected that the minority children would display an initial difficulty in adjustment (as measured by these traits) and a subsequent further decrease as a consequence of the desegregation experience. On the other hand, we felt that if our assumption that adjustment, at least in part, mediates achievement was tenable, then the child's academic achievement would be related to our measures, and long-term positive changes in adjustment and achievement might be expected.

Method

The personality measures consisted of paper-and-pencil items that were selected from various standard personality measures, such as those of Cattell (1965) and Edwards (1953). Items from the measures of general and school anxiety used by Sarason *et al.* (1960) to study classroom adjustment in both the United States and Great Britain were also included. Each of the five scales consisted of 15 items, each requiring a yes or no response. Specifically, the scales were the following: general anxiety (e.g., "Do some of the stories on television scare you?"); school anxiety (e.g., "Are you afraid when the teacher asks you questions in class?"); others' attitudes (e.g., "Do most of the other boys and girls like you?"); self-attitudes (e.g., "Do you ever wish that you were someone else?"); and need for school achievement (e.g., "Would you be happy if you got all C's on your report card?").

The five scales were administered orally during the second hour of testing, which followed the first hour by approximately one month. So that the child would not tire of the item format, items from the five scales were intermixed and distributed into two sets, one given early and the other toward the end of the hour. The need-for-school-achievement scale was administered only to grades 4–6 in the first year (1966), grades 5–7 in 1967, and grades 4–6 and junior high in 1969. The other four scales were administered to all grades in each of the three years (K–6 in 1966, K–7 in 1967, and K–9 in 1969).

Analyses of these scales were based on summary scores constructed for each scale by the summing of the scores on the 15 items for that scale. All items were scored so that the larger the child's total score on any of the scales, the more of the underlying attribute he was assumed to possess. Analyses were performed using both the entire sample and a select subsample consisting of only those children who were desegregated in 1966.[1] Since little additional information was provided by the use of this "cleaner" sample, only the analyses based on the entire sample are reported here except where noted. Other specific subsamples were also occasionally employed and their composition is noted where appropriate. An examination of the relationships between our various measures of adjustment and the child's actual school achievements is included.

---

[1] The analyses involving the entire sample included all Anglos and all minorities in the study. Thus these analyses did not take into account or differentiate between those minority children who were desegregated at different time intervals, i.e., some were desegregated in 1965, some in 1966, and some in 1967. In addition, the analyses included the minority children who were already in the receiving schools. (See Chapter 3 for more detail.)

Results

Evaluation of the Scales

Campbell and Fiske (1959) proposed a multitrait–multimethod matrix for assessing the convergent and discriminant validity of psychological traits. They suggested that different measures of the same trait should correlate more highly with each other than with measures of different traits involving separate methods and, ideally, that these validity values should exceed correlations between various traits measured by the same method.

The mean split-half reliability coefficients for each scale were computed from 10 random Spearman–Brown coefficients, corrected for length (Kuder and Richardson, 1937). With the possible exceptions of the self-attitudes scale for grades K–3 ($r = .48$) and the need-for-school-achievement scale for grades 4–6 ($r = .49$), the internal consistency estimates of reliability for the various scales were all within acceptable limits (range of $r = .61$ to $r = .84$ for grades K–3 and $r = .70$ to $r = .84$ for grades 4–6).

Consideration of the intercorrelations among the summary scores of the various scales, i.e., the heterotrait–monomethod estimates, showed much less cross-scale than intrascale correlation (range of $r = .29$ to .48 for grades K–3 and $r = .20$ to $r = .59$ for grades 4–6, with mean rs of .40 and .34, respectively). Thus, although the scales were interrelated, none of the intercorrelations appeared large enough to give serious question to the assumption that the various scales were measuring reasonably independent traits. Furthermore the interrelations were what one would expect. For example, general anxiety was positively correlated with school anxiety and negatively correlated with self- and others' attitudes. Sarason *et al.* (1960) reported a mean correlation between test anxiety and general anxiety of $+.56$ for grades 1–3 and of $+.59$ for grades 4–6, correlations similar to ours ($+.40$ and $+.57$, respectively). Since our scales were shorter, the intercorrelations should be somewhat lower. Whereas Sarason's younger children were in grades 1–3, the inclusion of kindergarten children in the Riverside School Study sample might also account for the relatively lower figures for the younger children in our sample.[2]

---

[2] The Campbell and Fiske validation process also involves obtaining estimates of the relative contributions of method variance. Such estimates require the construction of a

Predesegregation

On most of the direct school adjustment measures taken prior to desegregation, significant ethnic differences were found. Except for the need-for-school-achievement scale, the pattern of ethnic differences was consistent over all scales, with Anglos receiving the most "favorable" scores, Mexican-Americans receiving the least "favorable" scores, and Blacks falling in between (see Table 8.1). Individual contrasts indicated that Anglos differed from both the Blacks and Mexican-Americans, the marginal exception occurring between Blacks and Anglos for the others' attitudes scale (K–3) (p < .075 level). Also, in most cases the two minority groups differed significantly from each other, with Mexican-Americans scoring less "favorably" than Blacks.

These results may reflect poor school adjustment by the minorities as a result of what Lambert (1963) has labeled "norm conflict." That is, the minority child typically faces a conflict between the views of his family and neighborhood on the one hand and the views prevalent in the school setting on the other. The Mexican-American child may experience even more cultural norm conflict than a Black child since there is likely to be a sharper discontinuity for him between home and school. Added to this greater norm conflict may be other factors contributing to the less favorable scores of the minority children. Hauser (1971) concluded, after controlling for socioeconomic status, that race is a significant determinant of self-image. He found, for example, that Black males reported more themes of worthlessness, undesirability, uncertainty, and pessimism about the future. Also, in addition to greater norm conflict, the Mexican-American child may have a greater tendency toward "ethnic isolationism." For example, Ramirez, Taylor, & Petersen (1971) suggested that two characteristics of the Mexican-American culture foster and reinforce this isolation: (1) a suspiciousness of strangers and (2) a perceived threat to family and cultural ties. Such avoidance and rejection of the dominant "Anglo" culture might further abet his feelings of anxiety, frustration, and failure.

While these ethnic differences seem compelling, there may be a

---

multitrait–multimethod matrix that includes all of the intercorrelations resulting when each of several traits is measured by each of the several methods. Although we do not have other comparable measures of our traits against which we might further validate the present measures, the analysis we have considered does suggest that we are dealing with five traits that seem to be reasonably independent.

TABLE 8.1 Summary of School Adjustment Scores for 1966: Predesegregation

Scale	F[a]	df	p	Means[b,c]		
				Anglo	Black	Mexican-American
General anxiety						
K–3	26.13	2/1043	.01	7.04	<u>8.34</u>	<u>9.23</u>**
					—**	
4–6	48.01	2/531	.01	6.09	<u>8.66</u>	<u>9.66</u>**
					—**	
School anxiety						
K–3	43.89	2/1037	.01	4.25	<u>5.32</u>	<u>6.18</u>**
					—**	
4–6	22.02	2/526	.01	5.78	<u>7.46</u>	<u>8.20</u>*
					—**	
Others' attitudes						
K–3	27.06	2/1013	.01	12.54	<u>12.19</u>	<u>11.27</u>**
4–6	18.44	2/493	.01	13.44	<u>12.88</u>	<u>11.54</u>**
					—**	
Self-attitudes						
K–3	28.22	2/1024	.01	11.10	<u>10.67</u>	<u>9.84</u>**
					—**	
4–6	15.39	2/499	.01	11.23	<u>10.83</u>	<u>9.46</u>**
					—**	
Achievement need						
4–6	9.03	2/519	.01	<u>7.90</u>	<u>8.78</u>**	8.73

[a] For simplicity only the Fs for the ethnic variable are presented.
[b] The larger the score the more of that attribute the child reported (see text for more detail).
[c] The possible range of scores on all scales is 1–16.
* Underlined means are significantly different at the .05 level.
** Underlined means are significantly different at the .01 level.

problem in interpreting the results because of the wording of the items. For three of the four scales, excluding need for school achievement, there were not equal numbers of items worded so that agreeing with all statements generated a positive score on the trait for only half of the items. For general anxiety, school anxiety, and others' attitudes, any agreement response bias was confounded with a high score on the scale. Only on the self-attitudes scales were items approximately balanced for direction (seven versus eight).

Given this probable confounding, it could be argued that most of the minority–Anglo differences were not real differences. For example, if agreement response bias was correlated with social class, then anxiety differences, as measured by our scales, might simply reflect the confounding between ethnic group and social class, since a large majority of the Mexican-American and the Black parents, as compared with the Anglo parents, were classified in the lowest socioeconomic class. There were, however, several indications that agreement response bias did not contribute substantially to the obtained ethnic differences. Sarason *et al.* (1960) provided evidence that an agreement response bias did not contribute significantly to the scores on these anxiety scales. They further suggested that the correlation between test anxiety and social class could be expected to be positive but small. Also, since this number of positively and negatively worded items on the self-attitudes scale were balanced, racial differences on this scale could not be attributed to an agreement response bias, yet they were nevertheless obtained and were of the same order of magnitude. The argument against a confounding of the agreement response bias was further strengthened by the fact that on the others' attitudes scale, greater agreement response bias for the minority children would have yielded scores indicating more, not less, "favorable" attitudes toward them, which is opposite to the results obtained. Furthermore, the magnitude, direction, and consistency of the various intercorrelations between the scales suggest that systematic response bias was not a primary influence on the children's scores. In other words, one may interpret the scale score differences as reflecting real differences between the Anglos and the minority children. This interpretation is also supported by the analyses discussed below, which held socioeconomic status (SES) relatively constant.

Controlling for SES

Since ethnicity and SES are ubiquitously confounded, it is altogether possible that the scale score differences described above simply reflect social class and not ethnic differences. So that we could explore this problem, a number of analyses were performed comparing minority children with two select subsamples of Anglo children. One subsample consisted of the Anglo children in the lower 20% of the Anglo SES distribution, which permitted a comparison of minority and Anglo children who were approximately equal in SES, and the second consisted of Anglo children from the lowest 5% of the Anglo SES distribution.[3]

When these comparisons were made, most of the differences remained intact, although they shrank somewhat. It is interesting to note that the Mexican-Americans accounted for a large portion of the overall differences in most comparisons. As mentioned above, it may have been the greater "norm conflict" for Mexican-Americans than for Blacks that caused poorer school adjustment. On the other hand, the Anglo children in this sample may still have been at a higher SES level than the Mexican-American children but lower than the Black children. Ethnic differences still remained, however, in comparisons of the lowest 5% (SES) of Anglos to all minority children, but for the older children differences in general anxiety, self-attitudes, and need for school achievement were no longer statistically significant.

Since Anglos in the lower 20% SES subsample were better "adjusted" than the minority children, and since the lowest 5% of the Anglo sample, which was significantly lower in SES than the two minority groups, still maintained an overall, although considerably weaker, "adjustment" advantage, it is hard to argue that SES alone was the sole determinant of adjustment differences.

Effects of Desegregation

Several types of analyses were used to assess the effects of desegregation on school adjustment and its relationship to academic achievement. Differences in school adjustment between and within the ethnic groups were examined both one and three years after desegregation (1967 and 1969), allowing us to evaluate the consistency of ethnic group, sex, and grade differences and the consistency of the relationship of adjustment and achievement. Analyses of the child's pre- and post-

---

[3] The SES means for the Anglos were considerably higher than for the minorities: A = 55.01, B = 28.93, and M.A. = 17.60 (possible range of 1–96). However, the lowest 20% of the Anglos (SES) are more comparable to the minorities with a mean of 20.04 for the Anglos. Using this subsample, the SES level of the Mexican-American children, however, is still significantly lower than the one for this subset of Anglo children and the SES level of the Black children is above that of the Anglo children. The SES mean for the lowest 5% of the Anglos was 11.88, which is significantly below the means of the two minority samples.

desegregation adjustment scores using repeated measures were employed to examine the effects on school adjustment and achievement of longer periods in a desegregated classroom. Two types of effects are reflected in repeated-measures analyses: differences between ethnic groups with the effects of time changes removed, and effects that were due to, or interacted with, the time factor. These latter results were of particular interest, since significant changes over time provided information about developmental changes, and significant time by ethnic group effects provide data on the effects of desegregation. It is important to note, however, that desegregation effects revealed by these analyses were confounded with any other changes that might be occurring over time.

First Year of Desegregation

The data that are presented in Table 8.2 closely parallel those of 1966 (predesegregation). Ethnic differences existed for all scales, with the Mexican-Americans scoring least "favorably" and Anglos scoring most "favorably." Individual contrasts indicated that on all five scales

TABLE 8.2 *Summary of School Adjustment Scores for 1967 (First Year of Desegregation)*

				Means[b,c]		
Scale	F^a	df	p	Anglo	Black	Mexican-American
General anxiety	76.30	2/1467	.01	5.83	8.02 —**—	8.74**
School anxiety	53.68	2/1466	.01	4.53	5.59 —**—	6.38**
Others' attitudes	34.18	2/1393	.01	13.23	12.51 —**—	11.83**
Self-attitudes	29.30	2/1436	.01	10.42	10.07 —**—	9.43**
Achievement need	3.49	2/494	.05	6.80	7.38*	7.43

a For simplicity only the *F*s for the ethnic variable are presented.
b See footnote b, Table 8.1.
c The possible range of scores on all scales is 1–16.
* Underlined means are significantly different at the .05 level.
** Underlined means are significantly different at the .01 level.

Anglos were significantly different from both Blacks and Mexican-Americans. Furthermore, for all scales but one the minority groups differed significantly from each other, with Blacks scoring more "favorably" than Mexican-Americans. The only exception to this pattern was in need for school achievement, on which the two minority groups did not differ significantly.

In comparisons of the lower 20% (SES) of the Anglos with the minorities, all significant differences remained intact. Unlike the pre-desegregation results, however, most racial differences held fairly strongly when all the minority children were compared with the lowest 5% of the Anglos. The only exception was in need for school achievement, on which no significant ethnic differences occurred. There are several possible explanations for the postdesegregation ethnic differences obtained when SES was controlled. Proshansky and Newton (1968) argued that Black children in a newly desegregated classroom accept White prestige and increasingly withdraw into their own groups, the result being greater internal stress. These conditions do not exist for the White child since he is not negatively affected by the color–caste system. Minority children might therefore be expected to show a greater post-desegregation deficit in school adjustment compared with Anglo children. Also, lower-class Anglos may be able to maintain or even improve their self-concept in the desegregated classroom by comparing their academic performance with that of the newly arrived minority children, who are typically performing at a lower level academically. The addition of minority children provided a new "anchor point" with which to compare oneself as evidenced by the fact that achievement scores of the lowest 5% of the Anglo children were significantly higher than those of the minority children for both one and three years of desegregation (both $p < .01$).

Three Years Postdesegregation

The results were again similar to those found prior to desegregation, as can be seen from Table 8.3. The ethnic differences were the same in direction, and significant grade effects were obtained for general anxiety, others' attitudes, self-attitudes, and need for school achievement. These increases in school "adjustment" with age may, at least in part, have been a function of greater sophistication on the part of the older children, who had learned to give socially desirable answers. There were no significant race-by-grade interactions in 1969. Analyses

TABLE 8.3 Summary of School Adjustment Scores for 1969 (Third Year of Desegregation)

Scale	F^a	df	p	Anglo	Black	Mexican-American
					Means[b,c]	
General anxiety	69.61	2/1278	.01	6.04	8.31	8.91*
School anxiety	31.56	2/1275	.01	5.57	6.51	7.54*
Others' attitudes	28.51	2/1169	.01	13.49	12.83	12.11*
Self-attitudes	30.21	2/1238	.01	11.13	10.32	9.42*
Achievement need	4.73	2/1013	.01	7.30	7.82*	7.65

[a] For simplicity only the Fs for the ethnic variable are presented.
[b] See footnote b, Table 8.1.
[c] The possible range of scores on all scales is 1–16.
* Underlined means are significantly different at the .01 level.

comparing the lower 20% and the lowest 5% (SES) Anglos with all minority children indicated that most racial differences held up as they had in 1966 and 1967.

To further assess desegregation effects, we analyzed the child's score for each of the three years (1966, 1967, 1969) in a repeated-measures design. We expected the results to reveal ethnic group differences in adjustment, developmental trends (changes over time), and possible desegregation effects (time-by-ethnic-group interactions). As mentioned, any desegregation effects were confounded with anything else that might be occurring over time. Nonetheless some interesting results were obtained that were consistent with the ethnic, sex, and age differences discussed above.

Significant changes over time occurred for all of the adjustment measures. The most "favorable" change was found on the general anxiety scale, on which a decrease occurred following desegregation (1966 to 1967) and remained low after three years (1969). There was a similar initial drop in school anxiety during the first year of desegregation, but in 1969 the level increased beyond what it had been prior to desegregation. Following desegregation the children reported a small increase in favorableness of others' attitudes, which continued to increase in 1969. Self-attitudes decreased in favorableness following desegregation, but by 1969 they were back up to the predesegregation level. Only the need-for-school-achievement scale reflected consistently negative changes over time, dropping with desegregation and falling still lower in 1969.

Significant time-by-sex interactions were found on the general and school anxiety scales. In general, both sexes showed similar decreases in anxiety following desegregation (1967), but girls displayed much greater anxiety in 1969 than did boys. The time-by-grade interactions were also significant for the two anxiety scales. On both scales younger and older children showed a similar decrease in anxiety following desegregation, but in 1969 older children decreased further in general anxiety whereas younger children increased greatly.

Time effects alone do not provide us with as interesting information as do interactions of time with various other factors. Sex and grade-level changes over time, while interesting developmentally, are not particularly valuable in terms of assessing the effects of desegregation. Of special interest, however, is the significant ethnic-group-by-grade-by-time interaction ($p < .05$) obtained for general anxiety. All children decreased in general anxiety following desegregation. Two years later (1969) the younger children had increased whereas the older children continued to decrease. Furthermore in 1969 the younger Black children displayed a much larger increase in general anxiety than either the Anglos or the Mexican-Americans. In fact, the younger Blacks increased in general anxiety to a level that was both greater than the older Mexican-Americans and similar to that of the younger Mexican-Americans, whereas prior to this time they had been less anxious than both groups of Mexican-Americans. At least by our measure of general anxiety, the younger Black child appeared to be experiencing the most difficulty in the desegregated classroom in 1969.[4]

Sex and Grade Effects

Similar patterns of sex differences were obtained for each of the years both prior to and after desegregation. Girls showed far greater

---

[4] Difference scores created by subtraction of the child's predesegregation scores (1966) from his postdesegregation scores in 1967 and 1969 were also analyzed. As expected, however, these results were similar to those obtained from the repeated-measures analyses and are not reported.

general anxiety than did boys ($p < .001$) in all three years, a finding that agrees with findings by Bower (1960) and Sarason *et al.* (1960). Analysis also indicated that in every year the sex difference for Anglos was less than for either of the minorities ($p < .01$ for all three years). That is, Anglo girls reported less general anxiety than Black or Mexican-American girls and were close to the anxiety levels expressed by the Black and Mexican-American boys. Significant sex differences in school anxiety were also found for all three years, with girls reporting more anxiety about school than boys. Sarason *et al.* (1960) suggested that sex-related differences in anxiety may be a function of sex differences in defensiveness. If this is true, one might expect sex differences to be smaller on the school anxiety scale than on the general anxiety scale, assuming that boys would be less defensive about school work than about their general environment. The data supported this notion and followed a pattern similar to that obtained by Sarason *et al.* That is, while girls displayed greater anxiety on both scales, the pattern of differences was greater on the general than on the school anxiety scale. Few significant sex differences were found on the other scales.

Significant grade effects obtained on the school anxiety and others' attitudes scales were very similar across years. In general, older children were more anxious about school ($ps < .001$). In addition, following desegregation older children reported more favorable self-attitudes than younger children ($p < .01$), whereas prior to desegregation there was no significant age difference. Few significant grade-by-sex interactions were obtained other than on the school anxiety scale, on which younger children of both sexes were similar and lower in school anxiety than were the older children, and the older girls reported much greater school anxiety than did older boys both prior to ($p < .01$) and one year following desegregation ($p < .01$).

For the most part, the same effects for grade and sex seemed to hold for comparisons within each ethnic group. That is, in all three ethnic groups prior to desegregation, the girls displayed more general anxiety than boys, and the Black girls displayed more school anxiety than did the Black boys. No significant effect was found on Anglos or Mexican-Americans for school anxiety, but a significant grade-by-sex interaction was obtained for each of them. Anglo boys reported more school anxiety than Anglo girls in the lower grades but less in the upper grades, whereas Mexican-American boys displayed less school anxiety than Mexican-American girls in the lower grades but more in the upper grades. Only for the Blacks were sex differences obtained on any of the other scales; Black boys scored more favorably than Black girls on both the others' attitudes and the self-attitudes scales. Again these findings supported those reported by Bower (1960) and were consistent with the apparently greater acceptance of Black boys than Black girls in the desegregated classroom (see Chapter 10 on classroom social structure). In general the predesegregation sex differences recurred within all three ethnic groups, with girls displaying more general anxiety than boys (all ps < .05), but although significant (p < .05), the magnitude of the Anglo and Mexican-American sex differences in school anxiety seemed to decrease following desegregation. Few significant sex differences were found on the other scales.

Intraethnic grade comparisons revealed that prior to desegregation older Anglos scored more "favorably" than younger Anglos on three of the scales (general anxiety, school anxiety, and others' attitudes), and older Mexican-American and older Black children scored more "favorably" than their younger counterparts on two of the scales (Mexican-Americans: general anxiety and school anxiety; Blacks: school anxiety and others' attitudes, respectively, with all ps < .05). Following desegregation the grade effects were more or less comparable, with the following exceptions. One year after desegregation significant grade effects were obtained only for the Mexican-Americans; the older children were found to display more school anxiety (p < .01) yet they perceived others' attitudes toward them as more favorable than did the younger Mexican-Americans (p < .01). Whereas older and younger Blacks did not differ in the first year after desegregation, three years after desegregation older Blacks tended to score more "favorably" than younger Blacks in general anxiety, others' attitudes, and self-attitudes (all ps < .05). It is possible to interpret many of these age effects as reflecting childrens' increased defensiveness or awareness of what was socially desirable as they matured.

School Adjustment and Achievement

One of the primary aims of obtaining measures of school adjustment was to evaluate the relationship between the child's academic achievement and his level of adjustment in the school setting. To assess this relationship, the five school-adjustment indices were correlated with the child's achievement test scores. In general, the relationships between academic achievement and indices of school adjustment were relatively small, and significance ($p < .005$) was achieved only with the large sample size. Overall, however, these relationships, held for comparisons both between and within ethnic groups in each of the three years, and the directions and the relative sizes of the correlations were what one might expect. For example, in 1966 general anxiety and school anxiety were negatively related to achievement ($r = -.12$, $N = 1482$, and $r = -.24$, $N = 1473$, respectively), while others' and self-attitudes were positively related to achievement ($r = +.17$, $N = 1423$, and $r = +.21$, $N = 1435$, respectively). Furthermore, as might be expected, the relationship between school anxiety and achievement was stronger than that between general anxiety and achievement. All the correlations should be interpreted with caution, however, since their absolute magnitudes are small, accounting for relatively little of the total variance. Presumably, a number of other factors contributed much more to academic achievement than school adjustment as measured by our five paper-and-pencil scales. (See, for example, Chapter 5 on intelligence.)

To reveal significant interactions, we also assessed the relationship between adjustment and achievement using analyses of variance with relative level of achievement as one of the independent variables. Although causal relationships cannot be inferred from these analyses, the results were fairly clear. Table 8.4 summarizes the results for adjustment indices, with achievement (median split of the total achievement score standardized within grade), grade, ethnic group, and sex as the independent variables. As in the correlational analysis, school adjustment and achievement were related except for the need-for-school-achievement scale. As expected, children with low achievement test scores were more anxious both in general and about school and had less favorable self-concepts than high-achieving children. These relationships held up across all three years.

Prior to desegregation, low-achieving, Black and Anglo children reported more general anxiety than did their high-achieving counterparts, whereas for Mexican-Americans this relationship was reversed (all ps $< .05$). In 1966 low-achieving boys had less favorable self-attitudes than did low-achieving girls, whereas the reverse was true for high achievers, with boys having more favorable self-attitudes than girls

[5] See footnote 1.

TABLE 8.4   School "*Adjustment*" as a Function of Level of Achievement

Scale	F[a]	df	p	"Adjustment" means[b,c]	
				Low[d]	High[d]
General anxiety					
1966	5.57	1,1467	.05	8.58	7.57
1967	4.93	1,1019	.05	8.05	6.70
1969	10.90	1,938	.01	8.67	6.85
School anxiety					
1966	35.70	1,1458	.01	6.55	5.07
1967	28.46	1,1019	.01	5.86	4.41
1969	20.63	1,936	.01	7.31	5.71
Others' attitudes					
1966	14.89	1,1408	.01	11.80	12.66
1967	11.75	1,974	.01	12.06	13.04
1969	14.18	1,866	.01	13.00	13.55
Self-attitudes					
1966	32.02	1,1420	.01	10.00	11.04
1967	10.52	1,1000	.01	9.57	10.28
1969	25.51	1,914	.01	9.57	10.96
Achievement need					
1966	1.42	1,469	ns	8.45	8.30
1967	3.03	1,269	ns	7.29	6.76
1969	2.89	1,732	ns	7.79	7.39

[a] For simplicity only the Fs for the achievement variable are presented here. See the text for more detail.
[b] See footnote b, Table 8.1.
[c] The possible range of scores on all scales is 1–16.
[d] These adjustment means are for low and high achievers based upon a median split of achievement (see text for more detail).

($p < .01$). In 1969 low- and high-achieving boys were both more similar to each other and lower in general anxiety than were low- and high-achieving girls ($p < .05$). We want to remind the reader that these sex differences in anxiety may be a function of sex differences in defensiveness.

Adjustment and Change in Achievement

The effect of change in achievement across years on change in adjustment was also examined for additional information about the relationships between school adjustment and academic achievement. We expected any significant effects involving changes in relative achievement to throw some light on the relation between adjustment and achievement. Few effects were obtained, however, and most of these disappeared when we used the "cleaner" sample involving only those minority children desegregated in 1966 and those Anglo children present in the receiving schools at that time. Only changes in school anxiety and self-attitudes reflected important relationships with changes in academic achievement, particularly when we examined changes from predesegregation to three years postdesegregation (1969). Children who decreased in academic achievement increased in anxiety about school significantly more than did children who increased in academic achievement ($p < .05$). In addition, decreases in achievement were related to decreases in self-attitudes, and increases in achievement were related to increases in self-attitudes ($p < .05$). Although changes in academic performance and school adjustment were related, no differential effects appeared to be attributable to the race of the child, and unfortunately it is even very difficult to decipher the causal direction involved in these achievement–adjustment relationships.

Factor Analyses

Factor analyses were performed in an attempt to refine our measures of school adjustment. We expected the comparison of these results with those obtained from the entire group of children to clarify the influence of the different ethnic and cultural backgrounds of the children. A principal-axis factor analysis with *phi* correlations was carried out and also a varimax rotation to delineate clusters of relationships. A loading of .37 for each item was chosen as a cut-off criterion. As it turned out, if coefficients of less than .37 were selected, a number of questions loaded on more than one factor, making interpretation difficult. Using the .37 criterion eliminated about 40% of the original 75 items. Since on the basis of Ketcham and Morse's (1965) analysis it was expected that ethnicity and age would influence factor formation, a separate analysis was carried out for each ethnic group. The children were also divided into two age subgroups: kindergarten through third grade and fourth through sixth grade. The factors were interpreted for these different age levels by ethnic subgroups, both prior to and after desegregation.

The factor analysis of a total group of 994 children showed Factor I as a clear "general anxiety" factor with 14 items, all from the general anxiety scale. Factor II appeared to be an "others' attitudes" factor with 6 items, 5 of which were from the others' attitudes scale. Factor III had 4 school anxiety items, 3 self-attitudes items, and 1 others' attitudes items. The self-attitudes items included here pointed to a self-deprecatory attitude. The school anxiety and the others' attitudes items reflected avoidance of school and avoidance of a feared situation. Thus Factor III appeared to be a "self-diminishing and avoidance behavior" factor that could be subsumed under Anna Freud's (1946) "ego restriction" defense. The items that loaded on the factor reflected amazingly well her description of that mechanism: the person's diminished feelings lead him to avoid situations that elicit these feelings, thus restricting his scope of behavior and action. Factor IV appeared to be a "need for achievement" factor. The child evaluated himself with regard to the others. Although kindergarteners through third-graders were not administered the 15 achievement questions, the 4 items that loaded on this factor nevertheless reflected achievement since they represented the way the child compared himself with other children in accomplishment. The overall result for the 994 children was then quite clear: general anxiety (Factor I) was uppermost, followed by the evaluation by others (Factor II), self-diminishing and avoidance behavior (Factor III), and finally by achievement need (Factor IV).

If we now look at the results for the different ethnic groups, a different factor panorama emerges. For the Anglo children, there were a total of four factors, three of which appeared to be similar to three of the factors we named for the total group. Factor III, which did not emerge for the total group had 5 school anxiety items and very clearly represented specific fear of and avoidance of school. The self-denial and self-hatred that emerged when the total group was analyzed did not appear for the Anglo children taken separately. Factor II was somewhat better defined. There were 8 others' attitudes items that loaded on Factor II for the Anglos as compared with 5 for the total group. Factor IV also had an additional item loading on it. Thus for the Anglo children the factors were in order of importance: general anxiety, others' attitudes, school anxiety and school avoidance, and achievement through social comparison. Since the factors emerged more clearly than when the entire group of children was considered, it appeared that the factors derived from the total group reflected the influence of the different cultural backgrounds of the children and thus represented relatively "impure" factors.

The data from the 246 Black children yielded "general anxiety" as the first factor, with nearly all of the same 14 items as for the total group and for the Anglos. Factor II for the Blacks appeared to be "achievement and social comparison," with 5 items that constituted Factor IV for the entire group and for the Anglos. Having an evaluation of themselves was evidently more necessary to the Blacks than to the Anglos. Factor III was again a mixture of avoidance of the school situation and negative self-attitudes. Factor IV, evaluation by others, corresponded to Factor II for the Anglos, which suggested that this source of self-appraisal was less important for the Blacks than for the Anglos. The factors extracted for the Black children thus presented a more complex picture than did the Anglo factor structure. Did this imply a more differentiated "life space"? Social comparison seemed more salient for the Blacks than the judgment of others, whereas for Anglos the reverse appeared to be true: the judgment of others affected their self-appraisal more than the way they rated themselves. A fifth factor, not discussed above, represented aggressive impulses and fear of these impulses, which seemed to be absent in Anglos.

The factors for the 383 Mexican-American children also yielded a more complex picture than the one obtained for Anglos. Factor I was once again a "general anxiety" factor, represented here by 11 items instead of the 14 for the Anglos and the Blacks. It is curious that the missing items were those indicating fear that something would happen to them or to their parents. Factor II was a combination of self-evaluation and evaluation by others. This factor resembled Factor II for the Anglos more than Factor II for the Blacks, suggesting that, in contrast with the Blacks, for both the Mexican-American and the Anglo children the evaluation by others was more important than self-evaluation. For the Mexican-Americans, self-evaluations were salient, whereas for the Blacks, self-evaluation was far less important (relegated to Factor IV). Factor III contained school anxiety, avoidance, and self-deprecatory items. This factor revealed the Mexican-Americans as having at least as negative self-attitudes as the Blacks. It is interesting that these negative self feelings were already present in children this young. Factor IV contained three general anxiety items and one item that could be interpreted as hopes for a better situation. The three general anxiety items represented a concern that something bad would happen to them or their parents, which corresponded roughly to Factor V for the Blacks. We can only suggest the same tentative interpretation that the Mexican-American children had competitive and aggressive impulses and feared the damaging effect of these impulses. These were the items that involved aggressive tendencies toward the parents and that were absent in the general anxiety factor, suggesting that these impulses existed for the Anglos but played a less important role. Their association with hopes for a better situation also put them in a different context. Factor V for the Mexican-Americans was another social comparison factor. Thus, whereas social comparison as a source of self-appraisal was highly important to the Blacks (Factor II), it was not as important to the Anglos (Factor IV) and also seemed to be somewhat less important to the Mexican-Americans (split between Factor II and V). The factor structure for the Mexican-Americans, then, was as complex as that for the Blacks but seemed to be a cross between the Anglo and the Black structures.

Summary

Our attempt to validate the five scales suggested that the scales reflected distinct underlying traits related to adjustment. With the exception of need for school achievement, which appeared to provide little useful or interesting information, the other four scales all demonstrated that as compared with minority children, the Anglos were "better adjusted" to the school environment. They were, for the most part, lower in both general and school anxiety, and their self-concepts were more favorable as reflected by both their self-attitudes and their perception of others' attitudes toward them. Furthermore these results appeared to be a function of ethnic, over and above socioeconomic, differences since our analysis revealed that Anglos scored more favorably than minority children with SES controlled.

Analysis of developmental and sex information suggested that, in general, the girls were more anxious than the boys. However, the results might be interpreted to mean that the boys were more defensive. As expected, sex differences were smaller for school than for general anxiety, which lends support to the notion that the boys were more defensive about their masculine role in the general environment than they were in the school setting. Few consistent sex differences were found for the two self-concept scales. Grade effects were somewhat inconsistent across years, but in general, the older children had more favorable self-concepts than the younger children both on the others' attitudes and on the self-attitudes scales. Effects of grades on anxiety were more complex. Older children were more anxious about school than younger children prior to and one year after desegregation, but by 1969 this grade difference disappeared. Only in 1969 was a significant grade effect found for general anxiety, with younger children displaying more anxiety than older children.

Both the correlational analysis and the analysis of variance provided support for the relationship between adjustment and academic achievement. In all three years low-achieving children were more anxious both in general and about school than were high-achieving children. Lower achievers also revealed themselves as having less favorable self-concepts than higher achievers, both on the others' attitudes and on the self-attitudes scales. The relatively small magnitudes of the correlations between the scales and the achievement scores did suggest, however, that adjustment accounted for relatively little of the total variance associated with achievement.

Our analysis indicated that over time certain changes in school adjustment did occur. There were, however, very few differential changes that could be attributed to the child's ethnic group membership. Only one significant effect involving ethnic group was obtained by the use of a repeated-measures design. Over time younger Black children displayed a much larger increase in general anxiety than did either the younger Anglo or the younger Mexican-American children. Only school anxiety and self-attitudes appeared to reflect any relationships between changes in school adjustment and changes in academic achievement. On both scales children who dropped in academic achievement showed a decrease in their level of school adjustment. Thus a child's anxiety about school and his self-attitudes may have been mediators of his academic performance. Extreme caution must be exercised, however, when causal relationships are inferred from these analyses. There were no significant effects of ethnicity or interactions involving ethnicity for these analyses, which suggested that in terms of school adjustment the ethnic groups differentially changed very little in academic achievement as a result of the desegregation experience.

The factor analytic structure obtained from the *a priori* adjustment items when the entire group of children was used was quite clear. General anxiety, the uppermost factor, was followed by evaluation by others, self-diminishing and avoidance behavior, and finally achievement need. A somewhat different picture emerged for each ethnic group separately, reflecting the influence of the different cultural backgrounds of the children. The factors extracted for the Black children presented a more complex picture than did the Anglo factor structure. That of the Mexican-Americans was as complex as that of the Blacks, but it seemed to be a cross between the Black and the Anglo structures. In general, social comparison was a salient source of self-appraisal for the Blacks, whereas it was relatively less important to the Mexican-Americans and of even less importance to the Anglos, who relied more on the judgments of others.

In conclusion, the data suggested that the overall effects of desegregation were not great. That is, Anglos appeared "better adjusted" than did the minority children prior to desegregation, and they remained so after desegregation. The Black children were intermediate prior to bussing, and for the most part they remained in that relative position after desegregation. If anything, it appeared that younger Mexican-American children suffered the most upon desegregation and that older Mexican-American children gained the most. However, they remained "least adjusted" when compared to the children in the two other ethnic groups. In sum, the desegregation program in Riverside did not appear to have resulted in any consistent differential changes in adjustment for the three ethnic groups.

References

Bettelheim, B., & Janowitz, M. *Social change and prejudice.* New York: Free Press, 1964.

Bower, E. M. *Early identification of emotionally handicapped children in school.* Springfield, Ill.: Charles C Thomas, 1960.

California State Advisory Committee to U.S. Commission on Civil Rights. *Education and the Mexican-American community in Los Angeles.* 1968.

Campbell, D. T., & Fiske, D. W. Convergent and discriminant validation by the multitrait-multimethod matrix. *Psychological Bulletin,* 1959, *56,* 81–105.

Cattell, R. B. *The scientific analysis of personality.* Baltimore, Md.: Penguin, 1965.

Coleman, J. S., & staff. *Equality of educational opportunities.* U.S. Department of Health, Education, and Welfare. Washington, D.C.: U.S. Government Printing Office, 1966.

Coopersmith, S. *The antecedents of self-esteem.* San Francisco: Freeman, 1967.

Edwards, A. L. *Edwards Personal Preference Schedule.* New York: Psychological Corporation, 1953.

Festinger, L. A theory of social comparison processes. *Human Relations,* 1954, *7,* 117–140.

Freud, A. *The ego and the mechanisms of defense.* New York: National University Press, 1946.

Gerard, H. B., Blevans, S. A., & Malcolm, T. Self-evaluation and the evaluation of choice alternatives. *Journal of Personality,* 1964, *32,* 395–410.

Hauser, S. T. *Black and white identity formation: Studies in the psychosocial development of lower socioeconomic class adolescent boys.* New York: Wiley, 1971.

Katz, I. Factors influencing Negro performance in the desegregated school. *American Psychologist,* 1964, *19,* 381–399.

Ketcham, W. A., & Morse, W. C. *Dimensions of children's social and psychological development related to school achievement.* Cooperative Research Project No. 1286. University of Michigan, Ann Arbor, 1965.

Klausner, S. Z. Social class and self-concept. *Journal of Social Psychology,* 1953, *138,* 201–205.

Kluckholn, F. R., & Strodtbeck, F. L. *Variations in value orientations.* Evanston, Ill.: Row-Peterson, 1961.

Kuder, G. G., & Richardson, M. W. The theory of the estimation of test reliability. *Psychometrika,* 1937, *2,* 151–160.

Lambert, N. M. *The development and validation of a process for screening emotionally handicapped children in school.* Cooperative Report No. 1186. Cooperative Research Program of Office of Education of the U.S. Department of Health, Education, and Welfare, 1963.

Mosteller, F., & Moynihan, D. P. (Eds.), *On equality of educational opportunities.* New York: Random House, 1972.

Proshansky, A. J., Jr., & Newton, P. The nature and meaning of Negro self-identity. In M. Deutsch, I. Katz, & A. R. Jensen (Eds.), *Social class, race and psychological development.* New York: Holt, Rhinehart, and Winston, 1968.

Ramirez, M., Taylor, C., & Petersen, B. Mexican-American cultural membership and adjustment to school. *Developmental Psychology,* 1971, *4,* 141–148.

Sarason, S. B., Davidson, K. S., Lighthall, F. F., Waite, R. R., & Ruebush, B. K. *Anxiety in elementary school children.* New York: Wiley, 1960.

Schwartz, A. J. A comparative study of values and achievement: Mexican-American and Anglo youth. *Sociology of Education,* 1971, *44,* 438–462.

Silberman, C. E. *Crisis in Black and White.* New York: Random House, 1964.

Spence, J. T. Learning theory and personality. In J. M. Wepman & R. W. Heine (Eds.), *Concepts of personality.* Chicago, Ill.: Aldine Publishing Co., 1963.

Stotland, E., & Hillmer, M. Identification, authoritarian defensiveness and self-esteem. *Journal of Abnormal and Social Psychology,* 1962, *64,* 333–342.

Thorne, R. B. The effects of experimentally induced failure on self-evaluations. *Dissertation Abstracts,* 1954, *14,* 181–187.

9

Speech Anxiety and Linguistic Changes

Tora Kay Bikson, Harold B. Gerard,
Michel Thelia, and Erhan Yasar

Although comprehensive and systematic evidence about language competence and performance in elementary-school-aged subjects is not now available (*cf.* Chomsky, 1969), two points are well established in the existing literature: first, academic achievement is frequently both mediated by and tested in terms of verbal activities; second, verbal activities—and especially interpersonal communication—are reflective of and responsive to social contexts. In a desegregation situation, then, it is important to investigate ethnic differences in language behavior in order to assess their potential relationship to differential achievement. It is further important to understand how the social interaction situation affects the language behavior of the children involved and whether desegregation can be expected to produce long-term changes in verbal activities.

The studies discussed below approached such questions by investigating the speech characteristics of our sample children. We attempt here to assess the effects of desegregation by comparing pre- and post-measures of achievement-related speech properties and by examining the extent to which anxiety during speech-related tasks differentially affects verbal performance in the newly desegregated school situation.

The raw data used in the present investigation are the transcribed

Tora Kay Bikson, Harold B. Gerard, and Michel Thelia • University of California, Los Angeles, California. Erhan Yasar • Middle East Technical University, Ankara, Turkey.

contents of the Children's Apperception Test (CAT) (Bellak and Bellak, 1954) protocols collected in 1966, 1967, and 1969. The CAT test stimuli consist of black-and-white cartoonlike pictures depicting animals in various school, home, and play situations. Each child was instructed to make up stories to each of the pictures. His stories were tape-recorded and then typed in conversational form.

Normative Indices of Speech Sophistication

We shall first consider some readily quantifiable features of speech often thought to index language development and useful for obtaining a broad normative picture of the child's speech style in a school situation. For measures of this sort it was desirable to study a fairly large sample including all grades during all years studied. A subsample of 530 children was selected as shown in Table 9.1. Each transcription was transposed onto IBM cards and processed through a computer program that edited out errors, incomplete words, speech disturbances, and remarks by the interviewer. Four measures of speech sophistication were derived. They are described below.

Response Length. For children of 5 years and older, response length reflects not only verbal development but also social–situational constraints on performance (Cazden, 1966, 1967; Labov, 1970; McNeill, 1970). We measured the total number of complete words each child produced per picture both with and without social reinforcement from the interviewer, a variation we used in our procedure.

TABLE 9.1 Samples of Children Selected for Speech Study

Grade	Anglo	Black	Mexican-American
2nd	20	37	65
3rd	20	30	61
4th	20	32	61
5th	20	25	66
6th	20	15	38
Totals	100	139	291
Grand total:	530		

Word Length. Longer words have a lower probability of occurrence (Herdan, 1964; Yule, 1944; Zipf, 1932, 1949) and higher "information" value and are more "difficult" (Herdan, 1960, 1966). Also, difficulty rank on vocabulary tests is typically higher the longer the word (Lorge & Chall, 1963). Average word length, machine-scored as number of graphemes per word, is thus a suitable index of language development and—since no specific lexical contents are involved—ought to be free of cultural bias (Miller, 1953; Miller, Heise, & Lichten, 1951; Zipf, 1932).

Number of Different Words per Story. Standard vocabulary tests cannot be construed as semantic competence measures because the lexical sampling in those tests reflects cultural bias. The present method, on the other hand, yields a speaker-generated and open-ended vocabulary count free of such bias. The larger the number of different words in use, the lower the probability of occurrence of each and the greater the information value of each. Moreover, since verbal IQ and achievement tests are thought to depend heavily on standard vocabulary (Kingston & Weaver, 1970), comparisons of vocabulary ranges elicited in a common speech performance situation should provide a valuable supplement to the former sort of information. It must be noted, however, that number of different words is partially reflective of response length (Herdan, 1964).

Repetition Rate. While redundancy is unavoidably associated with response length in a fairly regular way because of the recurrence of function words (Fries, 1950), it is also thought to be inversely related to verbal sophistication and reflective of class differences in the "orientation to symbolize" (Bernstein, 1959, 1961). We computed repetition rate as the ratio of total words to different words per story.

Results

As expected, age constituted a highly significant influence on verbal output ($F = 6.65$, $p < .001$), with older children talking more voluminously (the second-grade mean was 82.26, while the sixth-grade mean was 121.55 words per story).[1] No main effects emerged for

---

[1] Response length was investigated by means of a four-way (school grade, ethnicity, story, and year) repeated-measures analysis of variance with year of administration as the repeated factor.

ethnicity, nor did ethnicity interact with grade, suggesting between-group developmental similarity. Of greater interest was the strong effect of the ethnicity-by-year interaction term on verbal production ($F = 3.33$, $p < .01$); shown in Table 9.2.

These data indicate both that minority students were more talkative than Anglos in the predesegregation interview and that their speech output was disproportionately depressed relative to Anglo output after desegregation. While the social dynamics behind these long-term outcomes are not clear, data are available concerning the effects of social context within the testing situation. In one of the testing sessions the second and third stories were reinforced (e.g., "That's a nice story," "You tell such good stories"), while the first and fourth were not reinforced. As expected, within an interview, social reinforcement was a significant source of variance ($F = 19.41$, $p < .001$), the first story (averaging 94.47 words) being considerably shorter than the last (averaging 107.95 words). Presumably, the effect of reinforcing the second and third stories was to increase output for the fourth story. While relaxation as the interview progressed would contribute to such an effect (*cf.* Goldman-Eisler, 1968), part of the influence of social reinforcement after the first story was probably to enhance relaxation. A separate analysis of variance using output differences between stories one and four—i.e., responsiveness to social reinforcement—as the dependent measure revealed no main effects for either ethnicity or desegregation. Thus verbal response length reflected only developmental changes and the effect of short-term social reinforcement. While the first two sources of variance produced common between-group results, the desegregation experience itself affected groups differently on this measure.

A similar analysis yielded quite different results for word length as a dependent measure. While age entered into no main or interaction effects, ethnicity was a significant determinant of word length, Anglo

TABLE 9.2   Word Count

	1966	1967	1969
Anglo	103.76	76.42	76.20
Mexican-American	138.50	90.42	78.38
Black	144.22	73.33	85.60

TABLE 9.3   Letters per Word

	First	Second	Third	Fourth
Anglo	4.067	3.882	3.927	3.828
Mexican-American	3.921	3.905	3.896	3.833
Black	3.982	3.857	3.876	3.799

children using longer words than minority children ($F = 3.56, p < .02$). While word length decreased overall throughout the interview, it did so much more rapidly for Anglo than for minority children, so that ethnic differences showed primarily on the first story (see Table 9.3). The effect of story order itself on word length was marginal ($p < .07$), in contrast with the strong main effects on response length. In the absence of either strong developmental or between-group effects for year, the importance of ethnic differences in word length relative to school achievement or desegregation was difficult to assess.

The third dependent measure, number of different words per story, yielded a strong age effect ($F = 10.42, p < .001$), older children employing a broader vocabulary range. No main effect emerged for ethnicity. Since the results closely resembled those obtained for response length, and since length increased vocabulary diversity (although not nearly so much as it increased repetition), it is important to determine whether or not the results for vocabulary size are simply a function of output volume. This question cannot be assessed directly here, since most segmenting procedures (e.g., Yule, 1944) require longer texts than those generated by our subjects. It should be noted, however, that story order had no effect on number of different words, in contrast with the strong effect on number of words. Furthermore, no year-by-ethnicity interaction occurred for number of different words, in contrast to its effect on number of words. Rather, in relation to number of different words, an interaction emerged for grade and ethnicity not seen for response length ($F = 2.03$, $p < .04$), as shown in Table 9.4.

Although overall ethnic differences were not statistically significant, there was a trend for minority children to use more different words than Anglos, a difference particularly apparent in the younger grades. These results were comparable to those reported by Entwisle (1966, 1968a, 1968b, 1970) and John (1963; John & Goldstein, 1964), who also used

TABLE 9.4   *Mean Number of Different Words per Story*

	Anglo	Mexican-American	Black
2nd graders	31.0	40.9	42.1
3rd graders	34.5	44.5	37.9
4th graders	43.9	48.6	58.9
5th graders	57.9	50.9	44.3
6th graders	59.9	51.9	64.3

open-ended vocabulary measures and who found young minority children employing substantially more different words than did their Anglo age-mates. That the differences obtained here for vocabulary range did not parallel those for response length and that they received support from researchers using word-association techniques led to the tentative conclusion that the number of different words used represented at least a partially independent aspect of language development. It further implied that minority children do not come to the desegregated school from a vocabulary-deprived background (*cf.* Bereiter, 1968; Raph, 1965), despite the fact that they fare relatively poorly on standardized vocabulary tests.

Analysis of repetition rate yielded no effect for age but a marked effect for ethnicity ($F = 8.82$, $p < .001$), minority children being more repetitive than Anglos. Because repetitiveness is closely related to length of response (Herdan, 1964), it was initially surprising to find no effect for age. A near-significant age-by-ethnicity interaction ($p < .10$), however, showed that while younger children tended to be less repetitive (and young Anglo children the least repetitive), only among Anglos was there a linear, age-related increase in repetition rate; minority repetition rates changed erratically from grade to grade.

Strong effects emerged for story order ($F = 7.59$, $p < .001$), repetition rate increasing from story one to story four, paralleling response-length increases. That repetition rate reflected response length is seen in two additional results: (1) year yielded a main effect for repetition rate ($F = 69.6$, $p < .001$), which decreased in much the same way that we saw total output decrease after desegregation; and (2) a year-by-ethnicity interaction ($F = 4.08$, $p < .005$) showed that repetitiveness decreased much more rapidly for minority than for Anglo children. Finally, year and story order interacted ($F = 2.09$, $p < .05$) so that increased repetitiveness from story to story diminished with successive years. These findings suggested that repetitiveness makes up a large part of the variance in differential response length. Also, the between-group difference in repetition rate does not imply a lack of verbal competence on the part of minority children (*cf.* contrary results for vocabulary counts); rather, such differences are more appropriately attributed to short- and long-term social constraints on performance.

Verbal Sophistication and School Achievement

The measures analyzed above were next examined in relation to school achievement. Verbal and overall achievement scores standardized within ethnic group were available, as were verbal class grades. Among the variables studied, only vocabulary size showed a positive and significant relationship to achievement: of 39 comparisons (vocabulary size in each of three years in relation to each of the achievement measures mentioned), 31 had r values of .10 or better ($.05 < p < .10$) despite an ethnic bias to the contrary (i.e., it was the minority students who used more different words but who fared relatively poorly on achievement measures). Given this bias, it is not surprising to learn that correlations improved markedly when only those achievement measures standardized within ethnic group were employed: on this basis, 12 comparisons with vocabulary size are possible, yielding an average r of .18 (significant at well beyond the .01 level). Over time, the relationship between achievement and vocabulary size became stronger, so that by 1969 vocabulary size correlated .16 with general achievement and .20 with verbal achievement, even though scores were standardized across ethnic groups. Similarly by 1969 vocabulary size correlated .17 with class grades on verbal-type subjects. Interestingly word length and achievement failed to correlate despite an ethnic bias in favor of such a relationship (i.e., Anglo children as a group received the highest grades and achievement test scores and also used the longest words).

The data presented above supply a broad, general description of Riverside children's speech over the years studied. In general, we can conclude that ethnic differences did exist, with minority children tending to speak more voluminously and repetitively, using shorter words and larger vocabularies than Anglo children, with no apparent overall ethnic differences in language proficiency. There appeared to be no ethnic difference in information load on responses, but there were differences in the way the information was distributed within responses, via word length and vocabulary diversity. We feel such differences ought to be construed as stylistic ones. Moreover, situational influences were demonstrably important in relation to response length and its concomitants. Social reinforcement was found to increase verbal output across groups, while desegregation disproportionately depressed minority responses. Ethnic differences in speech styles, particularly in relation to social–situational performance constraints, are investigated further in the studies discussed below.

Speech Anxiety

The large-scale normative study above unearthed no net language deficit for minority children. It is appropriate to inquire now whether differential performance constraints might not account for much of the discrepancy between minority and Anglo language behavior. Wolfram (1970), for example, pointed out that in most test situations the low-status speaker's fluency is affected by the nonindigenous and often threatening environment, but intervention of such performance constraints can often mask real competence (cf. critical review in Baratz, 1968, and Gordon, 1965). At present very little has been established about the range or determinants of communicative styles of children in spontaneous speech-performance contexts, in contrast with the large body of standardized testing norms. For this reason, Cazden (1970) termed it the "neglected situation in child language," commenting that "research on this enlarged question . . . has only begun."

Examination of situational constraints focused on fluency and anxiety in our verbal interaction situation. Briefly, performance research deals with the way basic language ability or competence is deployed in a specific verbal task in which extralinguistic individual, social, and situational parameters exert their influence as well (Cazden, 1967; Menyuk, 1970). For complex measures of this sort, machine coding was not possible. We therefore decided to sample a smaller number of subjects. Because so little is known about the properties of children's spontaneous speech bearing on our research interests, it was necessary to carry out the speech-performance investigation in two separate studies:

1. An experimental pilot study was conducted in a school outside the Riverside district so that we could manipulate anxiety independently of ethnicity. In this study, four story interviews were conducted as above with 64 randomly selected Anglo fourth-graders balanced for sex. Since our objective was to "bootstrap" measurements of fluency and disturbance, the main experimental factor was anxiety. In the high-anxiety condition a male "teacher" entered the testing room halfway through the picture series, i.e., after two pictures had been administered. He took a particularly stern attitude, and the child was told that the teacher would grade him carefully and strictly. Under low anxiety the child told stories about all four pictures without a midway anxiety induction.

2. Dependent measures developed and refined in the experimental pilot study were applied to a subset of data from the main Riverside sample, which included 20 Black, 15 Mexican-American, and 35 Anglo third-grade children, balanced approximately for sex, yielding a total *n* of 70. Part two of our analysis took, as its point of departure, the unedited tapes and transcriptions of pilot and field interviews, respectively.

In developing a set of language measures for investigating performance constraints on children's spontaneous speech in the desegregated school situation, we were guided by the sources cited above, who concurred in viewing language as reflective of and responsive to social–psychological properties of the verbal interaction situation. For selection of specific variables, we were influenced most by the work of Basil Bernstein (1959, 1961, 1962a, 1962b, 1970). We also relied heavily on studies by Frieda Goldman-Eisler (1952, 1954, 1955, 1958, 1961a, 1961b, 1961c, 1961d, 1968), in which psycholinguistic indices of intrapersonal processes (such as planning, outgoing affect, and caution) were investigated.

We do not present here the detailed results of the pilot study since their consideration would take us far beyond the immediate purpose of this chapter. Rather, we briefly discuss the results of using those measures that were subsequently applied to the sample of children from the larger Riverside study.

Fluency

We hypothesized that the first desegregated minority students might well make up a high-anxiety group, particularly in view of what previous research had revealed about the apprehensions of low-status speakers in cross-class communication situations involving either explicit or implicit social–linguistic evaluation by the co-communicator (*cf.* Katz, 1964, 1968; Labov, 1970; Sarason *et al.*, 1960; Williams, 1970). Anxiety, if it existed for the minority children, was probably greatest at the beginning of the school year in which they began to attend previously all-Anglo schools. If minority anxiety existed it would tend to manifest itself all through the testing session. However, as the results of the pilot study indicated, we could not expect simple between-group effects, for there was typically an order effect of relaxation and adaptation over time to the verbal task. Consequently, we had to expect order effects and order-by-condition interaction effects manifest throughout the session. In addition, on the basis of the pilot study results, more irregularity was expected for the minority than for the Anglo children.

Field Variables[1]

It seemed wisest to select only measures that could be taken from the typewritten protocols. Only if the results obtained from these variables resembled the experimental pilot data would it be worthwhile later to go to the voice tapes for timing of utterances and detection of breaths, hesitations, and other nonverbal events. From the fluency indicators we selected *utterance length,* measured in terms of words per utterance for each story. Not only is this fluency variable easy to measure, but it also correlates most strongly with the other fluency measures and its properties are well known (so that results here can be compared with those of many other researchers). In addition, utterance length is less problematic than either utterance duration or articulation rate since these latter two measures interact. Choice of words rather than syllables as units reflects convenience of analysis (all other measures require only words as units). Given that Anglo speakers use significantly more polysyllables than do minority speakers, the word as unit might be thought to bias the results; however, checking the pilot protocols from Anglo subjects revealed that even for this group the words-per-utterance and syllables-per-utterance measures correlated with one another at 0.95 or better.

---

[1] Field variables were selected from a factor analysis of the larger set of pilot variables on the basis of their reasonably high factor loadings and their susceptibility to scoring from typed protocols.

We next took, from the set of ready-coded outputs, *organizational expressions* (OE) such as "and so on," "and so forth," "and all that," "or whatever," "that's all," and "there's nothing else." We also recorded occurrences of *attention-getting expressions* (AE), such as "well," "now," "yes," "okay," "say," and "hey." In addition, we formed a composite variable, *introducers,* by joining two classes of positive and negative introducer expressions, PI and NI. Examples of PI are "you know," "I guess," "I mean," and "I think," and of NI are "I don't know," and "I can't think."

Finally, we selected the *subordination index* (SI), representing complex connectives (e.g., "He will come *not* always *but* often," and "They played well *after* he came"). These connectives were distinguished from simple run-on connectives, which were used either to begin or to link independent expressions (e.g., "and" and "so") and which could be omitted with no meaning change (e.g., "He came *and* I saw him"). In our pilot analysis, this index stood out among the specific classes of structural and lexical contents as potentially the most sensitive one for our purposes.

Utterance length proved to be very stable; between-story values of *rho* ranged from .67 to .80, which compared favorably with reliability coefficients for fluency measures taken from the experimental data. A repeated-measures analysis of variance with subjects nested under conditions (minority and Anglo) for the six stories revealed no overall between-group difference, but there was both an order effect ($F = 3.24$, $p < .01$) and an order-by-ethnic group interaction ($F = 3.34$, $p < .01$). Order effects were in the direction of increasing length from the beginning to the end of the interview for the minority children only. They began with utterances averaging *15 words* in length in the first story to utterances averaging *40 words* in story six, whereas Anglos began with *24 word* utterances and ended with utterances of *26 words* in average length. This suggested that there was a relaxation during the CAT administration for minority speakers whose initial extremely short utterances suggested caution and hesitation. If Goldman-Eisler's discussion of spontaneous speech parameters is tenable, our data lend support to the notion that the minority children initially face the verbal task with greater anxiety than do Anglo speakers. The dramatic change in fluency for the former suggests that, over time, affect comes to be channeled through verbal production.

The next item set we studied, ready-coded strings (OE, AE, PI, and NI), proved in general to be more reliable in the larger field sample than it was in the pilot study. Correlation matrices comprised of all possible between-story correlations of each variable with itself yielded relatively high *rho*s. Repeated-measures analysis of variance using the dependent variables in the ready-coded speech categories yielded results consistent with our predictions and were summarized by the outcome for the total set. There were no overall ethnic differences, but there was an order effect ($p < .05$) and an order-by-group interaction effect ($.05 < p < .10$), with the minority children exhibiting the more pronounced order effect. For the introducer variable (PI + NI) there was no between-group effect, but there was an order effect ($F = 2.5, p < .05$) and an interaction effect ($F = 2.2, p < .05$). Although the order effect was marked by a small overall increase (from a combined average of 1.67 to 1.86), in Anglos this effect appeared as an increase from story one to story four but tapered off at the end, whereas in minority children it exhibited a sharp increase in story two, followed by a drop and then another sharp increase. Thus although there was very little difference in the absolute scores on this variable from beginning to end, the minority speakers exhibited much more irregularity. While the AE variable failed to reflect significant effects, it did follow a similar pattern. That is, while there was virtually no change in Anglo scores from beginning to end (from 1.29 to 1.26), the minority scores changed considerably (from 1.0 to 1.46).

The analysis of "well-organized strings" showed a regularly emerging pattern in which the Anglo child changed very little and fairly regularly about his base line, while the minority speaker exhibited much more pronounced changes. Typically, Anglo scores showed a slight increase toward the middle of the interview followed by a slight decline, while minority scores increased from beginning to end. These results relate to our earlier discussion of fluency since it would appear that for minority speakers increasing fluency was achieved by increasing reliance on ready-coded strings. For minority speakers it seems that initial anxiety disrupted fluency by disrupting habitual output organization (it has already been noted that anxiety is generally thought to disrupt any complicated ongoing behavior). Decreasing anxiety was then manifested through increasing fluency mediated by the reappearance of ready-coded outputs, which presumably reduced tension by channeling affect through the verbal production process.

Finally, a repeated-measures analysis of variance of the use of complex connectives (SI) yielded no between-group or interaction effects, but there was an order effect ($F = 3.80, p < .01$), indicating an increasing use of complex connectives over time (with the exception of a drop for both groups on story three). Although there was no overall between-group effect, the Anglo mean was higher and the difference reached significance for the between-group comparison on story five ($t = 1.77$, $p < .05$; *cf.* similar t-test results for the high-anxiety pilot subjects).

From the analyses presented above, it is our tentative conclusion that the dependent measures developed in the pilot experiment give a reliable representation of some of the components of speech anxiety, applicable to a comparable interview situation with children from the different ethnic groups. In the field situation anxiety was manifest at the outset for the minority children, so it is not clear where the base line is for them on any of the dependent measures—the two groups did not show similar first-half interview behavior, which of course was a reflection of the tentative working hypothesis that minority speakers approach the verbal task in this type of school situation with greater anxiety. However, the direction of movement of scores on the dependent measures over time for the minority children paralleled that of the high-anxiety condition in the pilot. Further, the anxiety hypothesis was substantiated, as we saw above, by greater irregularity in (and higher standard deviation in) minority scores. Informally this interpretation was supported by the content of the stories: for the stimulus picture depicting a school situation, minority but not Anglo children explicitly expressed school anxiety (e.g., "He is ashamed of himself," "He doesn't want to read in front of the class," "He is thinking about a bad grade report"); Anglo children expressed other sentiments (*cf.* "He is bored," "He is thinking about a present he will get when he gets home").

It is a mistake, however, to anticipate that such anxiety will reflect itself in simple between-group differences. This is partly because there are wide individual differences in spontaneous speech (see Goldman-Eisler) and partly because spontaneous speech is an extremely complicated ongoing process about which very little is known, particularly in children.

While there is no clear-cut interpretation for the data on the ready-coded strings, their reliability within the field situation, and replication in the results of other researchers, suggests that different ethnic groups do rely on different kinds of ready-coded outputs. According to Bernstein, different quasi dialects arise in different subcultures from differing socialization processes. If that thesis is sound, one would expect all dialects (whether elaborated or restricted) to incorporate ready-coded strings, given that whatever is an ingrained product of socialization will be well organized in the sense that it will be a high-probability response under appropriate conditions (*cf.* Jones & Gerard, 1967). But if there is a difference between social dialects, then one would expect to see it highlighted in the use of differing well-organized strings. Such a difference is just the sort we found in our field data between ethnic groups (a difference not anticipated on the basis of our ethnically homogeneous pilot sample). The complexity of between-group linguistic differences was, however, notable even in the results of the competence-related measures analyzed in the first part of the paper, in which Anglos were found to use significantly more polysyllables while minority children used a greater number of different words, so that there were no overall language proficiency effects for ethnicity. These results are reminiscent of Schatzman and Strauss's (1955) interpretation of their interview data, in which perceived between-status message differences did not depend on differential information load but were rather seen to depend on having or not having shared (i.e., from the interviewer's point of view) rules for speech ordering and thought presentation. Moreover, whether it is awareness of this code difference between him and the interviewer or "evaluation apprehension," in part based on felt negative attitudes toward his speech or some other intervening performance variable, the lower-status speaker has been seen to experience greater anxiety, manifested in the disturbance of easy, well-organized speech.

That these differences in fluency represent responses to performance contexts rather than basic linguistic capability seems clear. In the speech anxiety analysis we found differences in kind rather than in quantity on the dependent measurement classes, and even quantitative differences appeared primarily as interactions rather than as main effects (indicating an eventual adjustment to the interview situation). These considerations suggest that use of some term other than *restricted* coding is needed to describe properties of dialects. That term seems to imply simple main effects for groups of the more-versus-less sort and seems to promote the notion that only restricted codes involve ready-coded phrases (whereas in fact a code is a code only because it embodies well-organized patterns). All dialects are regular, and mapping the intricate differences in communication strategies employed by different groups facing ostensibly similar verbal tasks bearing differential social–psychological parameters has barely gotten under way. Understanding such complex differences between minority and Anglo speech is important, particularly in the school situation, because of the predominance of verbal tasks and the differential anxiety they occasion for the students. At a time when there is a serious concern that the content of academic materials be "culture-fair," it is at least equally important to ensure that the medium be culture-fair as well.

References

Baratz, J. Language in the economically disadvantaged child: A perspective. *ASHA,* 1968, *10,* 143–145.

Bellak, L., & Bellak, S. S. *Children's apperception test.* Larchmont, N.Y.: C.P.S., Inc., 1954.

Bereiter, C. A nonpsychological approach to early compensatory education. In M. Deutsch, I. Katz, and A. R. Jensen (Eds.), *Social class, race, and psychological development.* New York: Holt, Rinehart & Winston, Inc., 1968.

Bernstein, B. A public language: Some sociological implications of a linguistic form. *British Journal of Sociology,* 1959, *10,* 311.

Bernstein, B. Aspects of language and language learning in the genesis of the social process. *Journal of Child Psychology and Psychiatry,* 1961, *1,* 313.

Bernstein, B. Linguistic codes, hesitation phenomena and intelligence. *Language and Speech,* 1962, *5,* Part 1, 31. (*a*)

Bernstein, B. Social class, linguistic codes and grammatical elements. *Language and Speech,* 1962, *5,* Part 4, 221. (*b*)

Bernstein, B. A sociolinguistic approach to socialization: With some reference to educability. In F. Williams (Ed.), *Language and poverty.* Chicago: Markham Press, 1970.

Boder, D. P. The adjective–verb quotient: A contribution to the psychology of language. *The Psychological Record,* 1940, III, No. 22, 310.

Busemann, A. *Die sprache der Jugend als Ausdruck der Entwicklungsrhytmik.* Jena, Germany: Fisher, 1925.

Cazden, C. Subcultural differences in child language: An interdisciplinary review. *Merrill-Palmer Quarterly,* 1966, *12,* 185–219.

Cazden, C. On individual differences in language competence and performance. *Journal of Special Education,* 1967, *1,* 135–150.

Cazden, C. The neglected situation in child language research and education. In F. Williams (Ed.), *Language and poverty.* Chicago: Markham Press, 1970.

Chomsky, C. *The acquisition of syntax in children from 5 to 10.* Cambridge, Mass.: The MIT Press, 1969.

Entwisle, D. Developmental sociolinguistics: A comparative study in four subcultural settings. *Sociometry,* 1966, *29,* 67–84.

Entwisle, D. Developmental sociolinguistics: Inner-city children. *The American Journal of Sociology,* 1968, *74,* 137–149. (*a*)

Entwisle, D. Subcultural differences in children's language development. *International Journal of Psychology*, 1968, *3*, 13–22. (*b*)

Entwisle, D. Semantic systems of children: some assessments of social class and ethnic differences. In F. Williams (Ed.), *Language and poverty*. Chicago: Markham Press, 1970.

Fries, C. *American English grammar*. New York: Appleton-Century-Crofts, 1950.

Goldman-Eisler, F. On the variability of the speed of talking and on its relation to the length of utterance in conversation. *British Journal of Psychology*, 1954, Gen. Sec., 45, 94.

Goldman-Eisler, F. Speech-breathing activity—A measure of tension and affect during interviews. *British Journal of Psychology*, 1955, Gen. Sec., 53.

Goldman-Eisler, F. Speech analysis and mental processes. *Language and Speech*, 1958, *1*, 59.

Goldman-Eisler, F. Individual differences between interviewers and their effects on interviewees' conversational behavior. *Journal of Mental Science*, 1959, *98*, 660.

Goldman-Eisler, F. A comparative study of two hesitation phenomena. *Language and Speech*, 1961, *4*, Part 1, 18. (*a*)

Goldman-Eisler, F. The continuity of speech utterance, its determinants and its significance. *Language and Speech*, 1961, *4*, 229. (*b*)

Goldman-Eisler, F. The distribution of pause durations in speech. *Language and Speech*, 1961, *4*, 232. (*c*)

Goldman-Eisler, F. The significance of changes in the rate of articulation. *Language and Speech*, 1961, *4*, Part 3, 1971. (*d*)

Goldman-Eisler, F. *Psycholinguistics*. London: Academic Press, 1968.

Gordon, E. C. Characteristics of socially disadvantaged children. *Review of Educational Research*, 1965, *35*, 377–388.

Herdan, G. *Type token mathematics*. The Hague: Mouton Press, 1960.

Herdan, G. *Quantitative linguistics*. London: Butterworths, 1964.

Herdan, G. *The advanced theory of language as choice and chance*. New York: Springer-Verlag, 1966.

John, V. The intellectual development of slum children: Some preliminary findings. *American Journal of Orthopsychiatry*, 1963, *33*, 813–822.

John, V., & Goldstein, L. S. The social context of language acquisition. *Merrill-Palmer Quarterly*, 1964, *10*, 265–275.

Jones, E. E., & Gerard, H. B. *Foundations of social psychology*. New York: John Wiley & Sons, Inc., 1967.

Katz, I. Review of evidence relating to effects of desegregation on the intellectual performance of Negroes. *American Psychologist*, 1964, *19*, 381–399.

Katz, I. Factors influencing Negro performance in the desegregated school. In M. Deutsch, I. Katz, and A. R. Jensen (Eds.), *Social class, race, and psychological development*. New York: Holt, Rinehart & Winston, Inc., 1968.

Kingston, A., & Weaver, W. Feasibility of Cloze techniques for teaching and evaluating culturally disadvantaged beginning readers. *Journal of Social Psychology*, 1970 82, 205–214.

Labov, W. Stages in the acquisition of standard English. In R. W. Shuy (Ed.), *Social dialects and language learning.* Champaign, Ill.: National Council of Teachers of English, 1965.

Labov, W. A note on the relation of reading failure to peer-group status in urban ghettos. *The Florida FL Reporter,* 7, No. 1, Special Anthology Issue: *Linguistic-Cultural Differences and American Education,* 1969, 54.

Labov, W. The logic of nonstandard English. In F. Williams (Ed.), *Language and poverty.* Chicago: Markham Press, 1970.

Lorge, I., & Chall, J. Estimating the size of vocabularies of children and adults: An analysis of methodological issues. *Journal of Experimental Education,* 1963, *32,* 147–157.

Maclay, H., & Osgood, C. Hesitation phenomena in spontaneous English speech. *Word,* 1959, *15,* 19.

McNeill, D. *The acquisition of language.* New York: Harper & Row, 1970.

Menyuk, P. Language theories and educational practices. In F. Williams (Ed.), *Language and poverty.* Chicago: Markham Press, 1970.

Miller, G. A. What is information measurement? *American Psychologist,* 1953, *8,* 3–11.

Miller, G. A., Heise, G. A., & Lichten, W. The intelligibility of speech as a function of the context of the test materials. *Journal of Experimental Psychology,* 1951, *41,* 329–335.

Opie, I., & Opie, P. *The lore and language of schoolchildren.* Oxford: Clarendon Press, 1959.

Raph, J. B. Language development in socially disadvantaged children. *Review of Educational Research,* 1965, *35,* 389–400.

Sarason, S. B., Davidson, K. S., Lighthall, F. F., Waite, R. R., & Ruebush, B. K. *Anxiety in elementary school children.* New York: John Wiley & Sons, Inc., 1960.

Schatzman, L., & Strauss, A. Social class and modes of communication. *American Journal of Sociology,* 1955, *60,* 329–338.

Siegel, S. *Nonparametric statistics for the behavioral sciences.* New York: McGraw-Hill, 1956.

Williams, F. Language, attitude, and social change. In F. Williams (Ed.), *Language and poverty.* Chicago: Markham Press, 1970.

Wolfram, W. Sociolinguistic premises and the nature of nonstandard dialects. *The Speech Teacher,* 1970, *19,* 177–184.

Yule, G. U. *A statistical study of vocabulary.* Cambridge, Mass.: Harvard University Press, 1944.

Zipf, G. K. *Selected studies of the principle of relative frequencies in language.* Cambridge, Mass.: Harvard University Press, 1932.

Zipf, G. K. *Human behavior and the principle of least effort.* Cambridge, Mass.: Harvard University Press, 1949.

10

Social Contact in the Desegregated Classroom

HAROLD B. GERARD, TERRENCE D. JACKSON, AND EDWARD S. CONOLLEY

As indicated in the first chapter, underlying the hopes and beliefs of most proponents of desegregation is the implicit assumption that the minority child will be accepted socially into the classroom of the receiving school. More than simply deriving the benefits of the supposed better curriculum and instruction in the receiving school, it is assumed that the minority child, through the medium of close contact with his Anglo peers, will come to adopt their achievement-related values (Katz, 1968) and will also come to view his own capabilities more positively (Katz, 1967).

Overriding these considerations is a long-established belief that a child, or an adult for that matter, cannot truly prosper in a socially uncongenial environment. The situation of the minority child entering a previously all-Anglo classroom is at best precarious. He is typically well behind his Anglo peers academically, especially in the upper grades; he is typically of lower socioeconomic status than they; he is in a new and unfamiliar situation; he has been bussed into school; and he may feel under pressure from home and school to do well in the new school. Given the likely handicap induced by these influences, it would seem to be of

HAROLD B. GERARD AND TERRENCE D. JACKSON • University of California, Los Angeles, California. EDWARD S. CONOLLEY • University of Southern California, Los Angeles, California.

paramount importance that the minority child find a welcoming atmosphere in the receiving classroom as represented by both peer and teacher acceptance.

Whether or not interethnic contact will have a beneficial outcome depends upon contextual factors such as mutually perceived status equality, intimacy, the intensity and pleasantness of the contact, and sanction and support within the larger social setting (Allport, 1954; Amir, 1969). To the extent that positive social support, as represented by these kinds of factors, is lacking in the newly desegregated classroom, we might expect the minority child to founder and fail. We suspect that the social climate of the classroom is the most important determinant of the child's success. In what follows we examine the effects of interethnic contact as it manifests itself in social choices.

Measuring interethnic contact in the Riverside schools presented a formidable problem. The sample children were in approximately 250 classrooms during each year of data collection. Direct observational measures were clearly impractical, given the large number of classrooms involved. The technique of sociometry (Moreno, 1934), however, provided a basis for inferring patterns of social interactions. The method assesses social attractiveness by asking each person in the group to make choices from among the other group members for preferred partners for specific activities relevant to the contact situation. Although somewhat imperfect, these choices have been found to reflect actual contact (Biehler, 1951; Byrd, 1951; Bonney & Powell, 1953; Shaw, 1971). The main reason for a discrepancy between sociometric choice and actual contact is that the chooser may express his desire for contact with others rather than his actual contact with them.

Sociometry has been applied to the study of multiracial classrooms for four decades, the general finding being that there is social cleavage along racial lines. In a study of a Brooklyn public school in 1932 in which the student body contained children of Italian, Russian, Jewish, German, and Black backgrounds, Moreno (1934) found that social cleavage along ethnic lines was quite pronounced by fifth grade. Criswell (1939) studied Whites and Blacks in a large number of elementary school classrooms in three New York public schools where the percentage of Black pupils ranged from 9% to 95%. Comparing the actual distribution of choices between and within ethnic cohort groups to that expected on the basis of the relative proportions of Blacks and Whites in the classroom, she found that White children exhibited racial self-preference from kindergarten on and that this self-preference increased in the upper grades. Black pupils, on the other hand, did not begin to show self-preference until fifth grade. Thus racial cleavage was manifested in the preference of Whites for Whites as early as kindergarten, but from the fifth grade on racial encapsulation was mutual. Loomis (1943) found sharp ethnic cleavage in sociometric choices between Anglos and Mexican-Americans in a high school and grade school in New Mexico.

Yarrow, Campbell, and Yarrow (1958) studied an integrated summer camp for 8- to 12-year-old children from low-income families. The children were assigned to cabins with equal numbers of Black and White children and the camp staff was racially integrated. Under these optimal conditions there was a significant decrease in the degree to which race was a criterion for friendship choice, but Whites remained the favored group. Campbell and Yarrow (1958), in another article based on the same study, reported that the Black girls were in a more disadvantaged position than were the Black boys. Jansen and Gallagher (1966), studying friendship in four racially integrated elementary school classrooms for gifted children, found that although there were sociometric choices crossing racial lines, three of the four classes contained Black cliques. Moorefield (1967) found that three-fourths of the Black children bussed into White schools in the Kansas City area were rated as "low-acceptance" by Whites in those schools. Shaw (1971), in a one-year longitudinal study of fifth-graders in a newly integrated school in Coral Gables, Florida, found few cross-ethnic friendship choices and low actual cross-ethnic interaction.

The Riverside Data

As described in Chapter 3, our sample included those minority children in the Riverside elementary school system who were desegregated in the falls of 1965, 1966, and 1967, and a matched sample of Anglos. Sociometric questionnaires were administered to all children in any elementary school class[1] attended by at least one Riverside School Study

---

[1] We did not attempt to collect sociometric data in the large junior or senior high schools, since the situation did not easily lend itself to sociometric measurement because the students attended departmentalized classes.

child for the years 1966, 1967, 1968 and 1969, and 1971. This meant that the sociometric data were collected from many more children than the original 1731, the actual number being approximately 6500 per year. In the questionnaire, which was administered in the spring of each year, each child was asked to give first, second, and third choices of whom from among his classmates he would prefer for friends, for schoolwork partners, and for members of a ball team. In our present analysis we have given all choices equal weight, whether first, second, or third choice. Avoiding arbitrary ranking of choices, particularly when choices are required, is recommended by Lindzey and Byrne (1968) and Campbell (1960). The sociometric questionnaire was self-administered by fourth-, fifth-, and sixth-graders and individually administered by an interviewer in the lower grades.

In presenting our own data, the amount of which is unprecedented in scope for longitudinal studies of interethnic contact, we will focus primarily on the effects of desegregation on the social status of the minority child by comparing his prior status in the segregated classroom with subsequent short- and long-term changes in status after he entered the previously all-Anglo classroom. As part of our investigation, we will compare, in a cursory way only, the social structure of Anglo and minority classrooms prior to desegregation with classrooms after desegregation.

The major thrust of the overall research program was to discover factors that may have influenced and mediated the minority child's achievement. In other chapters we examine arenas of influence such as the home, the teacher, and the child's personality. Since ethnic differences are necessarily heavily confounded with differences in both socioeconomic background and prior academic achievement, we shall attempt to examine separately the influence of these factors on social acceptance. In much of what follows we shall consider achievement effects of the social climate of the classroom, as indicated by the social acceptance of the minority child by his Anglo classmates.

In tracking down these achievement effects, we shall also examine the influence of the teacher on the minority child's social acceptance. Does she in any way set the climate tone for pupil-to-pupil interaction? Fortunately other data we have about the teacher enable us to explore this issue. In what follows we will, in a sense, be looking at a stepwise process: first how change influenced the minority child's social status on his achievement and then, backing up, how the teacher may have affected his social status.

Stratification

We attempted to determine if there were gross differences in the social structure of segregated and desegregated classes by comparing the skewness of the distribution of choices for each criterion (friendship, schoolwork partner, and play partner). In a perfectly unstratified class, each child would receive three choices. Degree of skewness provided an estimate of stratification, that is, the degree to which choices were distributed unequally among the children in a given classroom. A highly stratified classroom would be one in which a few children were overchosen (i.e., received six or more choices) and many were under chosen (i.e., received fewer than three choices).

Table 10.1 gives the percentage of pupils falling into three categories—underchosen, overchosen, and neither—on each criterion for 2224 Anglos in classes that contained no minority pupils, 696 minority students in classes in which there were no Anglos, and 3848 children in desegregated classes (which typically contained a relatively small number of minority students). The segregated minority classes tended to be less stratified; that is, they had significantly fewer children in the underchosen group than either the White or the desegregated classes for friendship ($p < .01$),[2] work ($p < .01$), and play ($p < .01$). The pattern was opposite for the percentage of pupils who were neither underchosen nor overchosen: minority classes had a higher proportion of children in that range on each criterion ($p < .01$ for all three). The distribution for overchosen children showed that minority classes had a smaller percentage of children receiving six or more choices on a single criterion, but this difference was significant only for the friendship criterion ($p < .01$).

This tendency toward a smaller proportion of underchosen children in segregated minority classes was an advantage enjoyed only by the Mexican-American children. The percentages of underchosen Mexican-American pupils on the friendship, work, and play criteria were 45%, 46%, and 49%, respectively. For the Blacks, who were typically in a

[2] Unless otherwise stated, confidence level estimates were based on analysis of variance.

TABLE 10.1   *Sociometric Choices Received in Minority, Anglo, and Desegregated Classrooms in 1966*

	Ethnic balance of classroom	Number of choices received[a]		
		0–2	3–5	6 or more
Friendship choices	Segregated minority	48.3[b]	41.8	9.8
	Segregated Anglo	55.0	32.2	12.7
	Desegregated	54.8	32.8	12.3
Work choices	Segregated minority	49.4	39.4	11.0
	Segregated Anglo	59.9	29.2	12.7
	Desegregated	58.9	28.8	12.2
Play choices	Segregated minority	56.1	30.8	13.0
	Segregated Anglo	62.6	23.1	14.2
	Desegregated	59.9	26.7	13.3

[a] We consider these three levels of choices received to reflect those who are underchosen (0–2), overchosen (6 or more), and neither underchosen nor overchosen (3–5).
[b] Percentage of pupils in segregated classes receiving 0–2 choices.

minority in the segregated classes, the corresponding percentages of underchosen children were 58%, 56%, and 59%. The pre-one (pre-desegregation)[3] segment of Tables 2A and 2B, 3A and 3B, and 4A and 4B also reflects this.[4] The mean friendship popularity for Blacks was

[3] Minority children were placed in Anglo receiving schools over a three-year span beginning in the fall of 1965. Comparison of popularity indices for each wave of desegregation gave no indication of any effect based on whether the minority pupils were in the first, second, or third group to be desegregated. Therefore, for the present analysis, in order to utilize as much data as possible, we have combined all three groups according to the years of desegregated schooling they had experienced by the time of each data collection in the spring of 1966, 1967, 1968, 1969, and 1971, regardless of the year in which the children were desegregated. This data structure covers a seven-year comparison from one year predesegregation to six years postdesegregation. For all years we list the total choices received on each criterion, and for all postdesegregation years we also give the number of choices received from Anglos.
[4] Since it was unwieldy to present marginals in the tables, these will be provided in the discussion itself.

2.38 versus 3.06 for Mexican-Americans ($p < .01$). The difference was less pronounced for the work criterion, with Mexican-Americans receiving 2.85 choices versus 2.59 for Blacks, a difference that was not quite statistically significant. Play choices presented a complicated picture. Among children in kindergarten through third grade in segregated minority classes, Mexican-Americans were more popular on the average than Blacks ($p < .05$). Among the older children, the boys received more choices than the girls. For play, the older Black boys were as popular as the Mexican-American boys, whereas the Black girls were less popular than the Mexican-American girls.

These data show a clear effect on cross-ethnic choice of the social arena within which the choice was made. The play criterion was a specifically defined activity in which criterion relevant skills were more important than ethnic membership. Friendship choice, on the other hand, was typically not tied to any specific activity, which made preference along ethnic lines more likely.

Overall, the segregated Anglo classroom had the greatest percentage of underchosen children. How can we account for this difference in the degree of stratification? Perhaps it rests on the greater heterogeneity in socioeconomic status and achievement in the Anglo classroom. If more advantaged children are socially preferred, the greater range of individual differences would result in a more stratified social structure. We shall return to this issue a bit later.

Social Status and Desegregation

Friendship

In comparing the friendship popularity of children in segregated classes during the year just prior to desegregation with their popularity after one year of desegragated experience (Tables 10.2A and 10.2B), we found no appreciable change for Anglos. Mexican-American boys and girls at both grade levels lost status after desegregation. The older Blacks appeared to be no lower after than before desegregation, whereas the younger Blacks, particularly the girls, lost friendship status.

One year after desegregation, Anglos were the most popular group for friendship, receiving 2.95 choices as compared with 2.29 for

TABLE 10.2A   Total Friendship Choices Received and Choices Received from Anglos by Younger Children (K–3rd Grade) Pre-One through Post-Four Desegregation

	Pre-one	Post-one	Post-two	Post-three	Post-four
Anglos					
Boys					
$N =$	45	189	124	86	25
Total	2.56	2.93	2.74	2.95	3.44
from Anglos		2.58	2.42	2.53	2.76
Girls					
$N =$	62	173	103	70	20
Total	3.32	2.99	3.06	3.64	2.50
from Anglos		2.60	2.52	3.00	2.05
Mexican-Americans					
Boys					
$N =$	139	135	97	48	20
Total	2.91	2.36	2.54	2.40	2.15
from Anglos		1.37	1.28	1.31	1.30
Girls					
$N =$	116	129	81	35	19
Total	3.14	2.24	2.32	2.43	1.79
from Anglos		1.75	1.28	1.63	0.79
Blacks					
Boys					
$N =$	60	103	55	33	12
Total	2.18	1.80	2.03	2.24	2.92
from Anglos		0.98	0.98	1.18	1.50
Girls					
$N =$	62	115	69	30	17
Total	2.68	1.30	1.48	1.57	2.12
from Anglos		0.53	0.68	0.73	0.56

Mexican-Americans and 1.74 for Blacks ($p < .01$). Anglos received 2.62 choices from other Anglos, whereas Mexican-Americans received 1.36 and Blacks 0.99 from Anglos ($p < .01$). In the lower grades, Mexican-Americans received more choices from Anglos than did Blacks ($p < .01$), but no difference existed in the upper grades. The low

TABLE 10.2B Average Number of Friendship Choices Received and Choices Received from Anglos by Older Children (4th–6th Grade) Pre-One through Post-Six Desegregation

	Pre-one	Post-one	Post-two	Post-three	Post-four	Post-five and six
Anglos						
Boys						
$N =$	67	86	67	67	91	75
Total	2.85	2.90	2.84	2.83	2.90	3.01
from Anglos		2.68	2.48	2.43	2.43	2.64
Girls						
$N =$	57	104	83	72	67	66
Total	3.03	3.00	3.29	3.04	3.09	2.98
from Anglos		2.70	2.93	2.59	2.78	2.70
Mexican-Americans						
Boys						
$N =$	116	104	101	64	55	59
Total	3.11	2.33	2.46	2.52	2.51	2.76
from Anglos		1.67	1.72	1.48	1.42	1.19
Girls						
$N =$	104	106	103	75	45	48
Total	3.13	2.24	2.52	2.15	2.56	2.25
from Anglos		1.39	1.48	1.23	1.31	1.10
Blacks						
Boys						
$N =$	43	46	46	41	27	41
Total	2.44	2.33	2.43	2.44	3.11	2.34
from Anglos		1.57	1.67	1.49	1.85	1.17
Girls						
$N =$	50	45	42	52	24	47
Total	2.20	2.11	1.48	1.94	2.21	2.17
from Anglos		1.47	0.76	0.77	1.75	0.91

friendship popularity of Black children in the lower grades could be due either to rejection by Anglo classmates or to self-isolation by Blacks, or to both. The observation by Campbell and Yarrow (1958) that the majority of children in an integrated summer camp initially rated as socially withdrawn were Black lends support to the reticence interpretation. Then again, Black reticence may have been due to feelings of rejection by Anglos.

Ethnic awareness and prejudicial attitudes appear to be less pronounced among younger than among older children (Horowitz, 1936; Clark & Clark, 1939; Pettigrew, 1967; Porter, 1971). This would imply that the younger minority child meets fewer social barriers in a desegregated class. Our data for friendship choice did not support this supposition. There appeared to be no age differential for Mexican-American children, whereas older Blacks received *more* choices than younger Blacks.

The pattern of friendship status for the second year after desegregation was similar to the one year postdesegregation pattern. Neither of the minority groups had increased in overall friendship popularity. Anglos were still the most favored group for friendship, receiving 2.97 choices as compared with 2.47 for Mexican-Americans and 1.83 for Blacks ($p < .01$). Anglos received 2.57 choices from other Anglos, whereas Mexican-Americans received 1.45 and Blacks 0.99 from Anglos ($p < .01$).

Data from the third year after desegregation continued to reflect a strong ethnic difference in friendship popularity favoring Anglos for total choices received: 3.11 for Anglos, 2.35 for Mexican-Americans, and 2.06 for Blacks ($p < .01$); and for choices received from Anglos: 2.64 for Anglos, 1.38 for Mexican-Americans, and 1.04 for Blacks ($p < .01$). Although the second- and third-grade minority children in the post-three column had experienced either no segregated schooling or at most only segregated kindergarten classes, their acceptance by Anglos was still quite low and was in no case significantly different from the status of the older minority children. The post-three friendship status of minority children did not change significantly from the previous two years.

By the post-four year there was no longer a strong ethnic difference in total friendship choices received. The number of choices received from Anglos did, however, continue to reveal a substantial difference, with 2.54 for Anglos, 1.48 for Mexican-Americans, and 1.53 for Blacks ($p < .01$). Generally higher scores for the older minority children were contributed to by a few heavily overchosen children. The increase was not general and did not occur for the small number of minority children in the third grade who had never been in segregated classrooms. The increase in minority friendship status without a commensurate increase in choices from Anglos was indicative of developing ethnic cleavage, since the minority increase could only be accounted for by an increase in choices received from other minority children.[5]

This same trend is seen even more clearly in the post-five and six column of Table 10.2B. These fifth- and sixth-graders had been in desegregated classes for most of their elementary school experience. Half or more of their friendship choices came from other minorities, which led us to infer a high degree of ethnic cohesiveness for friendship choices. Comparing this group to the post-one column for older minority children, we see that the extra years of desegregated schooling did not lead to greater friendship acceptance by Anglos.

Work Choices

Tables 10.3A and 10.3B show that after one year of desegregation the average total schoolwork choices received was 2.97 for Anglos, 1.86 for Mexican-Americans, and 1.55 for Blacks ($p < .01$). The averages for choices received from Anglos was 2.62 for Anglos, 1.24 for Mexican-Americans, and 0.94 for Blacks. As in the case of friendship, Mexican-

---

[5] We do not present the minority-to-minority data since there are problems in interpreting intra-subgroup choices where ethnic subgroups were typically small. After desegregation fewer than 30% of the minority children were in classrooms with four or more members of their own sex by ethnic subgroup. Cross-sex choices in the elementary grades are typically rare. Unless the child's sex by ethnic subgroup was four or more, he was forced to choose from among the Anglos in his class since he was asked to name three children for each criterion (friendship, work, and play). In addition, even when a given child's sex by ethnic subgroup was sufficiently large to enable him to made all three choices within his own subgroup, there may have been one or more children in the subgroup with whom he got along badly or with whom he was very competitive, which psychologically narrowed his range of choices further. There is probably some critical mass of same-sex cohorts required from among whom a child can comfortably choose three friends, work partners, or playmates without choosing one or more of them by default for want of a sufficient number of eligible candidates. Because of these constraints in the typical desegregated Riverside classroom, the minority child—Black or Mexican-American—was virtually forced to make one or more of his choices outside his own sex-ethnic cohort group. That this did occur no doubt implies greater ethnic cleavage than is suggested by the data we have tabled. Clearly if choices necessarily had to be made outside the child's sex-ethnic cohort group (nearly every child complied with the request to make three choices on each criterion), then the child's inclination to choose within his own subgroup was severely underestimated by our data. Subsequent analysis of first choices only revealed an increasing tendency over time to choose within his cohort subgroup.

TABLE 10.3A   Average Number of Work Choices Received and Choices Received from Anglos by Younger Children (K–3rd Grade) Pre-One through Post-Four Desegregation

	Pre-one	Post-one	Post-two	Post-three	Post-four
Anglos					
Boys					
Total	2.65	2.84	2.80	3.01	2.84
from Anglos		2.42	2.34	2.50	2.24
Girls					
Total	2.98	2.93	3.04	3.61	4.00
from Anglos		2.58	2.57	2.88	3.10
Mexican-Americans					
Boys					
Total	2.77	2.07	2.04	2.29	1.70
from Anglos		1.29	1.23	1.54	0.90
Girls					
Total	2.84	1.80	1.98	2.14	1.45
from Anglos		1.19	1.29	1.43	0.89
Blacks					
Boys					
Total	2.38	1.63	2.11	2.30	1.92
from Anglos		0.97	1.16	1.18	1.25
Girls					
Total	2.73	1.50	1.51	2.10	1.71
from Anglos		0.85	0.84	1.27	1.00

American children received more choices from Anglos than did Blacks. Comparing pre- and post-one means, we find that minority children lost work status. The higher work-status position of Anglos in the desegregated classroom was no doubt due, in part, to higher school achievement. We shall discuss achievement effects in a later section.

The average number of total work choices received by minorities in the post-two year continued to be far lower than the average for Anglos ($p < .01$). Black girls were underchosen (1.37) relative to Black boys (1.91), whereas Mexican-American girls (2.00) were roughly equal to Mexican-American boys (1.88). Among Anglos, girls were more often chosen as work partners than boys (3.22 versus 2.78). Post-two means for work choice received from Anglos showed little change from post-one, although Black boys were slightly higher in post-two and Black girls in the fourth- through the sixth-grade groups were somewhat lower. Neither of these changes, however, was statistically significant.

The table reveals that three years after desegregation Anglos still received more choices as work partners than did minority children. Anglos received 3.18 choices; Mexican-Americans, 1.96; and Blacks, 1.90 ($p < .01$). For choices from Anglos, Anglos received 2.63; Mexican-Americans, 1.22; and Blacks, 1.11 ($p < .01$). Three years after desegregation younger minority children did have a slight, although not statistically significant, work-status advantage over older children. The second- and third-grade minority children, with the exception of the Black boys, were nearly half a choice above the fourth- through sixth-graders.

TABLE 10.3B   Average Number of Work Choices Received and Choices Received from Anglos by Older Children (4th–6th Grade) Pre-One through Post-Six Desegregation

	Pre-one	Post-one	Post-two	Post-three	Post-four	Post-five and six
Anglos						
Boys						
Total	3.39	3.03	2.72	2.87	3.42	3.24
from Anglos		2.81	2.28	2.51	2.80	2.75
Girls						
Total	2.74	3.20	3.42	3.24	3.12	3.21
from Anglos		2.93	2.99	2.67	2.66	2.67
Mexican-Americans						
Boys						
Total	2.76	1.70	1.72	2.00	2.02	2.12
from Anglos		1.15	1.30	1.13	1.34	1.02
Girls						
Total	3.08	1.83	2.03	1.64	1.80	1.85
from Anglos		1.30	1.23	1.00	1.04	0.98
Blacks						
Boys						
Total	2.81	1.46	1.67	1.90	2.41	1.85
from Anglos		0.85	1.20	1.36	1.59	1.07
Girls						
Total	2.46	1.60	1.14	1.54	1.71	1.57
from Anglos		1.18	0.71	0.77	1.29	0.89

The four-year post data suggest that minority pupils, even after long-term contact, were not being fully integrated into the work structure of the classroom. Anglos still received more choices from other Anglos (2.71) than did Mexican-Americans (1.12) or Blacks (1.31) ($p <$ .01). Total work-partner choices received reflected much the same trend as in earlier years: Anglos, 3.30; Mexican-Americans, 1.82; and Blacks, 1.97 ($p <$ .01). Neither grade nor sex produced sizable post-four score variation. The third-grade children in the post-four year had never experienced segregated classes, yet they did not appear to be different from the older children, who, depending upon their grade, had experienced one or more years of segregated education early in their school careers.

The post-five and six data for older children reflected the continuation of ethnic barriers in sociometric work choices. Trends were the same as for previous years, with Anglos the most chosen group for both total choices ($p <$ .01) and choices received from Anglos ($p <$ .01). As was the case with the friendship choices, the long-term desegregated minority groups of post-five and six did not receive any more choices from Anglos than did the older minority children who had experienced only one year of desegregation.

Play

From Tables 10.4A and 10.4B we find that play choices received by minority pupils from Anglos in the post-one year were considerably higher for boys than for girls ($p <$ .01). Anglos were preferred play partners in kindergarten through third grade, but not in fourth through sixth grade ($p <$ .01 for the interaction). The number of choices received by minority pupils from other minority pupils was higher than the number of choices received by Anglos from minority pupils, but the means for total choices received, which reflected this, exhibited a significant grade-by-ethnic-group interaction—younger minority children, particularly girls, received fewer choices than did younger Anglos ($p <$ .01 for the interaction).

The post-one year found minority children doing well on the school playground, in sharp contrast to their schoolwork status, which was dependent on schoolwork achievement, in which they were low relative to Anglos. High play status existed principally for boys, which was presumably because of the higher value placed on excellence in team sports by boys as compared with girls. By post-two, only grade and sex remained as significant determinants of play status. Younger minority children still tended to receive somewhat fewer choices from Anglos, but minority boys in general were popular as play partners. Post-two scores showed that the high peer acceptance of minority children remained high, particularly for boys. The post-three through post-six data indicated that minority males in the fourth through sixth grades had the highest play popularity. There was a tendency for a certain few minority children to receive a large number of play choices, which may have reflected their possessing a high degree of athletic ability.

Socioeconomic Status (SES) and Social Position

Although the data revealed social status differentials favoring Anglos in two of the three social arenas studied (friendship and school-work), it is possible that these differences were attributable to factors other then ethnicity. According to Gronlund (1959), King (1961), and Lindzey and Byrne (1968), people seek out others within their own social stratum, and when they do choose out of their stratum, they tend to choose others of higher status. Since the minority communities in Riverside were distinctly lower in SES, perhaps the low relative status of the minority children in the desegregated classroom in both school-work and friendship may, at least in part, have been an effect of background SES. That is, if children tended to choose friends and work partners on the basis of their parents' SES, then minority children in the desegregated classroom were relegated to a low-status position because they tended to be considerably lower in SES than their Anglo classmates.

To examine the contribution of SES to social status, we divided the distribution of the Duncan (1961) SES index into six clusters. The lowest level included only minorities (no Anglos in our sample were that low in SES), levels 2 and 3 included Anglos and minorities of roughly the same average SES (the mean SES for minorities was actually slightly above that of Anglos for these levels), and levels 4, 5, and 6 covered the range of Anglo SES levels for which there were no corresponding minority clusters.

Table 10.5 presents total choices received on each criterion and number of choices received from Anglos by Anglos and by minorities in

TABLE 10.4A   Average Number of Play Choices Received and Choices Received from Anglos by Younger Children (K–3rd Grade) Pre-One through Post-Four Desegregation

	Pre-one	Post-one	Post-two	Post-three	Post-four
Anglos					
Boys					
Total	2.91	3.42	3.51	3.51	3.80
from Anglos		2.94	2.94	2.79	3.08
Girls					
Total	1.95	2.17	2.15	2.31	2.45
from Anglos		1.80	1.76	1.85	1.90
Mexican-Americans					
Boys					
Total	3.22	3.11	3.40	3.79	2.25
from Anglos		1.98	2.22	2.42	1.35
Girls					
Total	3.28	1.86	2.07	2.23	1.26
from Anglos		1.08	1.26	1.43	0.63
Blacks					
Boys					
Total	2.68	3.09	3.84	3.33	3.83
from Anglos		2.08	2.25	1.70	2.50
Girls					
Total	2.32	1.42	1.75	2.00	1.59
from Anglos		0.95	1.09	1.27	0.44

1966 (predesegregation),[6] 1967, and 1969 according to SES cluster. Since neither school grade nor sex interacted with SES, these factors are not included in the tables. In Anglo classrooms in 1966, social status was a positive linear function of SES ($p < .05$ for the linear trend for friendship and $p < .01$ for both work and play). The relationship between sociometric status and SES was not significant for segregated minorities, although it was slightly positive for Mexican-Americans on all criteria and slightly negative for Blacks.

In 1967 there was no relationship for Anglos between sociometric

[6] For this analysis we are including only those children who were desegregated in the fall of 1966 and 1967; they made up the majority of the sample (see Chapter 3).

TABLE 10.4B   Average Number of Play Choices Received and Choices Received from Anglos by Older Children (4th–6th Grade) Pre-One through Post-Six Desegregation

	Pre-one	Post-one	Post-two	Post-three	Post-four	Post-five and six
Anglos						
Boys						
Total	3.46	3.07	3.75	3.37	3.33	3.89
from Anglos		2.80	3.22	2.87	2.66	3.11
Girls						
Total	1.89	2.22	2.47	2.27	2.45	2.53
from Anglos		2.14	2.19	1.93	2.08	2.20
Mexican-Americans						
Boys						
Total	3.82	3.37	3.82	4.05	3.67	3.32
from Anglos		2.56	3.06	2.69	2.60	2.85
Girls						
Total	2.52	2.44	2.62	2.04	2.29	2.12
from Anglos		1.85	1.80	1.36	1.35	1.42
Blacks						
Boys						
Total	3.98	4.22	4.96	4.20	6.63	5.07
from Anglos		3.26	4.00	3.05	4.89	3.71
Girls						
Total	1.60	2.82	2.36	3.19	3.29	3.64
from Anglos		2.33	1.60	2.12	2.83	2.53

status and SES for either friendship or play; however, the linear trend for work choices remained ($p < .05$). Choices received by minorities from Anglos were not correlated with SES. Differences between ethnic groups within SES levels 2 and 3 for 1967 suggested that SES background alone could not account for ethnic differences in popularity. Anglos at level 2 received 1.05 more friendship choices from Anglos than did level 2 Mexican-Americans ($p < .01$) and 1.61 more friendship choices than level 2 Blacks ($p < .01$). Corresponding differences for work choices were 0.78 between Anglos and Mexican-Americans ($p < .05$) and 1.07 between Anglos and Blacks ($p < .01$), while play choices showed no such differences. Within level 3, Anglos exceeded

TABLE 10.5 The Effect of Socioeconomic Status (SES)[a] of Parents on Friendship, Work, and Play Choices Received in 1966, 1967, and 1969

	Anglos					Mexican-Americans			Blacks		
SES cluster =	2	3	4	5	6	1	2	3	1	2	3
N =	59	68	118	119	147	123	200	55	63	35	33
Total received 1966											
Friendship	2.51	2.44	3.25	2.77	3.49	3.02	3.13	3.24	2.54	2.43	1.97
Work	2.22	2.46	2.89	3.05	3.54	2.79	2.88	3.13	2.70	2.40	1.97
Play	1.85	2.28	2.48	3.38	3.29	3.15	3.57	3.56	2.46	3.17	1.88
N =	46	63	101	92	113	101	153	36	85	42	59
Choices received from Anglos 1967											
Friendship	2.56	2.33	2.61	2.71	2.71	1.65	1.51	1.39	1.09	0.95	1.07
Work	2.04	2.40	2.57	2.88	3.03	1.12	1.26	1.47	1.09	0.93	1.02
Play	2.43	2.03	2.37	2.38	2.70	2.27	2.10	1.83	2.12	2.71	2.00
N =	24	33	58	60	67	84	140	43	47	24	43
Choices received from Whites 1969											
Friendship	2.29	2.12	2.19	2.68	2.90	1.31	1.19	1.58	1.09	0.96	1.86
Work	2.08	1.97	2.64	2.97	3.03	0.92	1.10	1.77	0.89	0.96	1.47
Play	2.13	1.48	1.95	2.70	2.90	2.00	1.46	1.95	1.95	2.79	1.75

[a] SES is based upon the Duncan (1950) index, the higher the cluster number the higher the SES. There were no White families in cluster 1 and no minority families in clusters 4, 5, and 6.

Mexican-Americans by 0.97 choices for friendship ($p < .05$) and 1.07 for work ($p < .05$), with no difference for play choices. Level 3 Blacks were 1.26 friendship choices ($p < .01$) and 1.38 work choices ($p < .01$) below their Anglo classmates.

In 1969 the linear trends for Anglos were marginal, but level 6 Anglos did exceed the means for all other levels on all three criteria. Differences for Mexican-Americans were not significant for friendship and play choices received from Anglos, but level 3 Mexican-Americans did exceed their lower SES peers in work choices received from their Anglo classmates ($p < .05$). Level 3 Blacks received more friendship and work choices than lower SES Blacks, although the work choice difference did not reach statistical significance. For both friendship and work popularity, level 2 Anglos markedly exceeded minority children at that SES level. The comparison with Blacks at level 2 showed a 1.20 friendship choice advantage for Anglos ($p < .05$) and 1.12 work choice advantage ($p < .10$). The level 3 comparisons for friendship and work status of Anglos and minorities were not significant. The means for Anglos exceeded only slightly the averages for Mexican-Americans and Blacks on both friendship and work criteria.

Anglo children thus appeared to make SES social distinctions on each of the three criteria. Placing minority children in Anglo classrooms may have provided a lower anchor for SES distinctions, which, in turn, may have attentuated the relationship for Anglos. The more pronounced relationship between SES and work status was, of course, confounded by the correlation of SES with academic ability. Higher SES minority children were not more accepted initially by Anglos than were lower SES children, but by 1969 they did enjoy some advantage. The discrepancy in popularity between Anglos and minority children was greater the higher the SES of the Anglos. There was some evidence in the data that higher SES minority parents had greater contact with Anglos and that such contact fostered greater contact between their children and their Anglo classmates.

Peer Acceptance and Predesegregation Achievement

Several investigations have revealed that more popular elementary school children have both higher school achievement and higher IQ than do less popular children (Bonney, 1944; Grossman and Wrighter, 1948;

Laughlin, 1954; Thorpe, 1955). Particularly interesting is St. John's (1971*a*) study in Boston, which found that minority students who received higher ratings on friendship from Anglos had higher grades. We wished to determine if such a relationship between achievement and sociometric status held in our data and if the predesegregation school achievement of minority children influenced Anglo acceptance. In our examination of the relationship, 1966 standardized verbal achievement test scores were trichotomized within each ethnic group. These means were 90.86, 108.65, and 123.81 for Anglos; 81.83, 93.07, and 108.49 for Mexican-Americans; and 81.41, 93.53, and 108.59 for Blacks.

Referring to Table 10.6, we see that for Anglos in 1966 sociometric status was significantly related to achievement for friendship ($p < .01$), work ($p < .01$), and play ($p < .05$). Segregated minority children showed a similar pattern for the work criterion—a strong difference, with more than a full choice separating the means for upper- and lower-achievement thirds ($p < .01$). For play choices, higher sociometric status was enjoyed by the highest third only ($p < .05$). The same trend was seen for friendship choice but was not significant. The association between work status and achievement was as pronounced for minorities as it was for Anglos, whereas it was less so for play and friendship. Achievement thus appeared to be more broadly important among Anglos. Minority children were more discriminating, attributing importance to achievement only when it was relevant—in schoolwork—giving it less importance in choosing friends or play partners.

Let us now examine the achievement–social status relationship in the desegregated classroom. Table 10.6 presents the 1967 data for choices received from Anglos by Anglos and by the minority children desegregated in 1965 and 1966. For Mexican-Americans verbal achievement appeared to influence their being chosen by Anglos as a classwork partner, but the trend was weak. Blacks in the highest achieving third received more friendship and work choices from Anglos, although the differences were not strong ($p < .05$ for friendship and $p < .10$ for work). Play popularity appeared to be unrelated to achievement. The weaker trends notwithstanding, higher-achieving minority pupils were somewhat more likely to receive work and friendship choices from Anglo classmates than were their lower-achieving cohorts.

Comparing Anglo and minority children of equivalent verbal achievement (Anglos in the middle and lower thirds with minority children in the middle and upper thirds) reveals clear differences in

TABLE 10.6 *Verbal Achievement*[a] *and Choices Received for Friendship, Work, and Play in 1966 and 1967*

		Anglos			Mexican-Americans			Blacks		
		Low	Med.	High	Low	Med.	High	Low	Med.	High
	N =	184	174	191	136	156	144	67	72	60
Total received 1966	Friendship	3.14	3.05	3.72	2.98	3.08	3.32	2.18	2.15	2.85
	Work	1.92	2.85	3.99	2.36	2.85	3.28	2.12	2.22	3.72
	Play	2.31	2.80	3.27	3.21	3.23	3.83	2.52	2.07	3.52
	N =	139	152	147	129	106	88	81	90	79
Choices received from Anglos 1967	Friendship	1.92	2.63	3.08	1.44	1.65	1.73	0.78	0.87	1.62
	Work	1.77	2.57	3.49	1.08	1.32	1.57	0.83	0.82	1.49
	Play	1.72	2.52	2.86	1.79	2.33	2.20	1.96	2.11	2.59

[a] Based on 1966 scores trichotomized within ethnic group.

schoolwork popularity, favoring Anglos. In 1967 the difference between the work status of low-achieving Anglos and Mexican-Americans in the middle group was 0.55 ($p < .05$), and the corresponding difference between Blacks and Anglos was 1.03 ($p < .01$). The decrement between high-achieving minority children and the equivalent group of middle-achieving Anglos was even greater, the gap being 1.15 for Mexican-Americans and 1.19 for Blacks ($p < .01$) for both differences. Overall, the minority pupils in the highest-achieving third whose pre-desegregation achievement scores were comparable to the Anglo average were receiving fewer work choices from Anglos than the lowest-achieving third of Anglo students.

This relationship between achievement in 1966 and acceptance by Anglos still held in 1969, three years after desegregation, with no change other than a loss for the middle third of Mexican-Americans. Thus we see strong evidence of ethnic barriers that undoubtedly restricted social interchange between Anglo and minority children, as indicated by the considerably lower work popularity of minority children as compared with Anglos of equal academic ability.

Peer Acceptance and Changes in Achievement

The social threat of rejection by Anglo classmates may produce emotional interference with intellectual functioning (Katz, 1967; Pettigrew, 1967, 1968). A child's feeling of social isolation tends to reduce social comparison with the higher-achieving Anglo children. Social acceptance, on the other hand, is likely to induce the minority child to compare his performance with that of his Anglo classmates. Social comparison is manifested as effort toward improved performance (Festinger, 1954). A prerequisite for the child's attempting to improve his performance is the belief that the likelihood for eventual favorable comparison is fairly high, that is, that he has the potential to do well. We would thus expect that both Anglo peer acceptance (the lack of social threat) and relatively high ability (moderate to high probability of success) would lead to improved performance for the minority child in the desegregated classroom—or for any child in any classroom, for that matter.

Our data allowed us to make a longitudinal analysis of the same children over time, taking into account their predesegregation achievement and the degree to which they were accepted by their Anglo classmates. We categorized the minority children into those above and those below the median in predesegregation verbal achievement, assuming that a child above the median would be more likely to perceive himself as having a higher probability of academic success than would a child below the median. Acceptance by Anglo classmates, which we assumed to be negatively related to perceived social threat, was estimated by the number of schoolwork choices received by the child from Anglos.

Table 10.7A presents the one year postdesegregation data. Grade, sex, and ethnic group did not yield any independent effects and are therefore not shown. Furthermore the data for friendship and play popularity were very similar to the results for work acceptance and therefore are also not presented. From pre- to postdesegregation there was no effect of acceptance by Anglos on the achievement of the low-achieving minority children. For the initially higher-achieving minority children, on the other hand, there was an overall loss in achievement ($p < .01$) and an interaction between acceptance and pre- versus postachievement ($p < .05$, one tailed). Children above the median who were more accepted by their Anglo classmates did not drop significantly below their prior year's achievement, whereas those who were not accepted showed a performance decrement. In Table 10.7B we compare change in achievement from 1966 to 1969 (from pre to three years post) against three levels of the number of work choices received from Anglos during the entire three year post period. We found no reversal of the

TABLE 10.7A *The Relationship between Work Choices Received from Anglos and Standardized Verbal Achievement of Low- and High-Achieving Minority Pupils from Pre- to One-Year Postdesegregation*

		Low-achieving minority pupils		High-achieving minority pupils		
Number of work choices received from Anglos		0	1	2 or more	0	1	2 or more
$N =$	51	40	43	49	39	49
Pre		85.2	86.7	87.5	100.8	102.0	103.9
Post 1		86.3	86.7	88.0	90.7	95.3	99.1

TABLE 10.7B *The Relationship Between Work Choices Received from Anglos and Standardized Verbal Achievement of Low- and High-Achieving Minority Pupils from 1966 to 1969*

	Acceptance by Anglo classmates[a]					
	Low-achieving minority pupils			High-achieving minority pupils		
	Low	Medium	High	Low	Medium	High
$N =$	51	62	36	60	78	92
1966	86.1	85.8	86.3	101.1	103.2	106.6
1969	86.2	89.0	89.0	91.4	94.1	102.5

[a] Mean number of choices received from Anglos during four-year span. Low = 0.75, Medium = 2.99, High = 8.24.

short-term effects, although there was a slight, nonsignificant salutary effect for the lower-achieving children. For the initially higher-achieving group there was an overall decrease in achievement ($p < .01$) and the same interaction between acceptance and achievement change ($p < .05$), the high-achieving–low-acceptance children decreasing to a level that was only slightly higher than the average for the low-achieving–high-acceptance group, whereas the high-acceptance–high-achievement children appeared to be holding their own fairly well.[7]

If we assume that the child's prior performance conditions his performance expectations and that social acceptance is negatively related to social threat, our data support Katz's notions about the necessary and sufficient conditions for the academic well-being of a child in school, the necessary condition being a potential for success and the sufficient condition being the absence of social threat. Thus personal and situational factors combine in determining performance. There is another tenable interpretation. It may be that the higher-achieving minority child who happened to do well in the new classroom was accepted by his Anglo

[7] There were two possible contaminants here: statistical regression and the typical widening of the "achievement gap" that occurs irrespective of desegregation (see Chapter 4). These effects, however, would not have been expected to interact with peer acceptance since the 1966 achievement scores within each achievement group were similar for each level of subsequent peer acceptance.

peers, i.e., that achievement conditions acceptance rather than vice versa. Since our data are correlational, we cannot be sure of causal direction. Our intuition favors the hypothesis that acceptance affects achievement, although the process may be a complex circular one, with acceptance conditioning achievement and vice versa.

The Effect of Teacher Bias on Peer Group Acceptance

Lewin, Lippitt, and White (1939), in their classic study of group atmospheres, found that there was less interaction among children under an authoritarian leader than under either a democratic or a *laissez-faire* leader. Yarrow and Yarrow (1958) concluded from their summer camp study that the more comfortable and open the cabin counselor, the better the interethnic relations of the children in the cabin. St. John (1971*b*) identified a "fairness" component in a factor analysis of observers' ratings of teachers' classroom styles. Fairness had a significant positive correlation with the friendliness ratings by Anglos of minority children. In light of this kind of evidence, we can assume that a teacher's attitudes affect the degree to which minority and Anglo pupils interact.

Work by Bandura (1969) and Sarason (1968) suggests that modeling or imitation may be the mechanism mediating the relationship between the attitude of the adult authority figure and the child's behavior. The adult's attitude is expressed in his behavior, which is, in turn, mimicked by the child. We might therefore expect that a prejudiced teacher would, by her actions, induce a negative disposition in her Anglo pupils toward the minority pupils in the class. We derived a measure of teacher bias toward minority children from a factor analysis of the teacher's rating of each child in her class on a large number of bipolar semantic dimensions of differential attributes (see Chapter 11 for a detailed discussion of the method). One of the two principal factors that emerged from this analysis was the teacher's estimate of the child's academic talent and motivation (the other factor concerned how well behaved he was in class). When we compared the child's actual achievement in the previous year with the teacher's estimate of his intellect, it was possible to derive a discrimination index for each teacher reflecting how much she tended to over- or underestimate the intellectual capacity of her minority pupils relative to her Anglo pupils.

Table 10.8 shows the relationship between the teacher's discrimination index and the acceptance of the minority children by the Anglos in her class. The effect was strongest for the criterion of friendship choice ($p < .05$), was in the same direction but of a smaller magnitude for work, and was apparently not related to play choice. It is not possible to make a clear-cut causal inference, since the teacher discrimination index and the sociometric measure were based on data collected from the same children. There are at least three possible interpretations of the observed relationship. Teachers who perceive more friendly interaction between Anglo and minority pupils may also tend to assume similarity of ability between the groups; that is, Anglo acceptance causes perceived similarity rather than vice versa. This interpretation is somewhat farfetched but cannot be ruled out by our data. A second possibility is that teachers who are low in bias tend to use teaching methods, such as group projects, that encourage more interaction among their pupils. This is essentially what Lewin *et al.* (1939) found in their study of group atmospheres. An experiment by DeVries and Edwards (1972) found that the use of small biracial work groups in desegregated seventh-grade classes increased the number of cross-racial sociometric choices. In Chapter 10 we report that teachers who were low in discrimination were more likely to use small-group techniques to involve reticent children. The third interpretation, and the one we lean toward,

TABLE 10.8   *The Effect of Teacher Discrimination on Minority Friendship, Work, and Play Popularity with Anglos*

Sociometric criterion	Teacher discrimination index		
	Low	Medium	High
$N =$	138	129	156
Friends	1.64[a]	1.40	1.09
Work	1.26	1.15	0.96
Play	2.07	2.16	1.86

[a] The figures present the average number of sociometric choices received from Anglos.

is the modeling hypothesis, that the teacher sets the example in her treatment of the minority children in the class and the Anglo children follow suit. That we found no relationship between teacher bias and play status buttresses this interpretation, since on the playground the child's athletic prowess and not his teacher's attitude toward him was likely to determine his status.

Conclusions

The unprecedented amount of data we have examined points unmistakably to the conclusion that, with the exception of playground interaction, little or no real integration occurred during the relatively long-term contact situation represented by Riverside's desegregation program. If anything we found some evidence that ethnic cleavage became somewhat more pronounced over time. This was attested to by the fact that progressive improvement in the minority children's friendship and work status was due, by and large, to an increase in choices received from other minority children. There were exceptions to this, but the overall trend was certainly there. Furthermore younger minority children did not enjoy a status edge over the older children, which is what we might have expected, given the fairly well-accepted assumption that desegregation is more likely to be successful the younger the child. Nor can we assume that ethnic differences in social status were accounted for by either SES or achievement differences between Anglos and minorities since, within equivalent levels of SES and achievement, Anglos were still more popular than minorities.

The data did flag some hopeful signs. The social climate of the classroom, as reflected by peer acceptance and teacher attitude, appeared to influence the well-being of the higher-achieving minority child—what held for the minority child probably held for the Anglo child as well. We noted with some dismay that a favorable social climate, as represented either by high relative peer acceptance or a nonbiased teacher, was not able to raise the minority child's achievement but merely prevented any significant decline. In light of the achievement data presented in Chapter 4, any influence that prevents test scores from declining may, in fact, be salutary. The effect of these climate variables ought to be heartening to a social psychologist and should be encouraging from a social engineering standpoint, since it is just those sorts of influences that can be most tractably controlled.

There is an alternative interpretation for our findings that has to do with the fact that the minority children were bussed into receiving schools from the ghetto areas. The observed loss of friendship and schoolwork status by the minority children may not have been a result of desegregation per se but may instead have reflected their status as coming from relatively remote areas of the city. They were essentially strangers to the receiving school, in which the Anglo children already in the school had, by and large, enjoyed longstanding friendships with their classmates by virtue of living in the same neighborhood. Any group of children, minority or Anglo, may suffer the same status loss if they are bussed in from distant areas and are a small minority in the classroom. Children who are bussed into a school do not get an opportunity to interact with classmates after school or on weekends and may therefore find difficulty in establishing themselves socially in the classroom or as schoolwork partners (although it is our impression that elementary school children do not often do schoolwork together after school).

A test of this "stranger" hypothesis would require a comparison group of similarly bussed-in Anglo children, which we unfortunately did not have. The alternative interpretation must therefore stand as a possibility. Our feeling is, however, that it is not very tenable in the light of the relative absence of long-term status improvement. After spending six years in a school, it is not likely that a group of bussed-in children, minority or Anglo, would still be regarded as strangers.

One final comment. Ethnic cleavage may not necessarily be detrimental to the child's achievement. Cleavage does not preclude the possibility of the child's finding a congenial, nurturant social milieu in the classroom. Two basic conditions, it seems to us, must be satisfied, however, if a person is to prosper in a setting in which there is cleavage. One condition is that his subgroup not carry the stigma of inferior status with regard to activities important to the overall group. The second condition is that his subgroup be large enough for him to find congenial associations. The two conditions severely oversimplify the problem, but to discuss exceptions, the interaction between the conditions, and the influence of moderating variables would lead us too far into some fairly complicated conceptual terrain. The typical desegregated classroom in Riverside did not meet either of the above conditions. When entering the receiving classroom, the minority child was likely to be nearly two years behind academically and also found himself a member of a small ethnic subgroup of similarly academically disadvantaged cohorts. Under these adverse circumstances, the child's only academic salvation lay in social acceptance by the Anglo majority, so that he would have a sufficiently large, nonstigmatized, and congenial group against which to compare himself. It would be extremely difficult for him to improve his performance, as Katz predicted he would do, within his small, isolated, low-achieving ethnic clique. As a rider to or precondition of Katz's prediction, we can now say that only when there is Anglo acceptance will it be possible for the minority child to come to feel better about his own capabilities and, through healthy competition (comparison), to pull himself up to the Anglo performance standard, or at a minimum, to hold his own.

References

Allport, G. W. *The nature of prejudice*. Cambridge, Mass.: Addison-Wesley, 1954.

Amir, Y. Contact hypothesis in ethnic relations. *Psychological Bulletin,* 1969, *71,* 319–342.

Bandura, A. Social-learning theory of identification processes. In D. Goslin (Ed.), *Handbook of socialization theory and research.* Chicago: Rand McNally and Co., 1969.

Biehler, R. F. Companion choice behavior in the kindergarten. *Child Development,* 1951, *25,* 45–50.

Bonney, M. E. Relationships between social success, family size, socioeconomic home background, and intelligence among school children in grades III to V. *Sociometry,* 1944, *1,* 26–39.

Bonney, M. E., & Powell, J. Differences in social behavior between sociometrically high and sociometrically low children. *Journal of Educational Research,* 1953, *46,* 481–495.

Byrd, E. A study of validity and constancy of choices in a sociometric test. *Sociometry,* 1951, *14,* 175–181.

Campbell, D. T. A rationale for weighting sociometric choices. In J. L. Moreno and H. H. Jennings (Eds.), *The Sociometry Reader.* Glencoe, Ill.: The Free Press, 1960.

Campbell, J. D., & Yarrow, M. R. Personal and situational variables in adaptation to change. *Journal of Social Issues,* 1958, *14,* 29–46.

Clark, K., & Clark, M. The development of consciousness of self and the emergence of racial identity in Negro pre-school children. *Journal of Social Psychology,* 1939, *10,* 591–599.

Criswell, J. H. A sociometric study of race cleavage in the classroom. *Archives of Psychology,* No. 235. New York, 1939.

DeVries, D., & Edwards, K. *Student teams and instructional games: Their effects on cross-race and cross-sex interaction.* ERIC Document No. ED 070-808, 1972.

Duncan, O. D. A socioeconomic index for all occupations. In A. J. Reiss *et al., Occupations and social status.* New York: Free Press, 1961.

Festinger, L. A theory of social comparison processes. *Human Relations,* 1954, *7,* 117–140.

Gronlund, N. E. *Sociometry in the classroom.* New York: Harper and Brothers, 1959.

Grossman, B., & Wrighter, J. The relationship between selection rejection and intelligence, social status, and personality amongst sixth grade children. *Sociometry,* 1948, *II,* 346–355.

Horowitz, E. L. The development of attitude toward the Negro. *Archives of Psychology,* No. 194, 1936.

Jansen, V. G., & Gallagher, J. J. The social choices of students in racially integrated classes for the culturally disadvantaged talented. *Exceptional Children,* 1966, *33,* 222–226.

Katz, I. Socialization of academic motivation. In D. Levine (Ed.), *Nebraska symposium on motivation.* Lincoln: University of Nebraska Press, 1967.

Katz, I. Some motivational determinants of racial differences in intellectual achievement. In M. Mead, T. Dobzhansky, E. Tobach, & R. Light (Eds.), *Science and the concept of race.* New York: Columbia University Press, 1968.

King, M. B., Jr. Socioeconomic status and sociometric choice. *Social Forces,* 1961, *39,* 199–206.

Laughlin, F. *The peer status of sixth and seventh grade children.* New York: Bureau of Publications, Teachers College, Columbia University, 1954.

Lewin, K., Lippitt, R., & White, R. Patterns of aggressive behavior in experimentally created "social climates." *Journal of Social Psychology,* 1939, *10,* 271–299.

Lindzey, G., & Byrne, D. Measurement of social choice and interpersonal attractiveness. *The handbook of social psychology,* 1968, *2,* 452–525.

Loomis, C. P. Ethnic cleavages in the southwest as reflected in two high schools. *Sociometry,* 1943, *6,* 7–26.

Moorefield, T. E. The busing of minority group children in a big city school system. Unpublished doctoral dissertation, 1967, reported in M. Weinberg, *Desegregation research: An appraisal* (2nd ed.) Bloomington, Ind., 1970.

Moreno, J. L. *Who shall survive? A new approach to the problem of human interrelations.* Washington, D.C.: Mental Disease Pub. Co., 1934.

Pettigrew, T. Social evaluation theory: Convergence and applications. In D. Levine (Ed.), *Nebraska symposium on motivation.* Lincoln: University of Nebraska Press, 1967.

Pettigrew, T. Race and equal educational opportunity. *Harvard Educational Review,* 1968, *38,* 66–76.

Porter, J. A. *Black child, white child: The development of racial attitudes.* Cambridge, Mass.: Harvard University Press, 1971.

St. John, N. Thirty-six teachers: Their characteristics and outcomes for Black and White pupils. *American Educational Research Journal,* 1971, *8,* 635–648.

St. John, N., & Lewis R. The influence of school racial context on academic achievement. *Social Problems,* Summer 1971.

Sarason, I. Verbal learning, modeling and juvenile delinquency. *American Psychologist,* 1968, *23,* 254–266.

Shaw, M. *Changes in sociometric choices following forced integration of an elementary school.* ERIC Document No. ED 055 306, 1971.

Thorpe, J. G. A study of some factors in friendship formation. *Sociometry,* 1955, *18,* 207–214.

Yarrow, M. R., Campbell, J. D., & Yarrow, L. J. Acquisition of new norms: A study of racial desegregation. *Journal of Social Issues,* 1958, *14,* 8–28. (a)

Yarrow, M. R., Campbell, J. D., & Yarrow, L. J. Interpersonal change: Process and theory. *Journal of Social Issues,* 1958, *24,* 60–63. (b)

Yarrow, L. J., & Yarrow, M. R. Leadership and interpersonal change. *Journal of Social Issues,* 1958, *14,* 47–59.

11

Teacher Influences in the Desegregated Classroom

Eugene B. Johnson, Harold B. Gerard, and Norman Miller

The social atmosphere of the classroom is likely to have an effect on the well-being of pupils, regardless of their ethnic background. However, we expected the newly desegregated minority children in Riverside to be particularly vulnerable to such effects. The degree to which they were successfully integrated in the classroom would depend, in part, upon institutional supports (Allport, 1954). Since the teacher, as *the* principal authority in the classroom undoubtedly influences the play of such forces, we were anxious to explore her role in this regard.

Parents in Ocean Hill–Brownsville in New York fought against what they saw as an entrenched teaching bureaucracy. Parents in Canarsie opposed what they perceived as the ultimate lowering of educational standards and quality in their schools. Implicit in this social conflict and controversy is the increasing awareness that whose educational standards are being lowered depends on whose educational standards are being used as a yardstick. The cultural bias of methods of educational assessment (Kohl, 1965; Pearl, 1970) and the cultural bias of methods for assessing the sources of educational differences (Katz, Roberts, & Robinson, 1965) are under increasing attack.

Eugene B. Johnson • Brooklyn College, City University of New York, New York, New York. Harold B. Gerard • University of California, Los Angeles, California. Norman Miller • University of Southern California, Los Angeles, California.

Behind culturally biased measures lies social bias in educational practice. Students are not afforded the same treatment and consequently do not show the same level of educational achievement. This has been found in laboratory experiments (Johnson, 1972; Rothbart, Dalfen & Barrett, 1971; Rubovits & Maehr, 1971), in field experiments (Beez, 1968; Conn, Edwards, Rosenthal, & Crowne, 1968; Evans & Rosenthal, 1969; Meichenbaum, Bowers, & Ross, 1969; Rosenthal & Jacobson, 1968), in surveys (DeGroat & Thompson, 1969; Palardy, 1969), and in observational studies (Becker, 1952; Brophy & Good, 1970; Good, 1970; Hoehn, 1954; Mendoza, Good, & Brophy, 1972; Rist, 1970; Silberman, 1969). In field experiments, teachers' expectations are never manipulated in a downward direction and consequently we can never measure teachers' classroom behavior toward students expected to perform poorly. Yet these are the children primarily affected by social bias in the classroom (Johnson, 1972).

Observational data show that teachers' social biases affect their classroom behavior (Becker, 1952; Brophy & Good, 1970; Good, 1970; Hoehn, 1954; Mendoza, Good, & Brophy, 1972; Rist, 1970; Silberman, 1969), but there is no way to separate out the contribution of the behavior of the students themselves to those biases. Survey data consistently corroborate the effects of teacher expectations (DeGroat & Thompson, 1969; Palardy, 1969), but again it is difficult to separate teacher-based from student-based influences.

Given the technical difficulties of nonexperimental methods, an experimental approach might identify more effectively the sources of bias and their effects in interpersonal educational encounters. Yet most experimental research that has examined the influence of interpersonal expectations has done so not in learning contexts but with respect to experimenter bias (Adair & Epstein, 1968; Barber, 1969; Barber & Silver, 1968; Barber, Calverley, Forgione, McPeake, Chaves, & Bowen, 1969; Cooper, Eisenberg, Robert, & Dohrenwend, 1967; Duncan, Rosenber, & Finkelstein, 1969; Duncan & Rosenthal, 1968; Johnson & Adair, 1970; Marwit, 1970; Rosenthal, 1966; Trattner & Howard, 1970; Zoble & Seeman, 1970). There is probably less basis for predicting bias in an experimenter's behavior than in the behavior of a teacher (Johnson, 1972; Levy, 1969). Some research has found experimenter bias (Adair & Epstein, 1968; Cooper *et al.*, 1967; Duncan *et al.*, 1969; Duncan & Rosenthal, 1968; Marwit, 1970; Rosenthal, 1966;

Trattner & Howard, 1970; Zoble & Seeman, 1970) and some has not (Barber & Silver, 1968; Barber *et al.*, 1969; Johnson & Adair, 1970). The experimental research on the effects of expectations in learning settings generally supports the assumption of a self-fulfilling prophecy (Johnson, 1972; Rothbart, Dalfen, & Barrett, 1971; Rubovits & Maehr, 1971), though some of these findings are also confounded by experimenter bias (Johnson, 1972).

In their recent extensive review of the literature concerning the role of teacher expectations and bias, Brophy and Good (1974) concluded that although both naturalistic and experimental studies yield conflicting findings, the preponderance of evidence supports expectation effects. Further, this is more true of field experiments than of experimental studies. In a careful analysis of this now-extensive literature, they pointed to important distinctions between types of teachers and analytically differentiated among the expectation effects found with each type. *Proactive* teachers use expectations in planning individualized instruction but do not let the students' behavior or their own expectations interfere with the students' progress toward formulated goals. Passive (*reactive*) teachers have generally accurate and flexible expectations that are continually adjusted to students' behavior. The *overreactor* provides the strongest evidence of expectation effects that interfere with teaching progress, treating students as even more different than they really are, and consequently generating self-fulfilling prophecies.

The present research also focused on individual differences among teachers. It examined teacher bias in ethnically heterogeneous classes, utilizing an unobtrusive measure of ethnic discrimination. We will examine the effects of this bias on classroom grades as well as on standardized achievement test scores.

Methodology

So that we may study teacher effects, data will be presented for a subsample of children in the first year of desegregation for whom pre-desegregation data existed and who entered classrooms containing at least one Anglo and one minority child from the original Riverside sample. This subsample included 269 Anglo, 111 Mexican-American, and 72 Black children. There were 267 children in grades K through 3 and 185 in grades 4 through 6. The balance for sex was fairly good in each ethnic group.

The Measure of Teacher Discrimination

Teachers were asked to rate the sample children in their class-rooms on a series of semantic differential scales for each year in which data were collected.[1] A factor analysis of these ratings for the first year revealed two orthogonal factors, with all items having factor loadings of 0.60 or better. The first factor, accounting for 32.0% of the common variance, involved discipline and contained such items as disobedient–obedient, difficult to discipline–easy to discipline, and obstructive–cooperative. The other factor, reflecting intellectual competence and motivation, accounted for 17.3% of the common variance. Examples of items loading on this factor were good memory–poor memory, quick–slow, and intelligent–dull-minded.

Since the second factor, intellectual competence–motivation, pro-vided an index of the teacher's evaluation of the child's intellectual potential, we derived a measure of this evaluation by summing his teacher's ratings of him on each of the 13 scales loading on the factor. The data based on this index, which has a range of 13 (dull) to 91 (bright), are shown in Table 11.1 As indicated in the table, teachers judged minority children to be less bright than Anglos. Also, girls tended to be judged as brighter than boys.

Though both Mexican-American and Black children were judged to be less bright than Anglos, it might be expected that teachers would show considerable variation in the extent to which they saw an ability difference. This variation could be used as an index of teacher expecta-tion if it could be adjusted for the actual achievement of the children being judged. Teacher evaluations were standardized by grade and sex to eliminate sources of extraneous variation. Also, since Mexican-Ameri-cans and Blacks appear to be judged similarly but differently from An-

---

[1] The construction of an indirect attitude measure from the teachers' ratings of the children belonging to the different ethnic groups was suggested in a paper delivered by Norman Miller at the 1970 meeting of the Society of Experimental Social Psychology in Minneapolis, Minnesota, and entitled "Personality Differences Between the Black and White Children in the Riverside School Study."

TABLE 11.1 School Grade, Sex, Ethnic Group, and Teachers'
Judgments of "Brightness"

Ethnic group	Grade K–3		Grade 4–6	
	Male	Female	Male	Female
Anglo	59.93[a]	61.59	58.35	59.55
	(98)[b]	(80)	(46)	(53)
Mexican-American	49.88	52.62	47.75	47.36
	(33)	(21)	(29)	(28)
Black	47.52	49.65	43.08	52.31
	(23)	(20)	(13)	(16)

[a] Mean judgment of brightness (13 = dull, 91 = bright).
[b] Number of children in cell.

glos, the index was derived to reflect Anglo–minority comparisons. It should be noted that indices derived from Anglo–Black and Anglo–Mexican-American comparisons, analyzed separately, yielded results very similar to the analyses based on the composite reported in this paper.

Of the 297 teachers in the Riverside school system during the first year of desegregation, 145 had at least one Anglo and one minority child for whom data were available, 83 had at least two Anglo and two minority children, and 30 had at least three Anglo and three minority children. For each of these 145 teachers an index was constructed based upon the ratio of their average judgment of the brightness of the Anglo and minority children (standardized by grade and sex) in their classroom. If the "brightness index" was greater than 1.0, the teacher judged Anglos to be brighter than minority children. In fact, 78% of the teachers did have an index greater than 1.0. In those instances in which teachers did not judge Anglos to be brighter than minority children the differences in the opposite direction were small. Teachers did, however, differ considerably in the extent to which they saw a difference in ability between majority and minority groups.

If teachers based their judgments on actual school performance, we would expect a bias favoring Anglos, since in most classrooms a performance difference, as measured by standardized tests, favors Anglos. In order to correct for this "contamination of reality," teachers' judgments of ethnic differences in brightness were corrected for actual achievement differences as measured by tests administered in the previous year. For each teacher a ratio was constructed based on the average predesegregation achievement scores of Anglo and minority children (standardized by grade and sex). Dividing the "brightness index" by the predesegregation achievement index yielded a "discrimination" index reflecting the extent to which a teacher over- or underestimated ethnic differences in ability relative to actual achievement differences.

Results

Teacher Discrimination and Changes in Achievement

There were two ways of assessing the effect of the teacher's discrimination (as measured by the derived index) on the achievement of children in her class. One method, using the classroom as the unit of analysis, correlated achievement changes with the discrimination index. This procedure yielded a strong positive correlation between the teacher's discrimination index and the change in the achievement gap between the Anglo and the minority pupils in her class. A large pre to post increase in the achievement gap tended to obtain for teachers scoring high on the index, whereas little increase in the initial gap occurred for teachers scoring low. The effect was more pronounced for verbal achievement than for mathematical achievement. Moreover, the relationship obtained regardless of how many Anglo and minority children a teacher's brightness judgments were based on and regardless of whether predesegregation racial achievement differences were controlled or not.

There were two problems in using the classroom as the unit of analysis. First, correlational data obscured the influence of teachers on individual children. We were concerned with assessing the impact of the classroom on particualr individuals. Second, the correlational analysis precluded assessment of interactions between initial level of verbal achievement and either teacher discrimination or classroom context factors such as the initial achievement gap between minority and Anglo children at the start of the school year. So that we could examine possible influences of the initial Anglo–minority achievement gap, children were separated into three groups on the basis of whether predesegregation achievement differences between the Anglo and minority children in their classroom were large, moderate, or small.

Table 11.2 shows both initial verbal achievement and changes in verbal achievement (pre- to postdesegregation) as a function of ethnic group, teacher discrimination, and initial ethnic achievement differences in the classroom. It was important to consider first the initial verbal achievement scores and examine their interaction with the other inde-

TABLE 11.2   Ethnic Group, Initial Classroom Ethnic Differences in Verbal Achievement (on Standardized Tests), Teacher Discrimination, and Change in Verbal Achievement

Initial differences in achievement		Ethnic group		
		Anglo	Mexican-American	Black
High	High teacher discrimination	117.27[a] (22)[b] −2.14[c]	90.36 (14) −3.28	94.00 (8) −8.25
	Low teacher discrimination	118.26 (42) −2.36	87.67 (12) 0.00	90.00 (7) −1.00
Moderate	High teacher discrimination	106.69 (85) +2.08	95.78 (28) −6.68	95.67 (21) −6.28
	Low teacher discrimination	106.21 (76) +0.70	94.37 (35) −0.94	95.55 (18) +0.55
Low	High teacher discrimination	97.57 (21) +6.48	96.25 (12) −5.75	102.71 (7) −10.86
	Low teacher discrimination	100.52 (23) +0.26	93.40 (10) +0.70	93.45 (11) −5.82

[a] Predesegregation verbal achievement.
[b] Number of cases.
[c] Change in verbal achievement, pre- to postdesegregation.

pendent variables. There was, of course, a large ethnic difference in initial verbal achievement ($F = 41.44$, $df = 2/434$; $p < .01$), with Anglos showing initially higher levels of verbal achievement than either Mexican-Americans or Blacks. Fortunately there was no interaction between the initial Anglo–minority achievement gap and the teacher's discrimination index. This was critical because it indicates that assignment of minority children to classes was made independently of teacher characteristics. This being the case, we are able to draw inferences regarding teacher effects on the children that were not confounded by initial matching of teachers and children. Similarly teacher discrimination did not interact with ethnic group, which implies that within each ethnic group those children whose teachers were high in discrimination did not differ in initial verbal achievement from those whose teachers were low. Any teacher-induced differences in changes in verbal achievement could not therefore be attributed to regression effects. Also, extraneous sources of variance, such as grade and sex, showed nearly the same distribution for each ethnic group in classrooms classified as high and low in discrimination.

The verbal achievement change scores in Table 11.2 reveal a main effect for discrimination level ($F = 5.79$, $df = 1/434$; $p < .05$), an ethnic group main effect ($F = 8.20$, $df = 2/434$; $p < .01$), and most importantly, a discrimination × ethnic group interaction ($F = 5.17$, $df = 2/434$; $p < .01$). With teachers high in discrimination, Mexican-American and Black children showed larger decrements in verbal achievement (-5.24 and -8.46 respectively) than they did with low discrimination teachers (-0.08 and -2.09). The opposite appears to be true for Anglos, who appear to gain with high discrimination teachers ($+2.14$) and lose slightly with teachers who are low in discrimination (-0.46). In the main, teacher discrimination had a minimal effect on Anglo children relative to its effect on Mexican-Americans and Blacks. Finally, initial spread did not interact with discrimination or ethnic group, implying that the effect of discrimination was generalizable across classrooms differing in initial achievement spread.

In Table 11.3, which presents the same data controlling for initial individual verbal achievement, we find, in addition to the effects seen in Table 11.2, a three-way interaction ($F = 5.14$, $df = 2/440$; $p < .01$). A subanalysis revealed a strong discrimination × ethnic group interaction when only children initially high in achievement were considered ($F = 16.42$, $df = 2/440$; $p < .01$), but no such interaction for children low in

TABLE 11.3 *Ethnic Group, Initial Verbal Achievement (on Standardized Tests), Teacher Discrimination, and Change in Verbal Achievement*

Initial verbal achievement		Ethnic group		
		Anglo	Mexican-American	Black
High	High teacher discrimination	113.51[a]	101.74	104.53
		(98)[b]	(27)	(19)
		+0.58[c]	−10.85	−11.58
	Low teacher discrimination	111.95	102.81	103.92
		(123)	(21)	(12)
		−1.75	−3.62	+1.08
Low	High teacher discrimination	85.80	87.22	87.88
		(30)	(27)	(17)
		+6.96	−0.33	−3.18
	Low teacher discrimination	87.83	86.94	88.79
		(18)	(36)	(24)
		+9.72	+1.39	−3.08

[a] Initial verbal achievement.
[b] Number of children in cell.
[c] Changes in verbal achievement pre- to postdesegregation.

initial achievement. High-achieving minority children who had either high or low discrimination teachers showed changes in achievement that differed by almost a full standard deviation even though their initial verbal achievement scores were virtually identical. The discrimination effect was greatest for high-achieving Blacks, less for high-achieving Mexican-Americans, and nonexistent for Anglos. Teachers high in discrimination seem to induce an increasing divergence in verbal achievement between Anglo and minority children, while teachers low in discrimination do not.

How were these effects of teacher bias on achievement mediated? Did the biased teacher's behavior toward the minority child convey her attitude and discourage him in some way? Unfortunately we did not collect data on teacher–pupil interaction in the classroom, but we do have data, in the form of the teacher's grading patterns, that provide indirect evidence of the teacher's tendency to reward Anglo and minority children differentially. Table 11.4 presents the average verbal grades received by the three ethnic groups (standardized by school grade and sex with $\bar{X} = 100$, S. D. = 15). Anglo children received higher grades on the average than either Mexican-Americans or Blacks ($F = 18.70$, $df = 2/435$; $p < .01$). Also, as would be expected, teachers assigned higher grades to children high in initial verbal achievement than to those who were low (102.61 versus 90.49, $F = 62.07$, $df = 1/435$; $p < .01$). Most interesting, though, were three interactions. The differences in grades given to Anglo versus Mexican-American and Black children were smaller for teachers low in discrimination than for teachers who were high ($F = 5.27$, $df = 2/435$; $p < .01$). Also, although all teachers gave higher grades to high achievers than to low achievers, this initial achievement effect was greater for teachers who were low than for teachers high in discrimination ($F = 3.94$, $df = 1/435$; $p < .05$). Finally, there was a three-way interaction, suggesting that the influence of a child's ethnicity and initial achievement on a teacher's grading behavior differed for teachers high and those low in discrimination ($F = 3.81$, $df = 2/435$; $p < .05$). Although teachers high in discrimination were also sensitive to individual differences in achievement, giving higher grades to children initially high in achievement than to children initially low ($F = 19.24$, $df = 1/435$; $p < .05$), they differed

TABLE 11.4   *Ethnic Group, Teacher Discrimination, and Verbal Achievement Grades*

Teacher discrimination		Ethnic group		
		Anglo	Mexican-American	Black
High	High initial verbal achievement	112.34[a] (97)	95.89 (27)	93.21 (19)
	Low initial verbal achievement	97.07 (27)	84.18 (27)	91.82 (17)
Low	High initial verbal achievement	106.11 (122)	104.19 (21)	103.25 (12)
	Low initial verbal achievement	95.22 (18)	89.50 (36)	84.71 (24)

[a] Grades were standardized by sex and age ($\bar{x} = 100$, $sd = 15$).

from low-discrimination teachers in that the child's ethnicity modified the effect of initial achievement upon their grading. The interaction between ethnicity and initial achievement showed that high-discrimination teachers gave higher grades to high-achieving Anglos than to either high-achieving Mexican-Americans or high-achieving Blacks ($F = 16.26$, $df = 2/435$; $p < .01$). These teachers also discriminated by ethnicity when grading children initially low in achievement ($F = 6.35$, $df = 2/435$; $p < .01$), though Mexican-Americans suffered the most and Blacks the least. Looked at another way, teachers high in discrimination appeared to be sensitive to differences in initial achievement when evaluating Anglo and Mexican-American children (though they also discriminated against Mexican-American children), but they were insensitive to initial achievement differences when evaluating Black children. High- and low-achieving Black children received approximately the same grades. Teachers low in discrimination were not influenced in their grading by the child's ethnic background when grading children initially high in verbal achievement. On the other hand, when grading children initially low in achievement, these teachers were somewhat harsher on Mexican-Americans and Blacks ($F = 4.18$, $df = 2/435$; $p < .05$). Overall, in comparison to those high in discrimination, teachers low in discrimination were influenced in their grading more by achievement irrespective of the child's ethnicity.

Questionnaire Findings

A questionnaire was administered to teachers during the second year of desegregation to which 103 of our 145 teachers responded. Several questions concerned the use of a single educational standard in a desegregated classroom. Teachers low in discrimination were more likely to see a single educational standard as undesirable for a minority child's emotional adjustment (55.7%) than teachers high in discrimination (39.5%). There was also a tendency for teachers low in discrimination to see a single educational standard as less helpful to the minority child's educational adjustment (50.9%) than teachers high in discrimination (37.5%). When responses to these two questions, which were highly correlated, were combined into favorable, neutral, and unfavorable categories, there was a tendency for high- and low-discrimination teachers to differ in extreme response categories. These results are reported in Table 11.5 along with other questionnaire data.

TABLE 11.5 Responses of Teachers Classified as High and Low in Discrimination to Selected Questionnaire Items Administered the Second Year of Desegregation[a]

| | Is a single educational standard helpful to a minority child's educational and emotional adjustment? | | | Do you use small-group work as a means of motivating reluctant children? | | Do you use aspects of minority culture as a means of motivating minority children? | |
	Helpful	Neither helpful nor unhelpful	Unhelpful	Yes	No	Yes	No
High teacher discrimination	21 (44.6%)	8 (17.1%)	18 (38.3%)	3 (6.0%)	47 (94.0%)	17 (34.0%)	33 (66.0%)
Low teacher discrimination	14 (27.5%)	9 (17.6%)	28 (54.9%)	17 (32.1%)	36 (67.9%)	34 (64.1%)	19 (35.9%)

[a] χ^2 (Linear) = 3.44 ($p \geq .10$, $df = 1$) χ^2 = 11.18 ($p < .01$, $df = 1$) χ^2 = 9.36 ($p < .01$, $df = 1$)

Though the questionnaire findings were very tenuous and their interpretation *post hoc,* they do suggest an interesting explanation of teachers' grading behavior. If teachers high in discrimination more often employed a single educational standard, then they may have given different grades to high-achieving Anglo and minority children, since high-achieving Anglos did exceed the performance of their high-achieving minority counterparts. A teacher high in discrimination, once having differentiated her pupils by initial achievement, then proceeded to evaluate them within each ethnic group, also on the basis of initial achievement. Among Mexican-Americans and Anglos, low achievers received lower grades than high achievers, whereas for Blacks the relationship tended not to hold. This lack of differentiation for Blacks was likely to affect high achievers, since they were presumably not being rewarded for their performance. The effect of this lack of reward can be seen in the severe decrement they suffered in standardized test scores.

The teachers low in discrimination tended to give high-achieving Anglo, Mexican-American, and Black children the same grades, even though they did differ in standard achievement test scores. It is as if the teacher was compensating in her grading for cultural differences. At the same time, however, she was sensitive to individual differences in achievement irrespective of ethnic group. She tended, however, to use a single standard at the low end of the spectrum, giving lower grades to low-achieving Blacks and Mexican-Americans than to Anglos, which reflected actual differences in achievement.

Alternative Interpretations

The data reported suggest a relationship between teacher discrimination and changes in verbal achievement from pre- to postdesegregation. This relationship is consistent with the social psychological research that reports expectancy effects on performance. The differential grading patterns of teachers high and low in discrimination suggest an explanation for the effect of discrimination on verbal achievement that emphasizes the incentive value of grades. The questionnaire data on teachers' attitudes toward a single educational standard also suggest that teachers high and low in discrimination used different grading standards in the desegregated classroom.

There are three other tenable interpretations of the data. We can, for example, argue that the teacher's ethnic attitudes influence the self-esteem of her pupils, which, in turn, may influence achievement. As the data in Table 11.5 indicate, teachers scoring low in the discrimination index were significantly more likely to report using aspects of minority culture as a means of motivating minority children than were teachers high in discrimination ($\chi^2 = 9.364$, $df = 1$; $p < .01$), a procedure that might have enhanced the self-esteem of minority pupils. Given this tendency, minority children who had teachers low in discrimination might have participated more fully and would consequently have done better academically than children with high-discrimination teachers. However, an analysis of a measure of self-esteem changes derived from the children's questionnaire data failed to show any such effect of discrimination. Thus, though plausible, this explanation did not find empirical support.

Another possibility is that each teacher responded to achievement changes of her pupils that occurred spontaneously, independent of the influence of her biases or expectations. When the minority children in a particular teacher's class held their own or declined, her so-called discrimination index merely reflected that fact. This interpretation argues that a change in pupil performance determines a teacher's position on the index rather than vice versa. If we could have derived the teacher's index on one sample of Anglo and minority children and then determined how she affected performance changes of another sample of Anglo and minority children, we could have gotten around the possible contamination of reality on her index. This did not prove feasible with the data we had available. The fact, however, that high- and low-discrimination teachers did differ in questionnaire responses and grading practices does blunt the force of this possible explanation of the results.

A third explanation relates to the Coleman (1966) finding that integrated schooling was beneficial to minority achievement to the extent that the general socioeconomic status of the student body was high. Minority performance is presumably influenced by the predominant school norms. If teachers high in discrimination inhibit interracial contact (and therefore attenuate the influence of school norms) while teachers low in discrimination facilitate it, this difference in interethnic contact may mediate the influence of teacher discrimination on minority achievement. As indicated in Table 11.5, teachers low in discrimination were more likely to report using small-group settings as a means of involving reluctant children ($\chi^2 = 11.160$, $df = 1$; $p < .01$). Such teaching methods might have facilitated interracial contact. Furthermore, data reported in the next chapter support this interpretation; interethnic sociometric choices did vary as a function of the discrimination level of the teacher.

The present results suggest that teachers play a critical role in the success of a desegregation program. Their ethnic attitudes and teaching standards may mediate the success or failure of the desegregation experience of the children involved. This may occur through direct expectation of minority versus Anglo performance or may be mediated through sociostructural aspects of the classroom.

References

Adair, J. G., & Epstein, J. E. Verbal cues in the mediation of experimenter bias. *Psychological Reports,* 1968, *22,* 1043–1045.

Allport, G. W. *The nature of prejudice.* Cambridge, Mass.: Addison-Wesley, 1954.

Barber, T. X. Invalid arguments, post-mortem analyses, and the experimenter bias effect. *Journal of Consulting and Clinical Psychology,* 1969, *33,* 11–14.

Barber, T. X., Calverley, D. S., Forgione, A., McPeake, J. D., Chaves, J. F., & Bowen, B. Five attempts to replicate the experimenter bias effect. *Journal of Consulting and Clinical Psychology,* 1969, *33,* 1–6.

Barber, T. X., & Silver, M. Fact, fiction, and the experimenter bias effect. *Psychological Bulletin,* 1968, *20,* 1–29.

Becker, H. Social class variations in the teacher–pupil relationship. *Journal of Educational Sociology,* 1952, *25,* 451–465.

Beez, W. V. Influence of biased psychological reports on teacher behavior and pupil performance. *American Psychological Association Proceedings,* 1968, *3,* 605–606.

Brophy, J., & Good, T. L. Teachers' communication of differential expectations for children's classroom performance: some behavioral data. *Journal of Educational Psychology,* 1970, *61,* 365–374.

Brophy, J., & Good, T. L. *Teacher–student relationships.* New York: Holt, Rinehart, & Winston, 1974.

Coleman, J., & staff. *Equality of educational opportunity.* U.S. Department of Health, Education, and Welfare. Washington, D.C.: U.S. Government Printing Office, 1966.

Conn, L., Edwards, C. N., Rosenthal, R., & Crowne, D. Perception of emotion and response to teachers' expectancy by elementary school children. *Psychological Reports,* 1968, *22,* 27–34.

Cooper, J., Eisenberg, L., Robert, J., & Dohrenwend, B. S. The effect of experimenter expectancy and preparatory effort on belief in the probable occurrence of future events. *Journal of Social Psychology,* 1967, *71,* 221–226.

DeGroat, A., & Thompson, G. A study of the distribution of teacher approval and disapproval among sixth grade pupils. *Journal of Experimental Education,* 1969, *18,* 57–75.

Duncan, S., Rosenber, M., & Finkelstein, J. The para-language of experimenter bias. *Sociometry,* 1969, *32,* 207–219.

Duncan, S., & Rosenthal, R. Vocal emphasis in experimenters' instruction reading as unintended determinant of subjects' responses. *Language and Speech,* 1968, *11,* 20–26.

Evans, J., & Rosenthal, R. Interpersonal self-fulfilling prophecies: Further extrapolations from the laboratory to the classroom. *American Psychological Association Proceedings,* 1969, *4* (Part 1), 371–372.

Good, T. I. Which pupils do teachers call on? *Elementary School Journal,* 1970, *70,* 190–198.

Hoehn, A. A study of social status differentiation in the classroom behavior of nineteen third grade teachers. *Journal of Social Psychology,* 1954, *39,* 269–292.

Johnson, E. B. Pygmalion in the testing setting: Non-verbal communication as a mediator of expectancy fulfillment. Unpublished manuscript, 1972.

Johnson, R. W., & Adair, J. The effects of systematic recording error vs. experimenter bias on latency of work association. *Journal of Experimental Research in Personality,* 1970, *4,* 270–275.

Katz, I., Roberts, S., & Robinson, J. Effects of task difficulty, race of administrator, and instructions on digit symbol performance of Negroes. *Journal of Personality and Social Psychology,* 1965, *2,* 53–59.

Kohl, H. *36 children.* New York: New American Library, 1965.

Levy, L. Reflections on replications and the experimenter bias effect. *Journal of Consulting and Clinical Psychology,* 1969, *33,* 15–17.

Marwit, S. An investigation of the communication of tester bias by means of modeling. *Dissertation Abstracts International,* 1970, *30* (B1), 3390.

Meichenbaum, D., Bowers, K., & Ross, R. A behavioral analysis of teacher expectancy effect. *Journal of Personality and Social Psychology,* 1969, *13,* 306–316.

Mendoza, S., Good, T., & Brophy, J. The communication of teacher expectation in a junior high school. Unpublished manuscript, 1972.

Palardy, J. M. What teachers believe—what children achieve. *Elementary School Journal,* 1969, *69,* 370–374.

Pearl, A. The poverty of psychology—an indictment. In V. L. Allen (Ed.), *Psychological factors in poverty.* Chicago: Markham Publishing Company, 1970.

Rist, R. C. Student social class and teacher expectations: The self-fulfilling prophecy in ghetto education. *Harvard Educational Review,* 1970, *40,* 411–451.

Rosenthal, R. *Experimenter effects in behavioral research.* New York: Appleton-Century-Crofts, 1966.

Rosenthal, R., & Jacobson, L. *Pygmalion in the classroom.* New York: Holt, Rinehart, & Winston, 1968.

Rothbart, M., Dalfen, S., & Barrett, R. Effects of teachers' expectancy on student–teacher interaction. *Journal of Educational Psychology,* 1971, *62,* 49–54.

Rubovits, P., & Maehr, M. L. Pygmalion analyzed: Toward an explanation of the Rosenthal–Jacobson findings. Unpublished manuscript, 1971.

Silberman, M. L. Behavioral expression of teachers' attitudes toward elementary school students. *Journal of Educational Psychology,* 1969, *60,* 402–407.

Trattner, J. H., & Howard, K. A preliminary investigation of covert communication of expectancies to schizophrenics. *Journal of Abnormal Psychology,* 1970, *75,* 245–247.

Zoble, E., & Seeman, W. Can experimenter bias influence certain affective responses? *American Psychological Association Proceedings,* 1970, *5* (Part 1), 421–422.

12

Family Characteristics, Attitudes, and Values

VIVIAN TONG NAGY

Since family factors weigh heavily in determining a child's academic success, we examined their effects in our Riverside School Study.

Whiteman and Deutsch (1968) found that in a sample of fifth-grade Black and White children, the education and occupation of the head of the family correlated $+.45$ and $+.35$, respectively, with the Gates Reading Test scores of the children. In addition, they found two other socioeconomic status variables related to achievement: housing condition ($r = +.28$) and the number of children under the age of eighteen in the home ($r = -.29$). Vane (1970), Stodolsky and Lesser (1970), and Deutsch (1960) also reported depressed achievement among children of low socioeconomic status. Vane (1970) found that the achievement and intelligence of Black and White children in elementary school were not related to their ethnic identity but were significantly related to the occupation of their parents. Stodolsky and Lesser (1970) discovered that social class criteria of occupation, education, and neighborhood affect achievement within several ethnic groups.

Coleman (1966) reported that, overall, objective background factors (urbanism of background, migration, parents' education, structural integrity of the home, smallness of family, and items and reading material in the home) accounted for 10–25% of the variance in individual

VIVIAN TONG NAGY • Veterans Administration Outpatient Clinic, Los Angeles, California.

verbal achievement. For both Black and White children, the amount of variance accounted for by these background characteristics was relatively constant for children in grades 6–12. For the Mexican-Americans these characteristics accounted for more of the achievement variance in the lower grades.

Family Characteristics

The parent data in the Riverside School Study were obtained from interviews conducted with the parents in their homes in 1966, before the desegregation took place. In general, the mother was the primary source of demographic information about the family; mothers and fathers were interviewed separately on their attitudes and values. Interview data were collected from 976 of the total 1196 families that had children in the study. Of these 556 were Anglo, 254 were Mexican-American, and 166 were Black.

Occupational Position

The occupation of the head of the household (generally the occupation of the father) provided an index of socioeconomic position. The Duncan Socioeconomic Index for Occupations (1961) has a range from 0 to 96; the higher the index the higher the occupational position. The mean Duncan index values for the three ethnic groups were Anglo, 54.3; Mexican-American, 16.6; and Black, 26.1 ($F = 228.9$, $df = 2/973$; $p < .01$). Blacks tended to hold higher occupational positions than Mexican-Americans ($F = 21.2$, $df = 1/973$, $p < .01$), but this difference was relatively small as compared with the occupational advantage of Anglos over both minority groups.

Table 12.1 presents the cumulative percentages of each ethnic group over ascending deciles of this scale. The Anglo families were normally distributed over the entire occupational range, whereas more than 50% of the minority families were classified below the second decile. These figures clearly indicate major differences in the family backgrounds of the children in the study.

TABLE 12.1   Some Demographic Characteristics of the Three Ethnic Groups[a]

Duncan's socioeconomic index of occupations in deciles, in cumulative percentages:	Decile	Anglo	Mexican-American	Black
	1	2%	45%	33%
	2	14%	78%	63%
	3	16%	86%	72%
	4	28%	92%	77%
	5	43%	96%	85%
	6	54%	98%	88%
	7	73%	100%	96%
	8	85%	—	98%
	9	96%	—	99%
	10	100%	—	100%
Education, in years, in cumulative percentages:	0–8	3%	53%	16%
	9–12	41%	97%	72%
	12–16	80%	100%	94%
	16+	100%	—	100%
Family structure:				
Nuclear family		92%	77%	70%
Father absent family		4%	5%	15%
Nuclear family + extended kin		3%	9%	6%
Other		1%	9%	9%
Mean number of times moved in last 10 years		3.7	2.4	3.2
Residence: Mean number of persons/room		.82	1.22	1.09

[a] Sample sizes   Anglo: $N = 556$; Mexican-American: $N = 254$; Black: $N = 164$; total: $N = 976$.

Education

The amount of education acquired by the head of the household ranged from 0 to 25 years, with Anglos having 15.0, Mexican-Americans 8.6, and Blacks 12.4 ($F = 276.9$, $df = 2/1018$, $p < .01$). Anglos had more education than Blacks or Mexican-Americans ($p < .01$ by t for each comparison) and Blacks were more educated than Mexican-Americans ($p < .01$). Table 12.1 presents the distribution of parents in each ethnic group in each of four levels of educational achievement. In more than half of the Mexican-American families the head of the household did not have any high school education, compared with only 3% of the Anglos and 16% of the Blacks. Furthermore a much greater proportion of Anglo than minority parents had schooling beyond high school.

Compared to national norms, our Anglo and Black parents had considerably more education. Whereas for the country as a whole the median number of years of education were 10.7 and 7.9 for White and non-White males, respectively,[1] the medians in our sample were 13.5 and 11.9. The median for the Mexican-Americans in our sample, 8.3 years, was comparable to the national median of 8.1.[2]

In summary, it is evident that the three ethnic groups varied significantly on major socioeconomic determinants, with Anglo fathers having better jobs and more education than minority fathers. Blacks in Riverside were higher in socioeconomic status than Mexican-Americans. That the educational and occupational measures were closely related was supported by a high correlation ($r = .53$) between the Duncan index value and years of education for the heads of the households in this sample.

Other Demographic Characteristics of the Family

In addition to occupational and educational differences, the three ethnic groups differed in language use, geographic mobility, family structure, and housing conditions. In terms of language use, the average Mexican-American family spoke Spanish almost half of the time in the home. Response to the question "How many times has your family moved in the past ten years?" revealed greatest stability among the Mexican-American families ($p < .01$, see Table 12.1).

Although the traditional nuclear family structure, consisting of

---

[1] U.S. Bureau of the Census, *U.S. Census of Population: 1960*, Vol. 1, *Characteristics of the Population*. Part 1, United States Summary, Table 76.

[2] U.S. Bureau of the Census, *U.S. Census of Population*: 1960, *Persons of Spanish Surname*, Final Report PC(2)-1B, Table 3.

both parents plus children, existed for the majority of the families, small but significant proportions of the minority families consisted of either the nuclear family plus extended kin or of father-absent families (see Table 12.1). Of the Anglo families 92% consisted of mother, father, and children, compared to 77% of the Mexican-American and 70% of the Black families. The proportion of father-absent families among Blacks exceeded the other ethnic groups by a factor of 3, confirming other reports (Billingsley, 1968; U.S. Department of Labor, 1965).

Although most of the families resided in single-family dwellings, the occupational status difference among the ethnic groups was revealed in the average number of rooms in the family residences: Anglo, 6.2; Mexican-American, 5.4; and Black, 5.6. Also, as we noted in Table 12.1, both Mexican-Americans and Blacks lived under more crowded circumstances because their families were larger.

Ethnicity, Socioeconomic Status (SES), and School Achievement

As discussed in Chapter 4 there were clear ethnic differences in performance on standardized achievement tests, with Anglos performing at a level approximately one standard deviation above that of the minority children (107.93 for Anglos versus 93.88 and 93.97 for Mexican-Americans and Blacks, respectively). The relationship of SES to achievement was evident from the correlation of the child's standardized achievement scores with the occupational ($r = .37, p < .01$) and educational ($r = .40, p < .01$) status of his family.

Parental Attitudes and Values

In addition to socioeconomic factors, attitude and value differences have been previously found to be related to achievement and motivation for achievement (e.g., McClelland, 1961; Atkinson, 1964; Rotter, 1966). We examined the relationship between several parental value and attitude orientations that might have been expected to relate to the achievement of the child.

Anomie

Six items from the Srole anomie scale (1956) were included in both mother and father questionnaires (for example, "There's little use in writing to public officials because they often aren't interested in the problems of the average man"). Lower scores on the anomie items tend to reflect feelings of general despair and hopelessness in one's perception of the present and future state of society and one's general life situation.

In general, Anglo mothers and fathers expressed the least anomie among the parents ($\bar{x} = 18.54$ and $\bar{x} = 19.14$, respectively) and Mexican-Americans the highest ($\bar{x} = 14.88$ and $\bar{x} = 15.25$), with Blacks falling in between ($\bar{x} = 15.53$ and $\bar{x} = 16.24$). T-tests among the ethnic group means for mother as well as father respondents were all significant at better than the .05 level.

Since previous research has found that low SES respondents express higher levels of anomie than high SES respondents (e.g., Angell, 1962), it is possible that the anomie differences between Anglo parents and minority parents was primarily due to differences in socioeconomic level. To explore this possibility, a subset of low SES Anglo parents, the lowest 17% on the Duncan SES index ($N = 96$), were chosen for comparison with the minority parents. The average Duncan SES level for this subsample (17.35) fell well below the average for Blacks (26.08) and was quite close to the average for Mexican-Americans (16.60). While matching is always fraught with problems, comparisons of the attitudes and values of the minority with the Anglo parents in this low SES subsample promised to provide some indication of the contribution of SES to ethnic differences. On the anomie items, the low SES Anglos, like their higher SES Anglo counterparts, expressed less anomie than either the Mexican-Americans or the Blacks (low SES Anglo mothers, 17.70, and low SES Anglo fathers, 18.17), indicating that the ethnic differences were not primarily attributable to SES.

Internal–External (I–E) Control of Reinforcement

Perceived internal–external control of reinforcement (Rotter, 1966) reflects a person's sense of efficacy. Gurin, Gurin, Lao, and Beattie (1969) have identified two conceptually different components of the Rotter scale that have important implications for understanding the basic orientations of minority group members to their environment. An individual with high scores on the control ideology component (disagrees with statements such as, "The way the system works, there is no chance for you to ever really get ahead") believes hard work, effort, skill, and ability, rather than luck, produce success—the traditional Protestant ethic. The second component, personal control, refers to the person's feelings of control over the outcomes of his own life (e.g., "Many times you feel that you have little influence over the things that happen to you"). Strong feelings of personal control have been found to be related to heightened expectancies of success and to self-confidence in one's abilities in academic and job performance. Gurin *et al.* (1969), Coleman (1966), and more recently Collins (1974) provided support for this distinction. Collins found that Black college students were as likely to endorse beliefs in the Protestant ethic as were White students, yet, unlike Whites, they expressed a relatively low sense of personal control over their outcomes.

In our sample of mothers a high number of "disagree" responses to the four personal control items indicated a high sense of personal control (Anglo = 3.22, Mexican-American = 2.42, and Black = 2.80, $p < .01$ by F). For the four control ideology items the means were Anglo, 3.23; Mexican-American, 1.94; and Black, 2.66 ($p < .01$ by F). Relative to Anglo parents, Blacks and Mexican-Americans were considerably more external in their feelings of personal efficacy as well as expressing weaker general achievement philosophies. In addition, Mexican-American parents were more external than Blacks on both scales.

The response pattern of the minority parents to the control ideology measure was inconsistent with the Gurin *et al.* (1969) and Coleman (1966) findings. The Riverside School Study minority parents expressed weaker feelings of internal control on the control ideology measure than did the Anglo parents. The fact that our minority parents were of lower SES than the college students in the Gurin *et al.* study may account for these results. However, as in the case of the anomie scale, further analysis suggested that SES was not the primary determining factor. The Anglo parents who served as low SES comparisons on the anomie items were significantly ($p < .05$) more internal on both components (personal control: $\bar{x} = 3.16$; control ideology: $\bar{x} = 3.16$) than the parents in either of the two minority groups (personal control:

Mexican-American, $\bar{x}$ = 2.42; Black, $\bar{x}$ = 2.80; control ideology: Mexican-American, $\bar{x} = 1.94$; Black, $\bar{x} = 2.66$).

Thus our Mexican-American and Black parents believed that rewards for others as well as for themselves were more controlled by the environment than did the Anglo parents. Gross statistical control of SES differences between the Anglo and the minority parents did not eliminate differences in belief of individual or personal efficacy and influence.

Values for Children

Previous studies examining parental values for children have been primarily concerned with socioeconomic differences (Bronfenbrenner, 1958; Kohn, 1959, 1963). Bronfenbrenner (1958), in his comparative study of the differences in the overall character of parent–child relationships between middle- and working-class families over the 25-year period from 1928 to 1957, concluded that working-class mothers emphasized "traditional" values, such as *neat and clean, obedient,* and *respect for adults,* whereas middle-class mothers emphasized "developmental" values such as *happy, cooperative,* and *eager to learn.*

The Riverside School Study parents were asked to choose from the following list the five most desirable behavioral and personality characteristics in boys and girls: *good at sports, dependable, curious about things, happy, neat and clean, obedient, honest, good student, good manners, popular with other children, considerate of others, has self-control, nice looking, independent.* Since responses of fathers and mothers in each ethnic group were remarkably similar, as indicated by Spearman rank correlations (mean rank correlation = +.93), only the responses of the mother, the primary socialization agent, are presented here. Those data, for boys and girls separately, are presented in Table 12.2.

In general, Mexican-American and Black mothers expressed nearly identical preferences for girls; *neat and clean, honest, good student,* and *obedient* were the most frequently favored characteristics. However, in addition to *honest,* Anglo mothers chose *happy* and *dependable* more frequently than did the Mexican-American or the Black mothers. Interestingly, more Anglo and Black mothers than Mexican-American mothers chose *considerate of others* as a desirable trait for girls. Of all the

TABLE 12.2   Proportion of Mothers in the Three Ethnic Groups Choosing Each of 14 Attributes as among the 5 Most Desirable Characteristics for Elementary-Aged Boys and Girls

	Anglo		Mexican-American		Black	
	Boys	Girls	Boys	Girls	Boys	Girls
Good at sports	.15	.02	.43	.14	.42	.08
Dependable	.59	.60	.38	.36	.43	.35
Curious about things	.30	.28	.12	.11	.24	.17
Happy	.55	.64	.31	.39	.37	.42
Neat and clean	.26	.36	.46	.71	.51	.62
Obedient	.36	.36	.56	.62	.52	.50
Honest	.66	.68	.54	.63	.56	.54
Good student	.44	.45	.60	.59	.45	.54
Good manners	.28	.24	.47	.45	.34	.44
Popular with other children	.09	.12	.18	.17	.14	.20
Considerate of others	.70	.74	.37	.39	.41	.56
Has self-control	.35	.31	.31	.21	.39	.39
Nice looking	.01	.02	.07	.07	.01	.02
Independent	.20	.17	.14	.13	.12	.17

mothers, Anglo mothers attached the least importance to *neat and clean* and *obedient* for girls.

Mothers in the three ethnic groups also differed in the values desired in boys. The main difference was again between the Anglo and the minority mothers. *Considerate of others, dependable,* and *happy* were rated more highly for boys by Anglo than by either the Mexican-American or Black mothers. Minority mothers, on the other hand, stressed *obedient*—a characteristic relatively unimportant to Anglo mothers. The one characteristic unanimously selected by all three ethnic groups as particularly important for boys was *honest*.

In summary, the Anglo parents were primarily concerned that children be happy and also that they be dependable and show consideration for others, characteristics that are important for establishing good interpersonal relationships. This was as true for the low as for the high SES Anglos. By contrast, minority parents placed somewhat less importance on these characteristics and instead tended to emphasize behavior and appearance-related qualities, such as neatness, cleanliness, obedience, and good manners.

Important Functions of the Family

As compared with minority parents, Anglos placed greater importance on the interpersonal and emotional guidance and support functions of the family, while minimizing the more material values of

TABLE 12.3 *Mean Rank of Importance Assigned to the Functions of the Family by Mothers and Fathers in the Three Ethnic Groups*[a]

	Mother			Father		
	Anglo	Mexican-American	Black	Anglo	Mexican-American	Black
To be respected in the community	5.43 *	3.83 *	3.92	5.16 *	3.08 *	3.35
To have healthy and happy children	2.42	2.55	2.45	2.41	2.81	2.69
To have secure income and comfortable home	4.61 *	3.25 *	3.33	4.47 *	3.14 *	3.57
To have family members need and trust each other	2.63 *	3.54 *	3.36	2.82 *	3.71 *	3.40
To have high moral and religious standards	2.95 *	3.71 *	3.33	2.99 *	3.94 *	3.56
To assist each member to develop his abilities and personality	3.52 *	4.81 *	4.46	3.47 *	3.73 *	4.35
To be a place of safety from the outside world	6.40	6.26	6.58	6.62	6.26	6.56

[a] Low numbers indicate high rank value.
* Significant differences ($p < .05$) between the groups designated by the brackets, as determined by t-tests comparing mean ranks.

income, comfort, and respectability. The minority parents did not, however, believe that the essential functions of the family are to provide financial and social status or to enhance the emotional and psychological well-being of individual family members. These response patterns generally reflected ethnic rather than SES differences. When the responses of the parents in the low SES Anglo subsample were compared to those of the parents in the two minority groups, 17 of the 20 mean comparisons remained significant. (See Table 12.3.)

Relating these selections of important functions of the family with the parent choices of desirable characteristics for children is useful for a fuller understanding of the attitudes and orientations of these parents. Anglo parents selected the characteristics *considerate, honest, happy,* and *dependable* as the most desired characteristics for both boys and girls. This interest in the social and emotional adjustment and development of children was consistent with their emphasis on family member interdependance and guidance as basic functions of the family unit. The characteristics *neat and clean, obedient, good student,* and *good manners* were all chosen by more than 40% of both Mexican-American and Black parents; this emphasis on the proper appearance and social behavior of children was, in one sense, consistent with their emphasis, relative to Anglo parents, in the family functions on having a secure income and a comfortable home. All of these interests expressed a concern with more materialistic and tangible values. Mexican-American and Black parents appeared to be as focused on decorous and socially desirable behavior as they were on such values as honesty, considerateness, and the desire to have healthy and happy children.

Function of the School

In choosing from a list of six alternatives the three functions of the school that they considered the most important, most parents felt that schools should emphasize academic and achievement values: *teach reading, writing, and arithmetic* (chosen as one of the three most important functions of the school by 85% of all of the parents) and *teach how to study and learn on own* (71%). Next in priority were characteristics relating to the behavior of children: *teach how to get along with others* (55%) and *teach obedience and discipline* (43%). *Teach good character* (28%) and *teach practical things like handling money and traffic safety*

(13%) were perceived as the least important for schools to teach; perhaps the parents believed that these are best taught in the home.

However, there were some notable ethnic differences (χ^2s significant at $p < .01$). Anglo and Black parents, including the parents in the low SES Anglo subsample, especially emphasized the academic function of the schools. In addition, 73% of the Black mothers and fathers and 83% of the Anglo mothers and fathers (including over 70% of the low SES Anglo parents) regarded teaching children to study and learn on their own as an important function of the school. However, only 47% of the Mexican-American parents chose this as a primary function of the school. The emphasis by Mexican-American mothers, and especially fathers, on teaching children obedience—59% and 70%, respectively, compared to 36% of all Anglo parents, 43% of the low SES Anglo parents, and 40% of the Black parents—was consistent with the greater importance they placed on *obedient* as one of the five most desirable traits for both boys and girls to possess.

Important Characteristics of a Job

Like most of the attitudes and values examined above, those values considered most important in a job have been found to vary according to SES. Hyman (1953) and Centers (1949) found that lower SES individuals emphasize the economic advantages of a job situation as much as 2 to 1 over the more personal aspects. However, a more recent study failed to confirm this socioeconomic differentiation between low- and high-income Mexican-Americans (Grebler, Moore, & Guzman, 1970).

In ranking four characteristics of a job situation, Anglo mothers and fathers valued most highly *a job that is important and gives a feeling of accomplishment,* whereas Mexican-American and Black mothers and fathers placed more importance on *a job with good chances for advancement.* Parents of all three ethnic groups agreed that jobs with these two characteristics were more desirable than *a job that is secure* or *a job with a high income.* This fact is particularly noteworthy in the cases of the low SES Anglo and the Black and Mexican-American parents, for whom job security and income should have been particularly salient. Once again, the difference between the Anglo and the minority parents in their choice of most important aspects of a job cannot be readily attributable to the socioeconomic differences between them; the ranking of job characteristics by the parents in the low SES Anglo subsample exactly paralleled that of the total Anglo sample.

Discussion

The differences between the Anglo and the minority families on the attitude and value items cannot be accounted for by the fact that they differed socioeconomically. The Anglo parents in the lowest 17% of the SES distribution consistently expressed values and attitudes more like upper-class Anglos than like the minority parents.

The ethnic differences did make sense in that relative to the Anglos, minority parents were more likely to perceive a hostile environment and feel alienated from mainstream abilities to realize desired outcomes, a reaction consistent with feelings of low efficacy. Experiences of social discrimination might have contributed both to feelings of anomie and to helplessness in the face of society's control of their outcomes. The anomie and IE data for the Mexican-American parents may be partially accounted for by the influence of traditional Mexican and Mexican-American cultural values, which tend to induce a somewhat passive stance toward the world (Heller, 1966; Kluckhohn & Strodtbeck, 1961; Madsen, 1964). Unfortunately, apart from the anomie and internal–external items, we had no means of assessing the degree of adherence to these traditional values for the Mexican-American parents.

The feeling on the part of the minority parents, as compared with Anglos, of having little personal influence on the world around them as well as the belief that their status was not likely to change, is inconsistent with strong achievement-oriented attitudes that focus on personal effort. Although children's school performance is influenced by a number of factors (e.g., children's previous experience with rewards for achievement, peer influence, and classroom factors), it seems reasonable that the low achievement levels of our minority children may have been due in part to the transmission of weak achievement-oriented attitudes by their parents. The Anglo mothers and fathers may, by the same token, have exerted a positive influence on the achievement of their children through their own higher achievement orientations. These suggestions find some indirect confirmation in Chapters 6, 7, and 9. As shown in these chapters, the minority children did exhibit personality differences in the direction of lowered achievement motivation, differences consonant with the attitudes and values of their parents. This aspect of the data fit nicely with the implicit model underlying this discussion, namely, that parental socialization of achievement-oriented attitudes and values results in enhanced academic performance in the school setting. Interestingly, however, in spite of these relatively clearcut ethnic differences in the personality of children, the model broke down in that these differences in achievement motivation bore little relation to academic performance.

References

Angell, R. Preferences for moral norms in three problem areas. *American Journal of Sociology*, 1962, *67*, 650–672.

Atkinson, J. W. *An introduction to motivation.* New York: Van Nostrand, 1964.

Billingsley, A. *Black families in White America.* Englewood Cliffs, N.J.: Prentice-Hall, 1968.

Bronfenbrenner, J. Socialization and social class through time and space. In E. E. Maccoby, T. M. Newcomb, & E. L. Hartley (Eds.), *Readings in social psychology* (3rd ed.). New York: Henry Holt & Co., 1958.

Centers, R. *The psychology of social classes.* Princeton: Princeton University Press, 1949.

Coleman, J. S., & staff. *Equality of educational opportunity.* U.S. Department of Health, Education, and Welfare. Washington, D.C.: U.S. Government Printing Office, 1966.

Collins, B. E. Four components of the Rotter Internal–External Scale: Belief in a difficult world, a just world, a predictable world, and a politically responsive world. *Journal of Personality and Social Psychology*, 1974, *29* (3), 381–391.

Deutsch, M. Minority group and class status as related to social and personality factors in scholastic achievement. *Society for Applied Anthropology Monographs*, 1960, No. 2.

Duncan, O. D. A socioeconomic index for all occupations. In A. J. Reiss *et al.*, *Occupations and social status.* New York: Free Press, 1961.

Grebler, L., Moore, J. W., & Guzman, R. C. *The Mexican-American people.* New York: The Free Press, 1970.

Gurin, P., Gurin, G., Lao, R. C., & Beattie, M. Internal–external control in the motivational dynamics of Negro youth. *Journal of Social Issues*, 1969, *25* (3), 29–53.

Heller, C. S. *Mexican-American youth.* New York: Random House, 1966.

Hyman, H. H. The value-systems of different classes. In R. Bendix & S. M. Lipset (Eds.), *Class, status, and power.* Glencoe, Ill.: Free Press, 1953.

Kluckhohn, F. R., & Strodtbeck, F. L. *Variations in value orientations.* Evanston, Ill.: Row, Peterson & Co., 1961.

Kohn, M. L. Social class and parental values. *The American Journal of Sociology,* 1959, *64* (4), 337–351.

Kohn, M. L. Social class and parent-child relationships: An interpretation. *American Journal of Sociology,* 1963, *68,* 471–480.

Madsen, W. *The Mexican-Americans of South Texas.* San Francisco: Holt, Rinehart, & Winston, 1964.

McClelland, D. C. *The achieving society.* Princeton, N.J.: D. Van Nostrand Co., 1961.

Rotter, L. B. Generalized expectancies for internal versus external control of reinforcement. *Psychological Monographs,* 1966, *80,* 1–28.

Srole, L. Social integration and certain corollaries: An exploratory study. *American Sociological Review,* 1956, *21,* 709–716.

Stodolsky, S., & Lesser, G. S. Learning patterns in the disadvantaged. In M. L. Goldschmid (Ed.), *Black Americans and white racism.* New York: Holt, Rinehart, & Winston, 1970.

U.S. Department of Labor. *The Negro family: A case for national action.* Washington, D.C.: U.S. Government Printing Office, 1965. ("The Moynihan Report")

Vane, J. Relation of early school achievement to high school achievement when race, intelligence, and socioeconomic factors are equated. In M. L. Goldschmid (Ed.), *Black Americans and white racism.* New York: Holt, Rinehart, & Winston, 1970.

Whiteman, M., & Deutsch, M. Social disadvantage as related to intellective and language development. In M. Deutsch, I. Katz, & A. Jensen (Eds.), *Social class, race, and psychological development.* New York: Holt, Rinehart, & Winston, 1968.

13

Summary and Conclusions

NORMAN MILLER

This final chapter attempts to summarize and discuss the findings presented in the individual chapters composing this volume. Whenever relevant, we indicate how the findings bear on the hypotheses outlined in the opening chapter.

Native Ability

Chapter 5 confirms the typical finding of approximately one standard deviation of difference in measured IQ between Anglos and minorities (15 IQ points). Furthermore, while a rough equating of social class lowers this gap, there is still a residual difference of approximately 12.5 IQ points. Indeed, even if we take a most extreme subsample of Anglos who socioeconomically lie substantially below the minority groups, the direction of effect remains the same. The approximate difference of 11 IQ points provides persisting evidence of ethnic differences in measured intelligence. As pointed out in Chapter 5, the question of whether these differences should be attributed to genetic structures or to differences in experience remains unresolved. Regardless of the source of these differences, virtually no one questions that there are large differences *within* each ethnic group on measures of IQ. Furthermore the variation within each group does not seem, to be

NORMAN MILLER • University of Southern California, Los Angeles, California.

substantially less than that within another. Achievement within the two minority groups, however, is considerably more homogeneous than among the Anglos.

Added to this picture are several important features about the relation between ability (IQ) and academic achievement. Chapter 5 reports no difference in the strength of the relation (magnitude of correlation) between achievement and ability for minorities versus Anglos when all three measures of intellect are pooled and correlated with the standardized achievement measures. Yet in contrast to this latter outcome, the relation between the WISC and verbal achievement as presented by Gerard in the Chapter 1 showed flatter slopes for minorities than Anglos.[1] To add to this picture, for some IQ measures the correlation with achievement was higher for Blacks than for Anglos. And, interestingly, when SES was roughly equated, the correlation between IQ and achievement was higher for the minorities than for Anglos! In sum, our data show no clear-cut or overall difference in the relation between IQ and academic achievement among the three ethnic groups. Furthermore desegregation did not change this picture in any substantial way. Whereas the relation between IQ and achievement showed some evidence of decreased strength following desegregation, the relation between grades and IQ increased. (This latter result seemed to stem, quite naturally, from the normalized grading created by the desegregated classroom).

One thing is clear. The gap in the achievement of minority and Anglo children (as reflected in test scores expressed as grade equivalents) increased as they progressed through elementary school. This remained true regardless of whether their schooling occurred in a segregated or a desegregated setting. It argues against any simplistic interpretation of performance differences as due solely to initial differences in the innate intellectual capacity of the different ethnic groups.

Underlying Values (The Family)

One of the assumptions enumerated in the opening chapter is that *"The achievement gap is due to a difference in orientation toward*

---

[1] These two findings are not necessarily contradictory. The regression could be greater (slope steeper) for Whites, even though the correlations are of equal (or even lesser) magnitude. This would be expected given the smaller variance in the minorities in comparison to the Whites.

educational attainment within the Black and the White communities."
Underlying this assumption is the notion that the White community
stresses academic achievement more than the Black community or, more
specifically, that parents belonging to the two ethnic groups differ in this
regard. Indeed, the assumption of value mediation formed the basis for
the overall strategy of our research. Given this assumption, it then became important to use measures that tapped the sources of personality
development: the family, its values, and its attitudes. Likewise, it became important to measure the personalities of the children themselves
as well as the influences within the school setting that acted upon them:
teacher attitudes, peer acceptance, etc. In sum, the essence of this approach was that it put the child's personality in a pivotal position. It
looked for the influences that bolstered achievement motivation and
focused on achievement itself as a consequence of these achievement-
related personality structures. In this sense, our approach was in line
with that of Coleman (1966), with the emphasis upon the lateral transmission of values, or of Crain and Weisman (1972) in their survey
analysis of the relation between school integration, personality, and
achievement.

Needless to say, this is not the only model that could have been
chosen to guide the design of the Riverside study. For instance, an alternative that we considered, and perhaps mistakenly rejected, would
have focused primarily on the structural variables within the school and
classroom setting, examining directly such factors as differences in the
interaction patterns of minority and Anglo students within the
classroom, the degree of social support available to children of different
ethnic backgrounds, the degree of isolation of minority students because
of individual differences in teachers' attitudes and behavior, etc.[2]

Chapter 12 most clearly examines the parental influences upon the
child. The findings show virtually no difference in parental attitudes regarding the central function of the school. Mexican-American, Black,
and Anglo parents alike emphasized the importance of teaching basic
academic skills and the ability to study and learn on one's own. They

---

[2] Obviously, we did include some measures of these variables. However, we probably
chose to emphasize the former approach at least in part because of the prevailing research support for it. Undoubtedly such decisions are also reached to some extent as a
consequence of the skills and past experience of the principal investigators. Additionally, the implementation of the second approach implicitly required classroom in-
trusions and/or substantial physical renovations and monitoring systems that seemed
undesirable to the school district.

ranked various school functions identically. Indeed, in many respects Mexican-American and Black parents differed more than Blacks and Anglos.

On the other hand, the three groups did differ in their emphasis on other values. Minority parents emphasized more overt characteristics, such as *neat and clean, obedient,* and *good manners,* as most important for children to possess, whereas Anglo parents focused more upon less immediate qualities, such as *consideration, dependability,* and *adjustment.* Stated another way, minority parents emphasized qualities that would be more directly instrumental for success and acceptance of their child in the school setting. Since their children were being bussed into previously all-White schools, concern with their acceptance was appropriate. It is also possible that because of their lower social status, Blacks and Mexican-Americans paid more attention to appearances in general, especially when interviewed by predominately White interviewers, whereas the emphasis on less overt values exhibited by the Anglos only emerged as one of the luxuries provided by higher social status. In accordance with these value differences, when evaluating the important characteristics of future occupational opportunities, the minority parents emphasized opportunity for advancement, whereas Anglos emphasized opportunity for personal development and self-actualization.

On cursory examination, these differences might imply a stronger achievement orientation among minority parents—sensitivity and attention to the self-presentational behaviors necessary for acceptance in school, increased income, occupational advancement, and a higher status. They suggest a "have-not" orientation that is focused on getting ahead in the world by engaging in the more immediate behaviors designed to do just that. Minority parents seemed to be less concerned with the luxury of self-actualization than they were with more salient bread-and-butter issues. Yet to whatever extent these differences are interpretable as an orientation toward current problems, they are simultaneously interpretable as a focus away from more long-range and distant goals. This aspect is related to the quality that Mischel (1961) has centered on as one of the core features of achievement motivation: the ability to postpone gratification and to put aside current needs and desires for more distant aspirations. In this respect, it is interesting that the parents themselves differed in some personality traits that ordinarily seem related to achievement motivation. Minority parents, consistent with their socioeconomic position in life, perceived themselves as having less personal control over their outcomes and showed more anomie.

In sum, there is no clear evidence that the minority families placed less value on educational attainment. However, minority and Anglo parents did differ in ways that imply personality differences in the strength of achievement motivation among their respective children.

Personality Differences

The assumption of ethnic differences in personality, as already indicated, dictated the basic design of the Riverside School Study.[3] Furthermore, such differences are implicit in the hypothesis (presented in the opening chapter) that *"Achievement orientation deficits are reversible and are easier to reverse the younger the child."* In consideration of the validity of this hypothesis, it is important to note that if ethnic differences in personality do not exist to begin with, there is little point in attempting to assess their modifiability as a function of age and the desegregation experience. Second, even if they do exist, there is considerably less meaning to them if within-race differences in personality are unrelated to differences in academic achievement. We will examine these two underlying points in sequence.

Ethnic Differences in Personality

The comparison of family attitudes and values, as examined in Chapter 12, hinted that familial characteristics associated with ethnic membership were indeed likely to produce modal personality differences among the three groups of children. Chapters 6, 7, 8, and 9 however,

---

[3] In consonance with the model that we adopted in designing the Riverside School Study, we use the term *personality* to refer to motivational or generalized behavioral systems that show consistency over time and space. Further, many or most of these systems (sometimes spoken of as traits), are seen as mediating a child's scholastic or academic outcomes. In this sense they are viewed as occupying a causal role, and their development and emergence are assumed to precede temporally the child's academic performance. Of course, personality is often defined in terms of any of the dimensions of behavior along which individuals might consistently differ. As is apparent from our discussion, we treated intelligence and attitudes as separate from personality, although they can and indeed are appropriately viewed as components of personality by others. When speaking of ethnic differences in personality, we refer to behavioral manifestations of motivational systems on which the means of the three ethnic groups differed.

comment more directly on this question. Furthermore, two of these chapters are concerned with personality systems more commonly thought to underlie educational performance: achievement motivation (Chapter 6) and self-esteem and anxiety (Chapter 8).

These chapters show substantial evidence of personality differences among the three groups of children prior to desegregation. Chapter 7 reports ethnic differences in responsiveness to others (as indicated on a measure of preference for sitting at the front of the classroom) and responsiveness to peer pressure. The direction of difference could be interpreted as a greater need for approval among minority children, especially when viewed in conjunction with the greater anxiety (Chapter 8 and 9), less favorable self-concepts (Chapter 8), and greater self-ideal discrepancy (Chapter 7) also found among the minority children. In a related, though slightly different emphasis, when viewed in conjunction with the rod and frame data (showing greater susceptibility to the influence of the frame when attempting to position the rod vertically [Canavan, 1968]) and the internal–external control data (in which minority children reported less control over their environment), this collection of differences could be interpreted as indicating greater dependency among minority children. Other ethnic differences in personality added to a picture of the minority child as being less well adjusted than the Anglo. The goal setting of Anglo children during the ring-toss game showed greater consonance with actual performance (Chapter 6). Further, the minority child was more likely to derogate his ability in the face of failure (Chapter 6) and showed less tolerance for conflict (Miller, 1970).

Measures more closely related to achievement motives conformed to this picture. When presented with a hypothetical choice, an Anglo child was more likely than a minority child to choose a more valuable deferred reward in preference to a less valuable immediate one. Both the goal-setting differences and the greater externality of the minority children meshed with this picture of less achievement motivation. Descriptions of Anglo children by the psychometrists were more favorable in overall evaluation and depicted them as more active and expressive in the testing situation, and lastly, better groomed. Although these latter differences can just as appropriately be interpreted as differences in the psychometrists' perceptions of minority and Anglo children who, in truth, were equal on these dimensions, nevertheless they do fit with the overall differences that appeared in the less subjective task and objective test performance.

This picture of trait clusters concurs with the views and work of others. Coopersmith (1967), in speaking of the origins of low self-esteem, stressed dependency during infancy as the underlying state. He presented a general hypothesis of childhood dependency that includes a cognitive, information-seeking component. Dependency represents an attempt to establish self-worth and is produced and elicited by conditions that fail to provide stable evaluations. When one lacks internal benchmarks and self-definitions, external confirmation is sought; when one lacks feelings of personal competence, it is more difficult to deal with anxiety and threats when they arise. Hauser's (1971) careful comparison of lower-class Black and White males, using measures that provided clinical depth and richness along with procedures for objective assessment and evaluation, confirmed this direction of difference and argued that in the comparison of Blacks and Whites we are dealing with differences over and above the effect of social class. Furthermore, the weak internal control of Blacks that was seen by Crain and Weisman (1972) as the principal underlying component of their low achievement received some confirmation in our own data.

Turning to a different dimension of comparison, Chapter 9 shows linguistic differences between Anglo and minority children. In this case, however, the differences did not fall as clearly into the evaluative format characterizing the other personality differences (i.e., good–bad, adjusted–maladjusted, or consonant with middle-class versus lower-class values). For instance, minority speech showed a *greater* richness than that of Anglos as reflected in vocabulary size, though Anglos used more polysyllabic words. And though minority children were more repetitive, the analyses failed to reveal any overall difference in language proficiency.

Clearly then, there were modal differences in personality between the Black and Anglo children—indeed, between all three ethnic groups when the finer details of the data are examined. In general, the Anglo child exhibited more self-direction, more energy, and greater evidence of self-worth. These qualities seemed to feed into motivational systems generating scholastic achievement and ability to cope realistically with adversity and threat. A general summary such as this must, of course, gloss over many details, yet this description is apparently not simply (or primarily) a depiction of social class differences. Whenever the contribution of social class was examined (see Chapters 5, 8, and 12) ethnicity appeared to be the more potent source of differences.

The next question is whether desegregation produces any personality change. Not only does this question address the "achievement orientation deficit" hypothesis mentioned earlier, but it also comments on assumptions 4 and 10 in the opening chapter: *"Social influence will occur in any group so that the norms of conduct, beliefs, and values of the majority will influence the minority"*; *"Desegregation will increase the minority child's self-esteem."* The oft-cited hypothesis of lateral transmission of values also contains these two assumptions at its core (as does our initial underlying model depicting achievement motivation as the pivotal determinant of educational success and attainment). As explanations, they imply that personality *changes* must be in evidence.

In general, our data were most disappointing in this respect. There were few substantial changes reflected in the personality measures, particularly those anticipated to be most strongly related to achievement: the measures of achievement motivation, anxiety, and self-worth. Indeed, in some instances, the direction of effect was opposite to that expected. For instance, the younger Blacks showed an increase in anxiety (Chapter 8). We found no support for assumption 10 of the opening chapter: *"Desegregation will increase the minority child's self-esteem."* In general, desegregation disturbed the adjustment of the minority child but not the Anglo child (Chapter 7). Indeed, Chapter 8 shows that placing the minority child in the White receiving classroom, while raising his own anxiety and increasing his self doubts, had a salutary effect on those Anglos lowest in socioeconomic status. Perhaps the introduction of out-group members into the classroom decreased the salience of their own inferior position relative to their peers. In pursuing this issue further, we shall want to determine whether the Anglos lowest in socioeconomic status actually gain more peer acceptance when minority members enter their classes.

The Relation between Personality and Academic Achievement

The personality variables assumed to be most directly related to achievement motivation were even more disappointing. Desegregation did have the predicted effect on goal-setting behavior. In the ring-toss game the goal setting of minority children shifted toward realism, coming more into line with their performance. Furthermore, as would be anticipated (see assumption 3 in Chapter 1), this was primarily true for the first-graders in contrast to third- and fifth-graders. As implied above, however, this faint glimmer of the effect we predicted finds little additional confirmation in the other personality measures purported to be related to achievement motivation. The minority child's belief in whether or not he controls his own fate showed no change following desegregation, while tolerance for delayed gratification declined for all groups.

Even more fundamental to the question at hand, however, was the basic relation of these personality traits to academic achievement. Here the personality model failed completely. As reported in Chapter 6, goal-setting behavior and the tendency to delay gratification showed no consistent relationship with school achievement—either overall or within any of the three ethnic groups! Finally, the erratic relationship between fate control and self-attribution of ability hardly gave confirmation to the causal model relating actual scholastic achievement to underlying motivational variables.

The adjustment variables presented a somewhat more positive picture in showing some relation to school achievement. For instance, low-achieving children were shown to be more anxious in general and about school in particular (Chapter 8). Additionally, their self-concepts were less favorable as indicated by two self-report measures. This finding provided some positive support for assumption 11: *"Increased self-esteem will lead to increased achievement."* However, the low absolute magnitude of the correlations again virtually precluded assignment of a causal role to these personality measures (see Chapter 8). Virtually the same story emerges in the measures analyzed in Chapter 7. Though some significant relations in expected directions did occur (e.g., some confirmation of a positive relation between achievement and self-worth or happiness), the correlations accounted for a relatively miniscule amount of the variance in scholastic achievement.

These conclusions stand in sharp contrast to those of Crain and Weisman (1972). Because their work represents perhaps the most substantial published research on desegregation since the Coleman report and because many of the initial assumptions that guided their design were similar to our own, it is important to present and discuss their findings in the present context.

Crain and Weisman argued from their data that integration increased Black "security"; it supposedly promoted greater internal control and happiness while reducing anti-White anger and the defensively assertive consequences of low self-esteem. Furthermore these beneficial personality effects accrued only to those Blacks who experienced integration in elementary school, supporting assumptions 3, 4, and 10 in our introductory chapter.

In further contrast to our own data, integration was shown to have important consequences for educational and occupational achievement. Whereas 48% of Black men who attended segregated schools failed to complete high school, this was true of only 36% of those who attended integrated schools. Their figures were even more striking for migrants from the South (77% versus 45% dropout rate). The figures for college attendance and completion showed the same effect. Similarly, verbal achievement test scores were highest for those who attended integrated elementary and high schools, intermediate for those who attended mixed schools, and lowest for those with totally segregated schooling. While the differences for males are interpretable in terms of the different dropout rates for those attending integrated and segregated schools, the difference for females is too large to be attributable to such educational attainment differences.

Occupational achievement also showed this same beneficial effect. Alumni of integrated schools were more likely to enter occupations traditionally closed to Blacks; even controlling for educational attainment, they tended to earn more. Whereas attending an integrated elementary school was seen as primarily contributing to the development of personality traits associated with achievement and interpersonal effectiveness, the integrated high school was seen as supplying the values and normative supports for educational attainment and achievement. (Crain and Weisman termed this latter process the "context effect.") Most of the variance in these dependent measures of achievement was controlled by whether or not the Black student attended an integrated high school (in contrast to whether or not he attended an integrated elementary school). Additionally, Crain and Weisman argued that the high school also provided contacts that were instrumental in occupational achievement, terming this the "interactional effect of integration."

As indicated, Crain and Weisman's causal model relating family background and personality to educational achievement was identical to the one initially motivating our own research design. Arguing from the model, they saw the beneficial effects of integration upon educational achievement as deriving from personality and value changes caused by interaction with middle-class White children—both the "personality effect" and the "contextual effect," as they termed them, or the "lateral transmission of values" in the language of other researchers.

How can we account for this totally different conclusion from the one our own data yielded? There are several explanatory avenues. Self-selection is an important one in studies of desegregation (Pettigrew, 1969), and we will consider it first. As with the Coleman data, there is no completely satisfactory way of assessing their extent. Whereas Crain and Weisman explained their data in terms of apparent beneficial effects of the integrated school, they could not rule out the possibility that minority children whose parents voluntarily enrolled them in integrated schools differed at the outset from children in segregated schools. In other words, the self-selection interpretation assumes differences between the families of Black children enrolled in integrated and segregated schools.

Crain and Weisman did deal with some aspects of the self-selection explanation. Specifically they argued that Blacks in integrated schools did not have better backgrounds in terms of father's education, mother's education, size and stability of family, or origin of family. They showed that when these factors were controlled, the educational advantages that accrued from attending an integrated high school or elementary school still remained substantial. Black students in integrated schools apparently did not come from higher-status families than those in segregated schools. We do not wish to minimize these perfectly appropriate attempts to rule out dimensions along which self-selection might operate. The absence of some of the more obvious differences that we might expect to exist if self-selection were operating, however, does not rule out self-selection as an explanation of their findings. For instance, one of the points noted by Crain and Weisman (1972) themselves is that in many of the 25 metropolitan areas that they sampled, the Black population today, much less 30 years ago, was too small to fill a segregated high school. In 1968 all 12 grades in Minneapolis contained only 5255 Black students, clearly too few to fill a segregated high school. And in 1940, when most of Crain and Weisman's respondents were in school, the Black population there was one-fourth what it is today. On the other hand, a respondent growing up in Chicago would have found it extremely difficult to obtain an integrated education. It might be quite important to speculate about possible differences between Blacks who chose to migrate from the South to a city like Minneapolis and those who instead chose Chicago. Those choosing Chicago could more easily embed themselves in an all-Black ghetto; as a consequence of the difference in numbers, most could almost completely avoid interactions with Whites; differences in social and economic conditions between Blacks and Whites might consequently be much less salient; additionally the perceived social support available in Chicago would be much greater.[4]

The preceding example is not the only possibility. Crain and Weisman (p. 148) pointed out another instance of self-selection. A larger percentage of females attended integrated schools. A boy without older sisters had a 45% chance of attending an integrated school, whereas one with older sisters had a 58% chance. They suggested that parents look for "good neighborhoods" to protect daughters. Males born later into these families with daughters would then attend integrated schools. This implies that more of those students attending integrated schools had parents who were sensitive and responsive to the parental responsibilities of protecting their children. Such feelings of responsibility might well extend to other attitudes and dimensions of development that, when transmitted to the child via social influence and modeling processes, result in better academic performance. From the standpoint of this analysis, these beneficial effects would occur even though the educational level of these parents may not exceed that of parents who live in ghetto neighborhoods. The very combination of equal educational attainment of the two sets of parents (and presumably equal job status) in conjunction with the motivation by one set to defer at least some of their own immediate personal goals for the sake of their children (i.e., their pursuit of long-range goals and deferred gratification) implies that modeling effects between child and parent lead to better academic performance.

The point is that the attendant differences in values, attributes, and personalities of the parents who live in segregated or integrated areas and the differences in socialization, modeling, and social influence effects that ensue offer rival explanations of the effects Crain and Weisman at-

---

[4] Even if these differences did not cause different types of Blacks to migrate to the two cities, the differences between the cities could produce different experiences for the children growing up in them. These differences could, in turn, produce the observed educational effects, which might then mistakenly be attributed to integration. This, of course, would not be an instance of self-selection but, instead, a confounding of variables.

tribute to attending integrated as opposed to segregated schools. In other words, attending a northern segregated high school might predict Crain and Weisman's reported effects yet have little to do with the experiences provided by integrated education. Instead, their reported effects might stem from the differences in the values, aspirations, and personalities of those Blacks willing to move to the cities with smaller Black populations.[5] Such differences might well exist not only between metropolitan areas, as implicitly argued thus far, but also within them.

Although selection and/or confounding seems to be the best explanation of the discrepancy between our data on the one hand and both the Coleman and the Crain and Weisman data on the other, one serious alternative explanation remains: cultural change.[6] In this regard, it is important to note that although both studies were initiated in 1966, a substantial age difference existed between Crain and Weisman's respondents and our own. Their data were based on a cluster sample of 1651 Blacks between the ages of 21 and 45 recruited from 297 randomly selected city blocks in 25 different northern metropolitan areas. Their White sample consisted of 1326 respondents from an earlier National Opinion Research Center survey. Although they did not reveal the average age of either group, we can safely assume that their samples were at least a generation older than our own. Additionally, since the White comparison group was drawn from an earlier survey, it was quite likely even older than their Black one. A further consideration concerns whether or not the respondent was born in the South. Although we do not consider place of birth in our data, the vast majority of our Black children were not born in the South. Therefore comparisons between our Blacks and theirs might more appropriately focus on their northern-born, second-generation Blacks.

In contrast to our own data showing little in the way of strong

---

[5] This point is buttressed by the combination of two facts: (1) that an integrated high school predicts the size of the Black community better than does an integrated elementary school and (2) that in their data an integrated high school is more closely associated with beneficial effects than is an integrated elementary school.

[6] Whereas self-selection and other sources of confounding have received attention in prior discussions of studies of desegregation, the role of cultural change has not. Therefore, we will discuss it in more detail than we otherwise might. This more detailed examination, however, should not be interpreted as implying that we think it the most likely explanation. Rather, it constitutes one among several, any one of which (or all of which) might account for the differences between their data and ours.

relationships between personality measures and academic performance, Crain and Weisman cited internal control, for instance, as a critical predictor variable. We would like to suggest two propositions. First, as already implied, it seems likely that cultural changes have been occurring throughout the United States and further, that these changes constitute a shift in modal personality, one that minimizes the role of these personality structures in explaining other performance differences. Second, Crain and Weisman may have overemphasized the role of personality in accounting for their own results.

The notion of temporal changes in modal personality within a culture is not new. McClelland, in *The Achieving Society* (1961), argued that such personality changes presage changes in other cultural institutions. On the other hand, Barry, Child, and Bacon (1959), taking a Marxian view, contended that the causal relation flows the other way—that the basic personality found in a society represents an adaptation to the characteristics of the economic institutions. Regardless of whether personality changes initiate adjustment and evolution in other cultural institutions or, instead, flow from them, the notion of modal changes in American personality exists in several recent analyses of American society. All of these analyses argue for the decreasing importance of achievement motivation and related personality variables. For instance, Riesman's (1950) observational analysis of more than two decades ago, depicting the change from "inner directedness" to "outer directedness," implied a modal personality shift toward greater externality. People increasingly look toward the behavior and beliefs of others as the guide for their own behavior rather than relying on their own internalized values. His analysis likewise suggests a decreasing tolerance of delayed gratification; one is influenced more by what he sees in front of himself at the moment rather than finding direction from his internalized aspirations, imagined goals, and fantasies of the future. These changes seem to emerge naturally as a consequence of the migration from rural to urban centers. The increase in the proportion of the population dwelling in cities, where social influence factors are more pervasive, would at least partially explain this shift. On the farm one often had little choice other than his own or his family's standards. Likewise the greater pervasiveness of mass media in the urban center and their development and increasing intrusion over time into rural America must surely have facilitated such a change. Phillip Slater, in *The Pursuit of Loneliness* (1970), pointed to the important consequences that emerge when a culture shifts from economic scarcity to economic plenty. The result is an emphasis on consumerism—the ready availability of anything one wants at short notice. The 24-hour supermarket is the hallmark of this new culture. With any whim easily satisfied within minutes of its onset, there is little need for personality structures that will foster and sustain activity toward future goals. Charles Reich in *The Greening of America* (1970) presented still another analysis, which, although oriented toward a more popular audience, meshes nicely with these ideas. In his typology of the temporal change within America—Consciousness I, II, and III—we can see in his comparison of stages II and III the personality shift to which we are alluding. Consciousness II, the "establishment" culture from which the counterculture (Consciousness III) emerged in the 1960s, believes in a meritocracy of ability and accomplishment. In contrast with this striving in the service of the future, Consciousness III is the embodiment of the present, an openness and responsiveness to situational stimuli, a receptivity to new experience (p. 284).[7]

These observations have two implications for the Riverside and Crain–Weisman studies. First, they imply that the respondents in the two studies differed in modal personality—that Crain and Weisman's respondents, being a generation older than our own, possessed more of a system of personality ingredients that have long been eroding in America. Second, as this internal motivational system has dissipated across time and generations, it has been replaced by situational determinants of behavior.[8] As the asymptote of situational determinism is reached, individual differences in stable, enduring personality systems of internality, tolerance for delay, and achievement motivation occupy an increasingly weaker position in their ability to explain what people actually do—their educational achievement and attainment. In other words, the range or the dispersion of these individual differences decreases, and consequently they become increasingly irrelevant to the variation in achievement. Mischel (1968, 1973) has attempted to document this view in his analysis of personality. He concluded, in line with this argument, that the potency of specific personality traits as explana-

---

[7] See also T. Rozak, *The Making of a Counterculture.* New York: Doubleday, 1969.

[8] Westman and Miller recently documented this temporal trend in an analysis of changes in achievement motivation scores derived from thematic apperception tests. Analysis of mean scores of college students as reported in articles published over a 25-year span reveals a significant decrease in achievement motivation.

tions of the variance in human behavior has been exaggerated at the expense of situational determinants.[9]

There were some hints at such a process in the data of the Riverside study. As already indicated, our data showed little in the way of strong relations between personality measures and achievement. Indeed, the achievement-related personality measures related to actual scholastic performance less strongly than did measures of self-worth. Among the six achievement motivation measures, "four . . . appear to be virtually unrelated to achievement scores" (Chapter 6). Further ancillary data argue that we cannot attribute this failure to inadequacies in our instruments. An even more interesting hint appears in the delay-of-gratification measure. The hypothetical items indicated that in comparison with age-mates three years earlier, children from all three ethnic groups showed *less* tolerance for deferred gratification—clearly the kind of cultural change to which we earlier referred. It is surprising to find evidence for such a change over so short a time period. Moreover, other analyses of the behavioral data on tolerance for deferred gratification ("Would you like the small candy bar now or the large one later?") showed no ethnic differences. This was true for two qualitatively different measures (large deferred or small immediate candy bar and long deferred or short immediate play period with a preferred toy). The lack of ethnic differences, which implicitly reflect social class differences, again supports our temporal argument when these data are contrasted with Mischel's data collected 10 years earlier showing clear social class differences in the direction of greater tolerance for deferred gratification among those with higher socioeconomic status (SES). Direct analysis of social class effects upon these behavioral measures adds still more weight to this picture. Among White children there was an *inverse* relation between SES and tolerance of delay. High SES White children were more strongly oriented toward immediate gratification than their less advantaged age-mates (Miller and Zadny, 1969). This is exactly what is implied by Slater's (1970) analysis of the current American scene.

Closer examination of the Crain and Weisman data suggests they may have overstated the relation between personality and scholastic

[9] Mischel seems to imply that the greater importance of situational determinants of behavior is universal in both time and space. The preceding argument implies, instead, that the present importance of situational determinants may reflect temporally specific conditions and/or, ultimately, consequences of industrialization and cultural evolution.

achievement. While attending an integrated elementary school beneficially affected the development of internal control, it did not predict educational attainment or achievement very well. Rather, attending an integrated high school was shown to be the more potent determinant. In other words, though an integrated elementary education may have facilitated the development of personality traits that theoretically foster educational attainment, it was not a critical factor in increasing educational achievement and attainment. The decision to finish high school may have evolved from immediate social influence and from situational factors operating in the high school setting itself. Respondents who attended an integrated high school and a segregated elementary school were as likely to finish high school as those whose schooling was entirely integrated (p. 158). The data showing a strong association between high school integration and not fighting or being arrested provides another example of this contextual effect. Whereas these measures of hostility and social pathology are strongly related to the different normative pressures that distinguish the integrated and the segregated high school, they are unrelated to elementary school integration.

Situational Determinants of Academic Performance

Given our arguments above, the beneficial scholastic effects of desegregation are more likely to stem from the situational and social characteristics of the educational setting than from personality changes that might ensue from integration. Let us turn, then, to the data that most directly focus on such factors: the data reported in Chapter 11 on the effects of teacher attitudes and in Chapter 10 on the effects of the classroom social structure.

Teacher Attitudes

Our analysis of teacher attitudes compares teachers who substantially overestimated the difference in brightness between the minority and Anglo children in their class (relative to their true difference) with those whose overestimates were minimal or nonexistent. The relation between this and subsequent performance differences at the end of the school year showed that teachers' expectations of ability had important consequences for standard measures of verbal achievement. In the classes of teachers who exaggerated the intellectual inadequacies of minority children, they showed much larger decrements in verbal achievement test performance than did their peers in the classes of less biased teachers. Indeed, those in the classrooms of teachers low in discrimination showed slight gains in achievement. Moreover, it was the brightest minority children who seemed to suffer the most from the biased teacher. At the same time, Anglo children in the classes of the more biased teachers showed gains in achievement. We thus found increasing divergence in the verbal achievement of Anglo and minority children when instructed by a teacher who was relatively high in discrimination, whereas unbiased teachers did not induce such an effect. Taken together, these findings do not support assumption 6 in the introductory chapter: *"Salutary effects will also be mediated by teachers' influences, which will tend to normalize achievement in the classroom."* The increasing divergence in academic achievement between Anglo and minority children taught by biased teachers directly contradicted this assumption. Moreover, even in the classrooms of the less biased teachers, existing minority deficits were at best maintained at the same level and not reduced.

In consonance with these findings, the less biased the teacher, the smaller the difference in grades assigned to minority and Anglo children. Although high-achieving Anglo children did perform better on standardized tests than did high-achieving minority children, the less biased teachers tended to ignore these differences when assigning grades. This suggests that they used a double standard in grade assignment. On the other hand, teachers who showed substantial bias maintained these differences in their grading of Anglo and minority children.

Unfortunately the absence of direct observational data on teacher–pupil interaction makes it difficult to ascertain exactly how teacher attitudes produced the observed effects. One hypothesis is that teacher attitudes affect a child's feelings of self-worth and competence. Changes in self-esteem are wrought by translation of these attitudes into behavior toward the minority child. According to this hypothesis, lowered self-esteem takes its toll in lowered academic achievement. Yet we found no evidence that teacher expectancies acted through changes in self-esteem.

A second possibility is that teachers who are relatively high in bias create a classroom environment in which the minority child is less acceptable to his White peers (or finds them less acceptable to him). As a consequence, the minority child is influenced less by the White majority. He does not as readily accept their standards of academic performance; he does not internalize their middle-class achievement values, etc. This explanation specifies conditions for the "lateral transmission of values" hypothesis. In attempting to evaluate this explanation, we did find the differences in sociometric choices that might be expected if translation of teacher attitudes into peer acceptance were mediating the achievement decrements produced by more biased teachers.

In trying to understand this effect, we should not assume that it was the more biased teachers who treated minority and Anglo children differently. Alternatively, the less biased teachers might have done so. The data on grading shows that the less biased teachers tended to "overgrade" minority students. The "bending over backward" in order to be supportive of the minority students' academic plight may have reflected a more general predisposition on the part of these teachers to be differentially supportive toward minority students. If so, the failure of minority students to lose relative academic ground to Anglos in these classrooms reflected such differentially supportive behavior on the part of their teachers. This added support from the teacher might have arisen in the form of additional tutoring, instruction, special projects, etc.; alternatively, it could have focused on emotional support, consisting of warmth, encouragement, etc.; and lastly, it could have contained elements of both. Whatever the case, it might have enabled the minority child to overcome the stresses incurred as a consequence of desegregation and thereby at least have maintained his relative academic standing. On the other hand, the increasing achievement gap between minority and Anglo children in the classrooms of the more biased teachers may have occurred in the face of equal treatment toward the three ethnic groups. For these children, the lack of extra support may have permitted such factors as sociometric rejection, the strangeness of a new school, increased academic competition, lower grades, and a host of other negative experiences to exert their debilitating effect.

Assumption 9 of the opening chapter states that *"Teachers will treat children similarly regardless of ethnic background,"* or put another way, that the differences in teachers' behavior toward children in their class will not be organized along racial–ethnic boundaries and will not differentially effect their academic achievements. Regardless of which of interpretations of teacher effects is more tenable, they all clearly stand in contradiction to these expectations. Teachers appeared to behave quite differently toward children of different ethnic groups. Whether or not the debilitating effect of the more biased teachers on minority performance resulted from the low performance expectation communicated by the teacher in her behavior toward the minority child in her class must await more direct observation of teacher behavior.

Sociometric Configurations

As we have indicated a number of times, one of the core arguments for desegregation is that the social intermingling of ethnic groups provides the medium for the attitude and value changes that underlie gains in academic achievement for minority children. (Other explanations—curriculum, facilities, teacher attitudes, etc.—would not require desegregation as an essential ingredient for improved academic achievement among minority groups.) Earlier we argued retrospectively that the "lateral transmission of values" hypothesis contains serious flaws and that there is reason to suspect that its underlying assumption of a strong link between "personality" and "academic achievement" had little basis in Riverside, if not all of contemporary America. Further, our own data failed to support this link. Regardless, however, our sociometric data showed it to be basically irrelevant. Following desegregation, ethnic encapsulation increased over time for both friendship and work partner choices. Consequently, even if Anglo values were more achievement-oriented than those of minority children, and even if they were indeed internalized by minority children as they interacted with their middle-class Anglo classmates, the social interaction patterns implied by the sociometric data precluded much beneficial effect on academic achievement values. In other words, since minority and Anglo children appeared to interact less and less over time, this supposed primary mechanism for potential benefit could not operate to any great extent, if at all.

Closer inspection of the sociometric data does, however, reveal that if an increasing preference for affiliation with members of one's own ethnic group were not the rule, beneficial effects upon academic performance might indeed ensue from desegregation. Among the Anglo children sociometric status was positively related to academic performance. While Anglos who exhibited superior academic achievement received more nominations for choice as a work partner, even more important is the fact that they also received more friendship choices. Nominations for playmate also showed this same tendency. Although sociometric status choices for minority children were not as closely tied to academic performance, brighter minority children were more likely to be chosen as schoolwork partners by other minority children than were the less able ones. In the postdesegregation data, actual achievement was related to number of choices for work partner among all three ethnic groups.

These data lend further weight to our earlier discussion of the diminishing role of personality determinants in academic performance and emphasize further the importance of situational influences. It is unnecessary to see peer influences as producing their effects through a modification of basic personality structure. Rather they can be seen as a situational pressure that exerts an influence toward good academic performance. How might peer influences serve as a situational influence that does not operate through modification of the minority child's personality or value system? Modeling effects or observational learning could occur without the necessity of postulating alterations in personality. The rewards meted out in the school environment depend upon high academic achievement with sufficient frequency to sustain modeling effects based upon vicarious or observational learning. The higher status, teacher recognition and praise, and peer admiration obtained by the adequate or superior student, in combination with the lack of social support and acceptance of the academic dropout can combine in the middle-class school to reinforce directly academic performance.

Academic Achievement

Perhaps the most important goal of desegregation, and certainly the one paramount in the public's mind, is the potential educational benefit to minority groups. Chapter 4 examines this question most directly. Analysis of standardized reading achievement data offers a picture that provides little encouragement for those who see desegregation as a panacea for reducing the achievement gap that so ubiquitously characterizes minority academic performance. While the achievement of

Anglo children did not suffer, minority students showed no overall benefit. This failure to detect any general improvement cannot easily be attributed to the usual set of explanations drawn upon to account for a failure to confirm an expected hypothesis: small sample size, insensitive or inappropriate measures, insufficient time for the beneficial effects to manifest themselves, etc. Our data clearly represent one of the largest samples of minority children ever followed longitudinally. Furthermore, if beneficial effects upon educational achievement had occurred, it cannot sensibly be claimed that insufficient time had elapsed for them to be revealed; some of our children were followed from kindergarten through sixth grade. Likewise, our measures, standardized achievement tests, clearly possess the usual requisites of reliability and internal consistency. Their construct validity is further buttressed by the fact that they do yield meaningful differences as a function of factors other than the desegregation experience (e.g., ethnic group, grade). In sum, if there had been a beneficial effect of this particular desegregation program on achievement, it seems likely that we would have discovered it.

Where does this rather bleak outcome leave us? First, the absence of overall effects attributable to desegregation does not imply that desegregation is of little or no value, even in terms of academic improvement. Our analyses of situational factors (teacher attitudes and classroom sociometric structure) point to strong influences that may maintain or enhance minority achievement under some circumstances and erode it in others. The discovery that minority achievement is not automatically enhanced when minority and White children "rub elbows" may be a disappointment, but on further reflection this expectation seems hopelessly naïve, if not quixotic. In the absence of such a simple panacea, it is necessary on the one hand to consider mechanisms that might mediate beneficial effects and, on the other, boundary conditions under which these effects will occur. The teacher attitude and sociometric data suggest that boundary conditions do indeed exist and that under some circumstances desegregation will improve the academic performance of minority children while not hindering that of Whites. Furthermore, when taken in conjunction with our personality data, particularly those measures closely related to existing conceptualizations of achievement motivation, they argue that the beneficial effect depends upon more immediate and transitory environmental circumstances that must be maintained in the classroom setting (rather than the modification of basic personality structures). This interpretation is consonant with the major source of benefit attributed to integration by Crain and Weisman (1972). Likewise it is seen as following from the kinds of changes in modal character or personality that have been developing within the culture as a whole over the last century.

Classroom grades constitute another measure of academic achievement. Although the grade a teacher assigns to a child is contaminated by her biases and by certain nonacademically related behavior of the child. Nevertheless grades do represent a global measure of classroom behavior and performance. Beyond this, however, they undoubtedly have motivational consequences for the child's future school performance. Detailed analysis of changes in the grades received by minorities and Anglos after desegregation showed clear evidence of normalization both before and after desegregation. As time elapsed after desegregation, teachers gradually moved toward a common standard for all children. By the end of the third year of desegregation, the discrepancies between grades and achievement were negligible among all three ethnic groups. However, this is not either an innocuous or a clearly beneficial result. The achievement discrepancy between Whites and minorities inevitably implies that one consequence of desegregation (and the ensuing normalization of grading) is that minority children tend to receive lower grades than they did in the segregated classroom. While something can, of course, be said for the virtues of veridical performance feedback, it may nonetheless debilitate academic motivation. It is hard to see how minority students, after being enmeshed in a situation permitting direct daily comparison with many White classmates who display superior academic performance, could not help but feel discouraged, incompetent, and certain that the classroom is not a place where they can expect to attain praise, reward, and confirmation of their self-worth. Poor grades would clearly tend to negate or counterbalance any potential or possible beneficial effects of the desegregation experience.

Policy Implications

The optimism that characterized the early enthusiasts and policy makers who advocated integration and bussing as effective social engineering tools for minimizing if not eliminating the educational achievement gap between minority and White students must surely be tempered by the Riverside data. The lack of any overall effect of desegregation on achievement was striking not simply because it was unexpected but, additionally, because in many respects the Riverside situation seemed ideal for producing and showing a beneficial effect. Not only was the sample group studied of more than adequate size, but the longitudinal design clearly allowed sufficient time for the effect to appear were it indeed there to be detected. Furthermore the numerical domination of Anglo relative to minority children in some senses realized the theoretical ideal for maximizing beneficial effects.

Though in the main discouraging, certain aspects of our data point to important qualifying circumstances under which desegregation may enhance or deter educational achievement for minority students. The data on teacher attitudes confirm the suspicion that a child who elicits negative attitudes suffers educationally. The negative effect could simply stem from the extensive pressures on a teacher's time. A teacher's negative attitude toward a child, whether limited to that particular child or symptomatic of a more general attitude toward all members of a particular ethnic group, may prompt her to spend less time and attention on that child. Alternatively, or additionally, the quality of interaction with those children may be affected. Whatever the case, this certainly has implications for the selection and training of teachers. Perhaps insight into the effects of their prejudices might be self-corrective for some teachers. Additionally school systems as well as the institutions that recruit and train teachers should develop methods of detecting bias and negative expectations so that more careful selection could be initiated and remedial teacher training could be provided.

Another aspect of teacher behavior needing further study is the effect of normalized grading. When placed in the context of higher-achieving Whites—a pervasive consequence of any desegregation program—the average minority child tends to receive poorer grades than he previously did, undoubtedly eroding any interest in and/or positive attitude toward school. Katz (1967) maintained that excessive, covert self-critical comments are characteristic of Black children. He further argued that this consequence of an internalized negative self-evaluation underlies poor academic performance. In support of his argument, Dion and Miller (1973) showed that adult disapproval of Black children does indeed result in the development of less favorable self-evaluations. Furthermore, both the sociometric data and the ethnic pictures data (Green & Gerard, in press) suggest that group stereotypes

may be strengthened by integration, implying that the negative consequences of normalization of grading are likely to be exacerbated by the
social interaction between minority children and their White classmates.
In other words, the social comparison processes invoked for both
minority and White children by the postdesegregation changes in
normative levels of achievement, of which the children are certainly
aware, warrant consideration in this context. A minority child's daily
observation of the differences that exist on the average between minority
and Anglo students would act as an additional discouragement.

This view is, of course, quite contrary to the bootstrapping
assumptions presented in the introductory article—that competition
improves performance and that minority children will be motivated to
close the scholastic gap between themselves and Whites when they
perceive the differences that do indeed exist (see assumptions 7 and 8 in
Chapter 1). These processes seem especially unfortunate for the brighter
minority children. They, who have the most potential, are affected most
adversely by the teachers' attitudes, normalization of grading, and
White peer rejection. Desegregation removes them from a school setting
in which they were rewarded for their scholastic achievement into one in
which they can no longer receive as much implicit encouragement from
high grades. In support of these interpretations, Crain and Weisman
(1972) showed that those Blacks whose educational experience was
mixed—either in an integrated elementary school and a segregated high
school or vice versa—exhibited the lowest self-esteem and the least
internal control. By implication, inconsistent standards interfered with
the development of these dimensions of personality. Again, teachers
should be made aware that normalization of grading typically does occur and that the ensuing lower grades for the minority child may erode
motivation and subsequent academic performance. These considerations
argue for the elimination of the usual kinds of grading schemes that
permit invidious comparison.

The emphasis placed by our results on the importance of situational factors in conjunction with our arguments concerning their
increasing importance as our culture evolves highlights the importance
of social comparison processes and normative influences in the integrated school setting. Interestingly, whereas Crain and Weisman
spoke of this "contextual effect" as operating in the high school, our
results argue for its earlier importance in elementary school as well. In
stressing immediate social influence processes, we do not mean to argue

that the middle-class values of the high-achieving White children have no positive impact on the aspirations and achievement of minority children. Rather, if they do, it is most assuredly not mediated by changes in basic personality structures. Peer acceptance is apparently a most powerful reinforcer. If it were largely determined by academic performance, our arguments concerning the increasing responsiveness to external standards and situational influences would suggest that desegregation might be of value in spite of the invidious effects of academic comparisons that minority children might make between themselves and Whites.

However, the sociometric data offer only mixed encouragement in this direction. Indeed, the increasing ethnic encapsulation after desegregation constitutes a problem by itself. These data show in the most striking way possible that desegregating a school system will not automatically produce an integrated school. After children of different ethnic backgrounds are placed together within a common physical space, psychological boundaries emerge to reinstate the physical barriers that previously existed. Especially when considered in conjunction with those of Green and Gerard (in press), these data show the need to develop procedures and techniques that will promote cross-ethnic peer interaction and acceptance. Any dimension of minority student excellence that can be harnessed to generate increased acceptance should be used. Those areas of performance more closely related to the academic enterprise should be given special attention. For instance, the richer vocabulary of Black speech is clearly relevant to a commonly accepted dimension of scholastic achievement: verbal ability. The development of classroom curricula that specifically highlight this ability would constitute one vehicle for augmenting sociometric attractiveness for Blacks that is directly related to academic excellence. Another possibility might be the development of specialized curriculum materials that are specifically designed to promote minority student interest by building on aspects of their ethnic background.

In sum, our data show that desegregation is no simple panacea for counteracting the increasing achievement gap between White and minority students as they progress through school. Our findings suggest that major personality changes are not prerequisites for narrowing the gap and point instead toward the potential of situational factors in the educational setting that can be directly altered: teacher behavior and peer acceptance. In this sense our findings are encouraging; beneficial effects need not await basic changes in personality structures. They further show that simply implementing a bussing or desegregation program will not by itself achieve "integration" in the full sense of the word. Beyond desegregation, additional procedures must be developed to foster integration of the minority child into the classroom social structure and academic program.

References

Barry, H., Child, I., & Bacon, M. K. Relation of child training to subsistence economy. *American Anthropologist,* 1959, *61,* 51–63.

Canavan, D. Field dependency in Black, White, and Mexican-American elementary school children. Paper presented at American Psychological Association, Washington, D.C., 1969.

Coleman, J. S., & staff. *Equality of educational opportunity.* U.S. Department of Health, Education, and Welfare, Washington, D.C.: U.S. Government Printing Office, 1966.

Coopersmith, S. *The antecedents of self-esteem.* San Francisco: W. H. Freeman & Company, 1967.

Crain, R. L., & Weisman, C. S. *Discrimination, personality and achievement: A survey of northern blacks.* New York: Seminar Press, 1972.

Dion, K., & Miller, N. Determinants of task-related self evaluations in Black children. *Journal of Experimental Social Psychology,* 1973, *9,* 466–479.

Green, J. A., & Gerard, H. B. School desegregation and ethnic attitudes. In H. Fromkin & J. Sherwood (Eds.), *Integrating the organization.* Glencoe, Ill.: The Free Press, in press.

Hauser, S. T. *Black and White identity formation.* New York: Wiley-Interscience, John Wiley & Sons, 1971.

Katz, I. The socialization of academic motivation in minority group children. In D. Levine (Ed.), *Nebraska symposium on motivation.* Lincoln: University of Nebraska Press, 1967.

McClelland, D. C. *The achieving society.* Princeton: D. Van Nostrand, 1961.

Miller, N. Personality differences between the Black and White children in the Riverside School Study. Paper presented at the meeting of the Society of Experimental Social Psychology, Minneapolis, Minnesota, 1970.

Miller, N., & Zadny, J. J. Delay of gratification in Black, White and Mexican-American elementary school children. Paper presented at American Psychological Association, Washington, D.C., 1969.

Mischel, W. Delay of gratification, need for achievement, and acquiescence in another culture. *Journal of Abnormal and Social Psychology,* 1961, *62,* 1–17.

Mischel, W. *Personality and assessment.* New York: John Wiley & Sons, 1968.

Mischel, W. Toward a cognitive social learning reconceptualization of personality. *Psychological Review,* 1973, *80,* 252–283.

Pettigrew, T. F. The Negro and education: Problems and proposals. In I. Katz & P. Gurin (Eds.), *Race and the social sciences.* New York: Basic Books, 1969.

Reich, C. A. *The greening of america.* New York: Bantam Books, 1970.

Riesman, D., with Glazer, N., & Denny, R. *The Lonely Crowd.* New Haven, Conn.: Yale University Press, 1950.

Slater, P. *The pursuit of loneliness.* Boston: Beacon Press, 1970.

Author Index

305

Subject Index